THE COMPLETE BOOK OF COFFEE

THE COMPLETE BOOK OF COFFEE

The definitive guide to coffee, from simple bean to irresistible beverage

MARY BANKS with CHRISTINE McFADDEN, CATHERINE ATKINSON

LORENZ BOOKS

This edition is published by Lorenz Books
an imprint of Anness Publishing Limited
www.annesspublishing.com
www.lorenzbooks.com

Publisher: Joanna Lorenz
Editor: Margaret Malone
Designer: Ian Hunt (reference) and Jane Felstead (recipes and jacket)
Photography: William Lingwood (recipes), Louisa Dare (steps and equipment)
and Janine Hosegood (coffee bean samples)
Food for Photography: Carol Tennant (recipes)
Styling: HelenTrent (recipes)
Editorial Reader: Hayley Kerr
Production Controller: Ben Worley

A CIP catalogue record for this book is available from the British Library.

NOTES

For all recipes, quantities are given in both metric and imperial measures and, where appropriate, measures are also given in standard cups and spoons. Follow one set, but not a mixture because they are not interchangeable.

Standard spoon and cup measures are level.
1 tsp = 5ml, 1 tbsp = 15ml, 1 cup = 250ml/8fl oz

Australian standard tablespoons are 20ml. Australian readers should use 3 tsp in place of 1 tbsp for measuring small quantities of gelatine, cornflour, salt etc.

Medium eggs are used unless otherwise stated.

Contents

THE WORLD OF COFFEE	6
THE HISTORY OF COFFEE	8
COFFEE AROUND THE WORLD	54
THE ART OF COFFEE DRINKING	106

COOKING WITH COFFEE: THE RECIPES	154
CREAM DESSERTS AND HOT PUDDINGS	156
SOUFFLES AND MERINGUES	168
FRUIT DESSERTS	180
FROZEN DESSERTS	196
CAKE AND TORTE RECIPES	208
PIES, TARTS AND PASTRIES	220
SWEETS, BISCUITS AND BREADS	234
SUPPLIERS AND ACKNOWLEDGEMENTS	248
BIBLIOGRAPHY	251
INDEX	252

THE WORLD OF COFFEE

Everything you ever wanted to know about coffee is contained within this fascinating and beautiful book. Intended as a definitive guide to coffee, the reference section explores the history and cultural, political and economic impact of coffee across the world plus examines on a country-by-country basis the tastes and characteristics of coffee produced today. It also explains how to grind, brew and make the perfect cup of coffee. In the second half of the book, there are over 70 recipes demonstrating the wonderful versatility of coffee in the kitchen, with delicious souffles and meringues, puddings, fruit and frozen desserts, and enticing cakes, pastries and breads.

THE HISTORY OF COFFEE

This section traces the mysterious and conflict-ridden journey of the coffee bean from its Ethiopian birthplace, through Arabia and the Middle East, and on to Europe and the New World. The crucial role of the beverage in shaping the spiritual and social life of medieval Arabia and Turkey is examined, as is how, later, it became irrevocably entrenched in Western cultures. The vital role of the coffee house in the political, economic and cultural life across the world is covered, both historically and up to the present day. There is also a section devoted to the myriad methods of early coffee brewing and a discussion on coffee-drinking and coffee products.

THE GENESIS OF THE BEAN

Ever since its migration from north-east Africa to Arabia many hundreds of years ago, this vital bean has played a multifaceted role in moulding history. That short hop across the Red Sea helped alter social, political and economic life not only in Africa and the Middle East, but in mainland Europe, Britain and the Americas too. Coffee has made the fortunes and misfortunes of many, oiled the wheels of communication, inspired creative minds, stimulated the tired, and, for countless imbibers the world over, become a daily necessity.

Myths and Mysteries

So great was the mystique ascribed to coffee, that conjecture over the who, how and when of the invention of the beverage and the discovery of its properties was intense. Doctors, lawyers, poets and philosophers all had their pet theories and great kudos was linked to association with the so-called "discovery". As a result, in medieval Arabia and later in 17th-century Europe, stories and legends were rife.

Parched Corn or Black Broth

Those with a historical bent and a lively imagination traced the bean back to Old Testament tales, claiming that it was the same "parched corn" that Abigail gave to David, and Boaz to Ruth. Many were convinced it was the "black broth" of the Lacedaemonians, as the Spartans were then called. Petrus de Valle, a well-known Italian traveller, believed that coffee dated as far back as the Trojan war, suggesting that "the fair Helen with other ladies of Priamus's Court, used sometimes to drown the Thoughts of the Calamities she had brought upon her Family and Country, in a Pot of Coffee". Others thought that, in Homer's *Odyssey*, the substance called "nepenthes", which Helen mixed with wine and which "banishes sadness and wrath from the heart" was coffee.

Banesius, a late 18th-century writer, theorized in a treatise on coffee that since it was a medicine and most medicines were discovered by chance, the discovery of "this Liquor was as much a proof of fortuitous Experience as any of those (other medicines)".

Following this line of thought, Banesius went on to recount the ubiquitous fable of the dancing goats, in which an Arab or Ethiopian goatherd complained to the Imam of a neighbouring monastery that his flock "two or three times a week not only kept awake all night long but spent it frisking and dancing in an unusual manner". The Imam, concluding that the animals may have eaten something that was causing the reaction, went to the pasture where they danced. Here he found berries growing on shrubs, and he decided to try them himself.

Having boiled the berries in water and drunk the resulting brew, the Imam found that he was able to stay awake at night without any ill effects. Encouraged by what had been an enjoyable experience, he "enjoin'd the daily Use of it to his Monks, which, by keeping them from Sleep, made them more readily and surely attend the Devotions they were obliged to perform at Night time... It continued to keep them in perfect Health; and by this means it came to be in request throughout that whole Kingdom".

Dr James Douglas, in his scholarly work *Yemensis fructum Cofé ferens; or, a description and history of the Coffee tree* (1727), somewhat scathingly dismisses Banesius's story as having "too great an Air of Fable to be in the least depended on", stating that "those who are acquainted with the Nature of Vulgar Traditions, especially those of Eastern nations, will understand its thin credibility".

One of the many variations of the tale – this one by Sir Thomas Pope Blount – tells of how the Imam tried the coffee experiment upon "another sort of Beast, a sleepy Heavy-headed Monk". In a short time, the story goes, it had such a wonderful effect on him, that it "quite alter'd his Constitution, and hereafterwards became more quick, brisk, and airy than generally that sort of Cattle are".

Left: "Ruth on the Field of Boaz", wood engraving, from The Bible in Pictures, Leipzig, 1860 by Julius Schnorr von Carolsfeld (1794–1874).

Basic botany

Coffee comes from the fruit of an evergreen shrub, or tree, which flourishes in tropical and subtropical regions around the world. The trees produce delicate clusters of jasmine-scented blossoms, and fruit known as "cherries". Cocooned in each cherry, protected by pulp and parchment, are two coffee beans. Since approximately four thousand beans are needed to produce one pound of roasted coffee, few commodities require so much in terms of human effort.

Right: Coffea arabica, *botanical magazine, London, 1810.*

The Muslim View

The Muslims had another story which Dr Douglas describes as "still more wonderful, but equally groundless". The Muslims claimed that because of their special relationship with "Providence", and so that they would gain from so "beneficial a Liquor", the archangel Gabriel was sent to reveal to the prophet Mohammed "the Virtues and manner of preparing it" (coffee).

Yet another legend tells of the dervish Omar, known for his ability to heal the sick by prayer. Exiled from his home town of Mocha to a cave in the desert and nearing starvation, Omar chewed berries from shrubs growing nearby. Finding the berries too bitter, he roasted them, hoping to improve the flavour. Obviously a man of refined palate (and surprisingly well equipped with the necessary utensils), he decided the berries now needed boiling to soften them. He drank the resulting fragrant brew and was instantly revitalized, remaining in this state for several days.

A picturesque variation of the same tale states how Omar saw a bird of marvellous plumage in a tree, where it sang an exquisitely harmonious song. When he reached out for the bird, Omar found only flowers and fruit in its place. He filled his basket with these and returned to the cave, intending to boil a few meagre herbs for dinner. However, he boiled the fruit instead and created a savoury and perfumed brown drink.

Eventually – and both variations concur with this – patients from Mocha came to the cave for medical advice. They, too, were given the drink and, since this is a legend, they were of course cured. When news of the "miracle cure" reached Mocha, Omar was invited to return in triumph and was subsequently made the patron saint of the city.

Despite the vast literature assembled by many historians, no one has ever been able to say positively how and when the plant was discovered. Its origins therefore remain shrouded in legend in which truth and imagination are inexorably entwined.

Below: 1950s British advertisement referring to the story of the discovery of coffee's properties by goats eating the berries of a certain tree.

ODYSSEY FROM AFRICA

The coffee plant found its way from Ethiopia to Arabia sometime between AD 575 and AD 850. How it got there is not clear, but one possibility is that seeds were brought by African tribes-people as they migrated northwards from Kenya and Ethiopia to the Arabian peninsular. They were eventually driven back by spear-throwing Persians but they left behind coffee trees growing in what is now the Yemen.

Myths and Legends

Another possibility is that Arab slave traders brought the seeds back from their raids on Ethiopia; or, as is more likely, the responsibility lay with the Sufis – a mystical Islamic sect best-known for their "whirling dervishes". Classical Arabic literature endorses this, suggesting that it was a Sufi grand master, Ali ben Omar al Shadili, who brought coffee seeds to Arabia. Al Shadili had lived for a while in Ethiopia before founding a monastery in the Yemenite port of Mocha (Al Mukha). Since he later became known as the Saint of Mocha, he appears to be the same legendary Omar who discovered coffee berries while exiled in the desert, though the stories do not quite tie up.

According to Dr Douglas, a reasonably reliable account was unearthed in a collection of original manuscripts by Monsieur de Nointel, Louis IV's ambassador at the Arab ports. Written by an Arab in 1587, the document gives what was believed at the time to be the earliest account of the use of coffee and its subsequent spread through the Middle East. The author tells how the Mufti of Aden, while travelling through Persia in the mid-15th century, came upon some of his compatriots enjoying coffee. Returning to Aden in poor health, he remembered this liquor and thought it might help him recover. He sent for some, and found that it not only prevented sleep without any ill effects, but also "dissipated all manner of Heaviness and Drowsiness, and made him more bright and gay than he was wont to be".

Above: A Bedouin preparing coffee according to traditional Arabic methods.

Wishing to share the benefits with his dervishes, the Mufti gave them coffee before they embarked on their night-long prayers. He found that they, too, were able to perform "all their Exercises of religion with great Alacrity and Freedom of Mind".

Whatever the route and circumstances, there is firm evidence that the first cultivated coffee trees grew in monastery gardens in the Yemen, and most Arab authorities agree that the Sufi community was in one way or another responsible.

From Food to Beverage

As with the discovery of the plant and its journey to Arabia, the process of development from food to hot beverage is also a matter of historical speculation.

The comments of the early European explorers and botanists indicate that the Ethiopians chewed raw coffee beans – obviously appreciative of their stimulating effect. They also pounded ripe coffee cherries, mixed them with animal fat and moulded the resulting paste into pellets. This powerful cocktail of fat, caffeine and meat protein was a vital source of concentrated energy, particularly valuable in times of tribal conflict when warriors were required to give their all. The cherries were probably eaten as a ripe fruit, too, since the pulp is sweet and contains caffeine.

Early records also show that a wine was made from the fermented juice of the ripe cherries. The wine was called *qahwah*, meaning "that which excites and causes the spirits to rise", a term which was eventually used for both wine and coffee. Since wine was prohibited by Mohammed, coffee was nicknamed "the wine of Araby".

It seems possible that coffee was treated as a food in Arabia, too, and only later mixed with water to make a drink. The earliest version of the beverage was probably a liquid produced by steeping a few whole hulls in cold water. Later, the hulls were roasted over an open fire, and then boiled in water for about thirty minutes until a pale yellow liquid was produced.

By about AD 1000, the drink was still a relatively crude decoction made with green coffee beans and their hulls. It was probably not until around the 13th century that the beans were dried before use. They were laid out in the sun, and once dry, could be stored for longer periods. After that, it was a small step to roast them over a charcoal fire.

Right: Illustration showing the early Arabic method of brewing coffee over an open fire.

Early Uses

Initially, coffee was consumed only as part of a religious ceremony or on the advice of a physician. Once the medical men had observed coffee's beneficial effects, more and more of them started to prescribe it. Coffee was used to treat an astounding variety of ailments, including kidney stones, gout, smallpox, measles and coughs. A late 17th-century treatise on coffee and its uses quotes the work of Prosper Alpinus, a botanist. In his book on the medicines and plants of Egypt, Alpinus writes: "It is an excellent Remedy against the stoppage of Women's Courses, and they make often use thereof, when they don't flow so fast as they desire...it is a quick and certain remedy for those Women, who not having their courses are troubled with violent pains."

He goes on to describe how coffee was made: "This Decoction they make two ways: the one with the skin or the outside of the aforesaid Grain, and the other with the very substance of the Bean. That which is made with the skin is of more force then the other...

The Grain...is put into an Iron Instrument firmly shut together with the coverlid, through this Instrument they thrust a Spit, by the means thereof they turn it before the Fire, till it shall be well roasted; after which having beaten it into a very fine Powder, you may make use thereof, in an equal proportion according to the number of people that will drink it: Viz the third part of a spoonful for each person, and put it into a glass of boyling Water, putting a little Sugar thereto: And after having let it boyl a small time, you must pour it into little dishes of porcelain or any other sort, and so let it be drunk by little and little, as hot as it can be possibly indur'd".

Bun and bunchum

The African word for the coffee plant was *bun*, which then became the Arabic *bunn*, meaning both the plant and the berry. Rhazes (AD 850–922), a doctor who lived in Persian Iraq, and a follower of Galen and Hippocrates, compiled a medical encyclopedia in which he refers to the bean as *bunchum*. His discussion of its healing properties no doubt led to the belief that coffee was known as a medicine over a thousand years ago. Similar references appear in the writings of Avicenna (AD 980–1037), another distinguished Muslim physician and philosopher.

The word "coffee", meaning the drink, is a modified form of the Turkish word *kahveh* which, in turn, is derived from the Arabic *kahwa* (or *qahwah*).

Above: Portrait of Avicenna, Muslim physician, painting c. 17th century.

THE WINE OF ARABY

Above: On the steps of a Turkish coffee house, illustration, early 19th century.

Following the example of the Mufti of Aden and his monks, religious communities throughout Arabia took up the practice of drinking coffee. Little by little, however, its use spread beyond religious confines. Aden's citizens were among the first to take up the habit. Since the Mufti was a respected authority on Muslim law and presumably would not knowingly consume an illegal substance himself, they were keen to follow his example and try this new drink themselves.

Coffee-drinking took place in the mosque where, after the monks had had their fill, the Imam offered it to others who happened to be present. Served in this ceremonious manner against a background of devout chanting, coffee-drinking was seen as a wholesome and pious activity. However, everyone who tasted coffee liked it and wanted more, and it was not long before word spread of the rewards to be reaped from visiting the mosque.

Anxious to quell the trend, religious authorities tried in vain to restrict coffee consumption. Imams and monks were allowed to imbibe, but only in conjunction with their nightly prayers; physicians were also allowed to prescribe small quantities. However, as the less spiritually inclined continued to make late-night appearances at the mosque, and doctors increasingly began to prescribe coffee for all manner of ills, it was hard to curtail its use.

Recipients in the mosque found coffee a pleasant stimulant and conducive to sociability. Before long, the beverage was sold openly in the area, attracting a motley crowd of law students, night workers and travellers. Eventually, the whole city took up the practice, not just at night but round-the-clock and in the home too. Not surprisingly, the hot, strong coffee was particularly popular during Ramadan, when fasting is obligatory from sunrise to sunset.

Coffee Takes a Hold

The new drink quickly spread from Aden to neighbouring towns, and by about the end of the 15th century had reached the holy city of Mecca. Here, as in Aden, coffee-drinking at first centred around the dervish community at the mosque.

Before long, the citizens were also regularly drinking coffee at home and in public areas set apart for the purpose. They did so with obvious enjoyment as an Arab historian reports: "Thither Crowds of People resorted at all Hours of the Day, to enjoy the pleasure of Conversation, play at Chess and other games, dance, sing, and divert themselves all manner of ways, under the pretence of drinking Coffee".

As the centre of the Muslim world, Mecca's social and cultural practices were inevitably copied by Muslims in other major cities. Within a relatively short time, therefore, coffee-drinking took hold throughout much of Arabia, spreading west to Egypt, and north through Syria. The coffee habit was also established further by the Muslim armies who, at that time, were advancing through southern Europe, Spain and North Africa, and east to India. Wherever they went, they took coffee with them.

Coffee thus became an integral part of Middle Eastern life. So crucial was the drink to the smooth-running of society that, in many areas, marriage contracts stipulated that a husband should allow his wife as much coffee as she wanted. Failure to do so was grounds for a woman to sue for divorce.

Coffee in Persia

The coffee habit perhaps took root in Persia even before it came to Arabia. Persian warriors were said to have driven back the Ethiopians when they tried to settle in the Yemen. The Persians would have undoubtedly found to their liking the coffee cherries growing on the trees planted by the Ethiopians, and taken them back to their own country. The story of the Mufti of Aden also refers to coffee-drinking in Persia in the mid-15th century.

Coffee and religious devotion

The Muslims were convinced that the drink was a gift from Allah and were almost fanatical in their enthusiasm, as the following eulogy – or tirade – shows. Translated from the Arabic and printed, curiously, in the Transylvanian Journal of Medicine in the early part of the 19th century, the original is said to be the work of Sheik Abdal-Kader Anasari Djezeri Haubuli, son of Mohammed:

"O COFFEE! thou dispellest the cares of the great: thou bringest back those who wander from the paths of knowledge. Coffee is the beverage of the people of God, and the cordial of his servants who thirst for wisdom...
...Every care vanishes when the cup bearer present thee the delicious chalice. It will circulate fleetly through thy veins, and will not rankle there: if thou doubtest this, contemplate the youth and beauty of those who drink it...
...Coffee is the drink of God's people; in it is health...Whoever has seen the blissful chalice, will scorn the wine cup. Glorious drink! thy colour is the seal of purity, and reason proclaims it genuine. Drink with confidence, and regard not the prattle of fools, who condemn without foundation..."

From very early on, most major Persian cities boasted stylish and spacious coffee houses situated in the best parts of town. These establishments had a reputation for serving coffee quickly, efficiently, and "with abundance of Respect". As a rule, the political discussions and resulting disturbances usually associated with the coffee house scene were kept low-key; it seems the clientele were more interested in hedonistic pursuits. Persian coffee houses developed a reputation for talking, music, dancing and "other things of that kind", and there are even several reports of how the government was obliged to put a stop to "the infamous practices committed there".

An English traveller tells the tale of how the wife of the Shah tactfully appointed a mullah – an expert in legal and ecclesiastical matters – to make a daily visit to a particularly crowded and popular coffee house. His job was to sit there and entertain the patrons with civilized discussion of poetry, history and law. A man of discretion, he avoided controversial political issues, and disturbances were therefore rare. The mullah became a welcome visitor.

Having seen that the scheme was a success, other coffee houses soon followed suit and employed their own mullahs and story-tellers. These newfound entertainers sat in a centrally placed high chair "from whence they make speeches and tell satirical stories, playing in the meantime with a little stick and using the same gestures as our jugglers...do in England".

Coffee in Turkey

Despite having reached neighbouring Syria, coffee-drinking was relatively slow to spread to Turkey. However, following the expansion of the Ottoman Empire and the subsequent conquest of Arab Muslims, the Turks finally took to coffee drinking with a vengeance, as an English doctor writing from Constantinople confirms: "When a Turk is sick he fasts and takes Coffa, and if that will not do, he makes his will, and thinks of no other Phisick".

New watering holes According to a 16th-century Arab writer, the first two coffee houses in Constantinople were set up in 1554 by a couple of Syrian entrepreneurs quick to spot a trend. Their premises were impressively furnished with "very neat couches and carpets, on which they received their company, which first consisted mostly of studious persons, lovers of chess, trictrac, and other sedentary Diversions". Other equally opulent coffee shops quickly opened, sometimes to the dismay of the more pious Muslims. They were richly decorated and the clientele reclined on luxurious cushions while they were entertained with stories and poetry as well as singing and dancing by professional performers.

Despite the ever-increasing number of new establishments, the coffee houses were always crowded with people. Historians disagree as to the social standing of the clientele, some saying the coffee houses were frequented almost exclusively by "the lower orders", others claiming that they

Right: A Turkish domestic servant preparing coffee in the home.

appealed to all levels of society. As Hattox states in *The Social Life of the Coffeehouse*: "From the assumption that all classes went to coffee houses it does not of necessity follow that all classes went to the same coffee house."

The legal profession obviously found the coffee houses a useful place for networking, since the patrons of one establishment were said to consist mainly of travelling *cadhis* (judges) who were in Constantinople looking for work; the professors of law or other sciences, as well as students coming up for graduation and eager to secure a prestigious job. Even the chief officer of the Sultan's palace and other high-ranking members were seen to drop by.

The travelling English – writers, botanists, doctors – had never seen anything like the coffee houses and wrote extensively about them. Henry Blunt in his *Voyage to the Levant* recounted with amazement: "for there upon Scaffolds half a yard high and covered with Mats, they sit crosse-legg'd after the Turkish manner, many times two or three hundred together, talking, and likely with some poor Musick passing up and down".

Sir George Sandys wrote somewhat disapprovingly: "there sit they chatting most of the day, and sip of a Drink called Coffa...in little China Dishes, as hot as they can suffer it, black it is as soot, tasting not much unlike it...which helpeth, as they say, Digestion, and procureth Alacrity. Many of the Coffa-men keeping beautiful Boys, who serve...to procure them Customers".

Coffee at home The Turks drank as much coffee at home as they consumed at the coffee house. A French traveller observed: "as much money must be spent in the private families of Constantinople for coffee as for wine at Paris". Sir Henry Blunt wrote in a letter to a friend: "for besides the innumerable store of Coffa-houses, there is not a private fire without it all day long".

Blunt went further, extolling the many therapeutic benefits of drinking coffee: "they (the Turks) all acknowledge how it freeth them from Crudities caused by ill Diet, or moist Lodging, insomuch as they using Coffa Morning and Evening, have no Consumptions which ever come of Moisture; no Lethargies in aged People; or Rickets in Children, and but few Qualms in Women with Child: But especially they hold it of singular prevention against the Stone and Gout."

Left: Large numbers gathered in the coffee houses to gossip and sip coffee.

CUSTOM AND RITUAL

Once coffee had started to lose its religious associations, coffee houses, or *qahveh khaneh*, sprang up all over the Middle East. There were also hole-in-the-wall coffee shops, and strolling vendors who heated coffee over small spirit lamps and filled the dishes of passers-by.

At the same time, coffee-drinking had become equally well established in the home. No social interaction was complete without it. Coffee was served by barbers before haircuts, by merchants before and after bargaining, at chance meetings between friends and at the most formal of banquets. European travel writers were astounded by the level of consumption. One wrote: "They drink coffee not only in their houses, but even in the publick streets as they go about their business, and sometimes three or four people, by turns, out of the same cup".

A Better Brew

By the early 16th century, whole coffee beans were roasted on special stone trays, and later on metal plates. Once roasted, the beans were boiled for thirty minutes or more, producing a strong dark liquor which was stored in vats until needed. As demand increased, however, preparation and brewing techniques improved. Coffee was freshly made with pulverized beans and boiling water. Sugar and delicious spices, such as cardamom, cinnamon and cloves, were added to improve the flavour. Although the use of roasted beans had become common practice, coffee made with the lightly roasted cherries (with the bean removed) was still highly prized in the Yemen where the coffee trees grew. Known as "Sultan's coffee", it was drunk mainly by those of the highest rank, or by visitors to whom it was served as a testimony of respect and honour.

Café à la Sultane

"*The manner of making the* Café à la Sultane *is this. They take the husks of perfectly ripe fruit, beat them, and put them in an earthen Pan over a Charcoal-Fire, keeping them constantly in motion, and only toast them until they change Colour a little. At the same time Water is set to boil in a Coffee-Pot, and when the Husks are ready, they throw in both the outer and inner Shells separately, about three times as many of the first as of the last; then boil them up in the same manner as common Coffee. The Colour of the Liquor is pretty much like that of best English Beer. The Husks must be kept in dry Places till they are used; for the least Moisture spoils the Taste of them.*"
Dr James Douglas, 1727.

Above: A strolling street vendor of coffee, Istanbul, early 18th century.

Life in the Coffee House

As the coffee houses proliferated, so did competition for customers. The coffee house masters tried to attract clientele "not only by the goodness of their Liquor, neatness and dexterity of their Servants" but also by sumptuous surroundings and entertainment. Musicians, jugglers and dancers were employed, and puppet shows were provided as well.

When customers grew bored with what the house had to offer, and conversation began to flag, they would make their own entertainment. Poets would be asked to recite, or, if a dervish was present, he would be invited to deliver a light-hearted sermon.

Backgammon, chess and various card games were also popular. Gambling almost certainly took place, as did drug use. Coffee had become popular with opium users, and there were always two or three *narghiles* (water pipes) available for the leisurely smoking of hashish or tobacco while customers waited to be served.

The British ritual of buying rounds of drinks in pubs undoubtedly has its roots in the Turkish coffee house. If a customer saw someone he knew about to order a coffee, he would shout a single word *caba*, meaning "gratis", which indicated to the proprietor that he was not to take the man's money. The newcomer, in turn, would individually greet all those already present before taking his seat. If an older man arrived, everyone would rise in respect and the best seat would be vacated for him.

It was customary to drink coffee as hot as the mouth could bear, so it was sipped, or more probably slurped, from a small china dish – handles were to come later. Early English travellers were probably amused, or even repelled, by this strange, rather exotic habit. One wrote: "they are sometimes near an hour on one dish...and it is none of the least diversions which strangers find among them, to hear this Sipping-Musick in a publick Coffee House, where perhaps some hundreds are drinking at a time".

Above: Turkish coffee house, lithograph, 1855.

Coffee Drinking in the Home

In 16th-century Constantinople, there was no house, rich or poor, Turkish or Jewish, Greek or Armenian, where coffee was not drunk at least twice a day, and usually more often – twenty dishes a day was not uncommon. It became a custom in every home, no matter how humble, to offer coffee to visitors and it was considered unspeakably ill-mannered to refuse it. At formal banquets, guests were offered coffee immediately upon arrival, and they were plied with it continually for the duration of the feast, which could have lasted as long as eight hours.

Though coffee-drinking had become an accepted part of everyday life, it nevertheless continued to maintain its magic. The way in which coffee was served in the home was always ceremonious. There was a requisite exchange of courteous greetings, enquiries after health and family, the praising of God, and elaborate rituals, similar in complexity to those of the Japanese tea ceremony. Melon seeds and dates might be served alongside the coffee to add to the enjoyment.

Most well-to-do households kept coffee stewards, whose sole responsibility was to attend to the preparation and serving of coffee. The chief steward, known as the *Kahveghi*, had the privilege of an "apartment" – probably little more than a cupboard – situated next to the coffee hall where visitors were received. The hall was decorated with richly coloured rugs and cushions, and gleaming ornamental coffee pots. Coffee was served with great decorum on silver or painted wooden trays large enough to hold up to twenty porcelain coffee dishes. These were always half-filled, not only to prevent spillage, but so that the dish could be held with the thumb below and two fingers on the upper edge.

Very grand households also kept pages, or *Itchoglans*, who, at a nod from the head of the household, took the coffee from the stewards and, with impressive dexterity, handed it to visitors without either touching the rim, burning themselves or spilling a drop.

Above: Wealthy households had servants whose sole duty was to prepare the coffee.

Lord Byron on coffee

The Victorian poet's view of Turkish coffee comes across in this poem:

And Mocha's berry, from Arabia pure,
In small fine china cups, came in at last;
Gold cups of filigree, made to secure
the hand from burning, underneath them placed.
Cloves, cinnamon, and saffron, too, were boiled
up with the Coffee, which, I think, they spoiled.

COFFEE AND CONFLICT

When a seemingly exclusive group of people are seen to be enjoying themselves and getting a little lively, especially at night, other groups tend to feel threatened. So it was in 16th-century Arabia when the political and religious leaders could not fail to ignore the good times being had in the coffee house. As Hattox states in *The Social Life of the Coffeehouse*, the relaxed clubby atmosphere inevitably led to caffeine-induced airing of news, views and grievances concerning the state. Even worse, attendance at the mosque was in decline now that coffee could be obtained elsewhere.

The first place to experience the crackdown was the holy city of Mecca, where an assembly of muftis, lawyers and physicians declared that coffee-drinking was not only contrary to religious law but caused physical harm. The level of argument that went on demonstrates the passion which coffee aroused and the conflict it provoked amongst those anxious to be seen to be taking the politically correct line.

The Suppression of Coffee Drinking

The story goes that the Governor of Mecca was scandalized by the behaviour of a group of coffee-drinkers in the mosque who were legitimately preparing themselves for a long night of prayer. At first the Governor thought they were drinking wine, which was of course forbidden by Muslim law. Even when assured otherwise, the Governor concluded that coffee made people drunk or at least prone to acts of civil disorder, and he decided to prohibit its use. However, he first summoned a group of experts and asked for their considered opinion.

The legal experts stated that coffee houses were indeed in need of some reform, but that there was a fine line as to whether coffee beverages themselves were genuinely physically harmful, or whether they were simply a catalyst that adversely affected people's behaviour. Not wishing to take final responsibility for such a serious and delicate issue, they declared that the decision should rest with the physicians.

Two Persian brothers – practising physicians in Mecca – were summoned; it was no accident that one of them had written a book discouraging the use of coffee. Medical practice in those days was based on the concept of bodily humours, and the brothers accordingly declared that *bunn*, from which coffee was usually made, was "cold and dry" and therefore harmful to health. Another doctor present argued that *bunn* "scorched and consum'd the Phlegm", and could not possibly have the qualities attributed to it by the Persian brothers.

After protracted debate, everyone decided to play safe, and agreed that it would be prudent to declare coffee an illegal substance – as the Governor had intended all along. As a result, many of the assembled company eagerly confirmed that coffee had indeed "disordered their senses". One man inadvertently declared that when he drank coffee he experienced the same effects as wine produced – a laughter-provoking comment since he would have had to break Muslim law in order to know. When questioned, he imprudently acknowledged he had drunk wine and was duly punished.

Right: As coffee houses grew in popularity, it was not long before the relaxed behaviour of the coffee drinkers attracted the notice of religious and political leaders.

The Mufti of Mecca, a holy man and a lawyer by profession, heatedly opposed the decision but was alone in defending the drink. Ignoring the Mufti, the Governor signed a declaration outlawing the selling or drinking of coffee both in public and in private. All stores of the seditious berry were burnt; the coffee houses were shut down and their owners pelted with the fragments of broken pots and cups.

The declaration was sent to the Sultan of Egypt, who, much to the Governor's embarrassment, was astonished to hear of the condemnation of a beverage which the whole of Cairo found wholesome and beneficial. Moreover, Cairo's doctors of law, who had much greater status than those at Mecca, found nothing illegal in the use of it. The Governor was duly reprimanded and told he could use his authority only to prevent disorders that might take place in the coffee house. Coffee-drinking, which in any case had been going on behind closed doors, was restored. A year later, the Sultan condemned the Governor to death for his crime against coffee; the two Persian physicians subsequently met the same fate.

Arguing the finer points of Islamic law in relation to coffee became increasingly bizarre and esoteric. In Constantinople, for example, religious zealots claimed vehemently that the process of roasting reduced coffee to charcoal, and to use such a base article at the table, was grossly impious. The Mufti agreed and declared that coffee was illegal.

As usual, the ban was never entirely followed. People gradually reinstated coffee-drinking at home, and, having given up hope of enforcement, the officers of the law started to grant permission for coffee to be sold in private. Eventually, a less scrupulous Mufti was appointed and the coffee houses were opened again.

Next, a tax was introduced forcing Constantinople's coffee-house owners to pay an amount proportionate to business done. Despite this hefty contribution to government coffers, the price of a cup of coffee remained as low as ever – a sure indication of the vast amount served.

Above: The ritual of coffee drinking encompassed grinding, brewing and serving.

In the years to follow, repeated attempts at suppression were made throughout the Middle East by political and religious leaders. Each time the usual string of complaints met with the usual anarchistic resistance. Lacking popular support and faced with divided opinion among the lawyers, physicians and religious experts, the attempts consistently failed. By the end of the century, coffee-drinking was a deeply rooted habit throughout the Middle East that no level of prohibition could budge.

MIGRATION OF THE TREE

Towards the end of the 16th century, reports from travellers and botanists of a strange new plant and drink began to reach Europe from the Middle East. As the reports grew in number and frequency, European merchants started to realize the potential of the new commodity. Already involved with Middle Eastern trade, the Venetians were quick to exploit this opportunity, and the first bags of coffee beans arrived in Venice from Mecca in the early 1600s.

The Arab Monopoly

Supplying coffee to the Venetians was the start of a lucrative export business for the Arabs, and one which they guarded jealously for almost a century. Great lengths were taken to ensure that no bean capable of germination left the country; beans were either boiled or parched, and visitors were kept well away from the coffee plantations. Until about the end of the 17th century, the Yemen was the only centre of supply for the European coffee trade.

Dutch Enterprise

Around the time that the Venetians took delivery of their first consignment of beans, Dutch merchants began to examine the possibility of coffee cultivation and trading. They already had a considerable amount of information from the botanists, and the merchants saw no reason why the Arabs should maintain their monopoly. At the time, the Dutch were probably Europe's most proactive traders and in possession of the best merchant ships. It comes as no surprise, therefore, to learn that a Dutch merchant managed to steal a coffee plant from Mocha and bring it unharmed back to Europe.

By the middle of the century, cultivation trials had been set up in the East Indian Dutch colony of Java – hence the well-known Mocha-Java blend of bean – and by the 1690s plantations had been established in rapid succession in the neighbouring island colonies of Sumatra, Timor, Bali and Celebes. The enterprising Dutch East India Company had also begun large-scale cultivation in Ceylon, where the plant had already been introduced by the Arabs.

The Universal Coffee Nursery

In 1706, Dutch growers in Java sent home the first crop of beans and a coffee plant, which was carefully transplanted in the Amsterdam Botanical Garden. This consignment, though small, was to play a key role in the annals of the coffee trade. Amsterdam became the trading centre for coffee grown in the Dutch colonies, and the plant produced berries from which seedlings were later taken to the New World. Dr James Douglas, an 18th century scientist, regarded these plants as the ancestors of coffee plantations in the West, and named the Amsterdam Botanical Garden "the universal coffee nursery".

The Tree for the King

In 1714, the burgomaster of Amsterdam presented the King of France, Louis XIV, with a healthy five-foot coffee tree

Above: Arab merchants strictly controlled the trade of Mocha coffee produced in Yemen.

Above: Once Dutch traders broke the Arabian monopoly, coffee soon spread to all parts of the world. Painting by H Vroom, 1640.

grown in the Botanical Garden. The French had not been blind to the commercial success of the Dutch, and had in fact smuggled seed from Mocha to Réunion Island off Madagascar. They had been less successful with propagation at home, however, so "The Tree", as this specimen from Amsterdam became known, was received with the utmost gratitude and respect. It was planted in the Jardin des Plantes where a greenhouse had been especially built, and entrusted to the care of the Royal Botanist.

It was Louis XIV's secret ambition that the seeds from The Tree would be the progenitors of future coffee plantations throughout the French colonies. His wish came true, for The Tree flowered, bore fruit, and became the ancestor of most of the coffee trees presently growing in Central and South America.

Cultivation in the New World

The question as to whether it was the Dutch or the French who first introduced coffee cultivation to the New World has long been a matter of dispute. In the year following delivery of The Tree to the French, the Dutch sent coffee plants from the Amsterdam Botanical Garden to their territories in Guiana in northern South America. A short time later – the date is not certain – a French naval officer, Gabriel Mathieu de Clieu, determined to bring coffee cultivation to the New World, procured with great difficulty one or more coffee seedlings from the Jardin des Plantes. Historians disagree as to whether it was a single plant or several.

De Clieu set sail with his precious cargo to the island of Martinique, north of Guiana. The journey was long and arduous. Not only did a fellow passenger repeatedly try to destroy the seedlings, even managing to rip off some of the leaves, but the voyage itself was fraught with danger and difficulty. There were terrifying storms, attacks by pirates, and finally the ship was becalmed for days on end. Though the water supply had almost run out, de Clieu shared his scanty ration with his precious plant. Miraculously, both survived, and the seedling was transplanted in the officer's garden. Kept under armed guard, the tree flourished and grew to maturity, and de Clieu was rewarded with his first harvest in 1726.

Fifty years later, there were nearly nineteen million coffee trees in Martinique and de Clieu's dream was well on the way to fulfilment. From the two coffee-growing centres of Martinique and Dutch Guiana, cultivation radiated throughout the West Indies and Central and South America.

ESTABLISHING PLANTATIONS

Wherever the European colonists went, they took coffee with them, though the Catholic missionaries and religious communities undoubtedly played a key role in its migration too. With their natural interest in botany, monks were curious about the plant, and, as in the early days in the Yemen, coffee trees were often nurtured and studied in monastery gardens.

Initially, France was Europe's major supplier of coffee. The French took the plant from Martinique to the islands of Guadeloupe and Saint Domingue (now Haiti), and from 1730 onwards, cultivation spread rapidly throughout the French Antilles.

Meanwhile, coffee production had advanced into a large number of other countries. The Spanish took it to Puerto Rico and Cuba, and later to Colombia, Venezuela and westwards to the Philippines. From Dutch Guiana (now Surinam), cultivation spread to French Guiana, and from there in 1727 the Portuguese introduced it to Brazil, destined later to become the world's largest producer. In 1730, the British introduced coffee to Jamaica where the highly prized Blue Mountain beans are still produced.

By around 1830, the Dutch colonies of Java and Sumatra were the chief suppliers of coffee to Europe. Financed by the British, India and Ceylon tried to compete, but could not budge the Dutch. In the mid 1800s, a coffee blight called *Hemileia vastatrix* swept through the whole of Asia and wiped out the supply, giving Brazil a long-awaited opportunity. Within a few years Brazil had become the world's leading coffee supplier, a position it still holds today.

The Final Stage of the Journey

By the end of the 19th century, coffee had spread both east and west in a belt lying roughly equidistant between the Tropics of Cancer and Capricorn. The Dutch, French, English, Spanish and Portuguese had between them managed to establish thriving coffee plantations in all their territories which lay within the zone.

The final stage in coffee's journey took place in the early 1900s in German East Africa (now Kenya and Tanzania). German settlers planted coffee on the slopes of Mount Kenya and Kilimanjaro – ironically only a few hundred miles from coffee's original home in Ethiopia. Coffee had completed its nine-century circumnavigation of the world.

The effect of the slave trade

The Portuguese and Dutch imported massive numbers of African slaves to Brazil and Java. Coffee production more than doubled, while it fell in other areas.

in £m	1832	1849
Brazil	80.6	180.0
Java	40.3	100.0
French and Dutch West Indies	17.9	6.0
Venezuela	13.4	20.0

From *Coffee As It Is, and As It Ought To Be.* P.L. Simmonds, 1850

Above: Workers on a South American coffee plantation. 19th-century engraving by F. M. Reynolds.

PLANTATIONS IN BRAZIL

In the early 1700s, Brazil had yet to start growing coffee. In 1727, when invited to help settle a boundary dispute between Dutch and French Guiana, the Brazilians were glad to mediate since it gave them a potential opportunity to procure some of Guiana's closely-guarded coffee seedlings.

The story goes – and there are several versions – that Francisco de Mallo Palheta, a dashing army captain and well-known womanizer, was despatched to Guiana to arbitrate. Once there, he proceeded to ingratiate himself both with the Governor and his wife, with whom he had a brief affair. The boundary dispute resolved, the time came for Palheta to leave. The Governor's wife presented him with a bouquet as a token of thanks for his services, both political and amorous. Hidden among the flowers were cuttings of a coffee plant. Here the versions vary; some say he was openly presented with a thousand seeds and five living plants. Whatever the truth, Palheta returned to Brazil with the cuttings, seeds or plants.

Cultivation started on a small scale, mainly for local consumption. However, the plant adapted itself so well to the local topography, soil and climate that cultivation grew to an intensive scale. By 1765 the first shipments of beans had been exported to Lisbon.

Pioneer Planters

The first planters had to hack away areas of mosquito-infested jungle in sweltering heat. They not only had to plant the coffee seedlings, but, more importantly, food for themselves. Next, they had to get a roof over the heads of their family, slaves, machinery and harvests. Since the forest encroached on all sides, they were completely isolated, so the early *fazendas*, or estates, were the nuclei of human life in the rainforest.

As the taste for coffee spread among Europe's and America's expanding urban populations, the planters grew more wealthy, the *fazendas* larger and life became more comfortable. It was a time of unprecedented prosperity.

As Stanley Stein points out in *Vassouras, a Brazilian Coffee County, 1850–1900*, coffee cultivation in Brazil had a colossal impact on economic and social life. From an economic view, coffee cultivation created an unhealthy dependence on a staple crop subject to the fluctuations of a world market. The crop was also subject to the vagaries of the weather. Cold winds blowing in from the Andes brought severe frosts, and on several occasions the plantations were nearly destroyed.

Socially, coffee cultivation sired a new aristocracy – the coffee barons with their massive *fazendas* and autocratic lifestyle. It also resulted in an unprecedented influx of African slaves, which not only stratified society but also changed forever the ethnic makeup of central Brazil. However, it can be argued that the ultimate cause of these devastating changes was not the cultivation of the plant itself but the insatiable demand from Europe for the drink.

Coffee and slavery

The *haciendas* and *fazendas* – the massive estates of the Spanish and Portuguese colonies – grew on the back of slave labour. Between 1840 and 1850, more than 370,000 African slaves were openly smuggled into Brazil. Slavery was abolished in Spanish-speaking colonies by the 1850s, though it continued through to 1888 in Brazil.

Above: Coffee bean collection, painted by Francisco Miranda, 1750-1816.

THE COFFEE TRADE

Despite the Arab monopoly, coffee beans began to infiltrate Britain and mainland Europe from very early on via the botanists' pockets. By the early 17th century, coffee beans could be found in the cabinets of interested botanists throughout the continent. Small sacks of beans were also brought in by private individuals already familiar with the drink – merchants, diplomats, business people and travel writers, for example, but it was not long before coffee attracted the attention of merchants.

The First Shipments

Since Venetian merchants had long sailed the waters of the East, and were doing much business in Constantinople, it is widely accepted that they were the first to import coffee to Europe. The precise date is not known, but the first shipment of beans must have arrived in Venice around the early 1600s.

Hot on the heels of the Venetians, the Dutch started shipping coffee; trade records mention coffee beans from Mocha as early as 1616, though it seems they confined shipments to their colonies in Asia and the New World, since it was not until 1661 that the Netherlands received its first substantial consignment of beans. Coffee was also introduced very early on into Austria and Hungary, making an overland entrance via the northern extremities of the Turkish Ottoman Empire.

Following the shipping routes, coffee reached all the major European ports – Marseilles, Hamburg, Amsterdam and London – by around the middle of the 17th century, though it was some time before regular lines of supply were firmly established. It arrived in the 1660s in North America, probably via Dutch colonists in New Amsterdam (renamed New York after the British took control in 1664). A century later, coffee made the reverse journey across the Atlantic when Brazil started shipping it to Lisbon.

Above: In some cases, merchants instructed workers to throw the coffee beans into the sea to avoid the lowering of coffee prices. Illustration, Brazil, 1932.

The Coffee Trade Evolves

In its journey from plantation to cup, coffee inevitably passed through the hands of the brokers and merchants. Coffee-trading attracted speculators and entrepreneurs right from the start, though it was a precarious business subject to cycles of boom and bust.

In the early days, supplies were often erratic due to adverse weather conditions which affected both the crop itself and the means of transport. The arrival of the next shipment was always uncertain, and when it did arrive, the merchants were forced to pay whatever the ship masters demanded. The artificial price manipulation combined with erratic supply, forced coffee into the status of a luxury.

By post-Industrial Revolution days, shipping and the machinery associated with coffee grew more sophisticated.

Telecommunications came into being, enabling crop forecasts to be sent by cable. As supply and distribution systems developed, more and more traders entered the market. Many of them formed syndicates which attempted to corner sections of the market and force prices up, and from the 1860s onwards, organized Coffee Exchanges were set up in major coffee-trading centres such as New York and Le Havre.

Coffee Auctions

Shapiro tells us in *The Story of Coffee*, that bags of coffee were sold in London at what were known as candle auctions. Bids were accepted for lots as long as a lighted candle set up in front of the auctioneer continued to flicker. Once the candle went out, the lot went to the last bidder. In the United States, before the New York Coffee and Sugar Exchange was set up, coffee merchants would roam the streets in particular areas, taking bids and then selling the bags to the highest bidder at the end of the day.

Coffee merchants could be formidable figures. A young American, entering the trade, described them thus: "I ask you to picture those silk-hatted, frock-coated, bewhiskered and highly dignified gentlemen, whom one approached with awe and trembling knees, (they) were the importers and jobbers of coffee who carried large and assorted stocks of East Indian, Central and South American growths for sale to the wholesale grocers, and to the large traders".

Processing the Product

In 17th-century Europe and North America, coffee beans were at first sold unroasted and unground. American consumers bought green coffee by the bag or half bag, and roasted it on a pie plate in the oven, or in a frying pan over the fire. The British appeared to be fussier; one former planter stated that "the care of roasting the beans and grinding is thought by many masters of families too delicate and important a task to be entrusted... to any servant".

The invention of the coffee mill in 1687 contributed to the beverage's widespread use, but brought with it the problem of adulteration. Because of the colour and powerful aroma of ground coffee, it was easy for unscrupulous vendors to "take it down". Among the substances used were roasted rye, grated burnt crusts, roasted acorns, sand, clay and sawdust. Even worse were the East London "liver-bakers". The same British planter complained: "They take the livers of oxen and horses, bake them and grind them into a powder, which they sell to the low-priced coffee-shopkeepers. Horse's liver coffee bears highest price". He pointed out that it could be identified by allowing coffee to cool. A thick skin then formed on the top.

Above: Roasting imported coffee beans in an English factory, black and white engraving, 1870.

COFFEE AS MEDICINE

Once in Europe, coffee beans moved first from individual botanists' cabinets to the apothecaries' shops, where they became a vital part of the pharmacopoeia used by 17th-century doctors, chemists, herbalists and even midwives.

Coffee was looked on as a medicine not only because of its high price, but perhaps because of its strong taste – a "black, nasty Hel-burnt Liquor" as one person wrote. Hahnemann, founder of homeopathy, stated firmly: "Coffee is strictly a medicinal substance...No one has failed to be disgusted for the first time he smoked tobacco. No healthy palate ever found strong coffee, without sugar, palatable on the first trial".

The doctrine of bodily humours taught by the herbalist Galen (AD 131-200) continued to dominate European as much as Islamic medicine. The theory stated that the four humours – yellow bile, black bile, phlegm and blood – were reflected in a person's physical makeup. If the humours became too unbalanced, illness would result. In turn, each humour was linked to two physical qualities – heat, cold, moistness or dryness. Food, drink and medicines were thought to possess these qualities, and were administered to correct imbalances.

As is generally the case with coffee, there was disagreement. Some physicians claimed its qualities were cold and dry, others that they were hot and dry. Still others argued that the qualities of the coffee husks were different from those of the bean. This confusion is evident when we see the variety of ailments for which coffee was prescribed.

A somewhat tongue-in-cheek booklet, written in 1663, gives examples of "Persons, and Places of their Abode, who were cured (by coffee) when left off by the Physitians". These included "Benjamin Bad-cock (who) drank Coffee in Layden, and his Wife... remained barren four years, after which he left drinking Coffee, and in three quarters of a Year she had a goodly chopping Boy", and "Anne Marine of Rotterdam...troubled with a Corn on her upper Lip, the more it was cut, the bigger it grew, so that she at last drank Coffee, and the Corn dropt into the Dish as she held it to her Mouth".

On a more serious note, a French doctor, having collaborated with colleagues, asserted that among its many therapeutic effects coffee counteracted drunkenness and nausea, promoted the flow of urine and relieved dropsy, smallpox and gout. The French Larousse encyclopedia stated that coffee was particularly indicated for all men of letters, soldiers, sailors and workers who were staying in hot surroundings, and, strangely, for the inhabitants of countries where cretinism was rife.

Coffee and creativity

Still more enthusiastically, Balzac in his *Treatise on Modern Stimulants* writes: "The coffee falls into your stomach, and straightaway there is a general commotion. Ideas begin to move like the battalions of the Grand Army on the battlefield when the battle takes place. Things remembered arrive at full gallop, ensign to the wind."

Above: Honore de Balzac, French author. Painting by L. Boulanger, 1809-1867.

Coffee as a Stimulant

Certain after-effects of caffeine did not go unnoticed. One respected medical man wrote: "When I awake I have the intelligence and activity of an oyster. Immediately after our coffee, the stores of memory leap, so to speak, to our tongues; and talkativeness, haste, and the letting slip something we should not have mentioned, are often the consequence. Moderation and prudence are wholly wanting".

More positively, a Dr Thornton asserted: "A cup of Coffee strengthens and exhilarates our mental and bodily faculties; and nothing can be more refreshing either to the studious or the laborious".

Other eminent writers also wrote appreciatively of coffee's power to stimulate creativity. Balzac, Zola, Baudelaire, Victor Hugo, Molière and Voltaire were among its most ardent imbibers. Both Voltaire and Molière are quoted as replying to the remark that coffee was a slow poison: "I have drunk it upwards of fifty years, and unless it were very slow indeed, I would certainly have been dead long ago".

The effects of over-indulgence gave rise to considerable medical comment. Hahnemann refers to the "coffee disease" which results in "an unpleasant feeling of existence, a lower degree of vitality, a kind of paralysis". Other negative effects were reputedly melancholia, piles, headaches and a reduced libido.

There was concern, too, about the harmful effect coffee might have on children and nursing mothers. It was thought to be a major cause of tooth decay and rickets in children, and "a rattling of the breast" in nursing mothers.

Amongst coffee's opponents was Sinibaldi, an eminent Italian medical writer. He stated: "The commerce which we have opened with Asia and the new world, in addition to the smallpox and other diseases, has brought a new drink, which has contributed most shockingly to the destruction of our constitutions...it produces debility, alters gastric juice, disorders digestion, and often produces convulsions, palsy of the limbs and vertigo."

Above: The stimulating and invigorating properties of coffee are shown in a positive light in this advertisement from the Pan-American coffee bureau in the 1950s.

The medical debate was to continue for many years, as doctors, pursuing new avenues of insight, argued the pros and cons of coffee, claiming it to be alternatively therapeutic and detrimental to the body and mind. This debate still continues today.

Coffee and healthy skin

As a country where green tea has been the national beverage for nearly 1,000 years, Japan was understandably slow to take up coffee drinking. It was not introduced until the 19th century and even today is still a relatively undeveloped market.

Apart from drinking coffee, however, Japan is home to the slightly unusual practice of lying in the roasted coffee beans. It is thought that the coffee contains elements beneficial to healthy skin.

Right: Absorbing coffee's nutrients via the skin.

COFFEE CONSUMPTION DEVELOPS

Having escaped the confines of medicine and developed into a social activity, coffee-drinking spread through Europe during the first half of the 17th century. However, it was not until about 1650 onwards that we begin to hear more of when, how and by whom coffee was sold and drunk.

The people largely responsible for its growth were not necessarily the merchants, the aristocracy or well-healed professional travellers. As Shapiro states in *The Story of Coffee,* it was the "countless unnamed peddlers who spread through the streets of Europe carrying on their backs the gleaming tools of their trade – coffeepots, trays, cups, spoons and sugar. These men bore the steaming, potent gospel of coffee beyond the boundaries of the East to the as yet uninitiated West".

At first, however, the new beverage fell under harsh criticism from the Catholic church. Fanatical priests claimed – with somewhat hazy logic – that if Muslims were forbidden wine, which was sanctified by Christ, then coffee must be a substitute invented by the devil. Pope Clement VIII in the 16th century eventually brought the dispute to an end by sampling coffee for himself and declaring it a truly Christian beverage. Once word of papal approval became known, coffee-drinking flourished freely throughout Europe.

Above: Coffee vendor, Paris. Illustration by M. Engelbrecht, c. 1735.

Social Change and the Birth of the Coffee House

The reasons for coffee's swift and almost universal popularity were more complex than papal approval or mere availability. In *Drugs and Narcotics in History*, Porter and Teich suggest that the timing was also important. The period between the 17th and 19th centuries was one of profound social, cultural and intellectual change. Coffee was simply a timely adjunct; people took to it because they were ready for it.

Firstly, there was an urge to establish some sort of private life outside the constraints of the family, and new gathering places were therefore needed. For the aristocracy the cultural life of the courts was gradually declining and this created another need for a new type of venue.

Secondly, the period was a time of progressive ideas – the age of Enlightenment in France, and later, the rise of the libertarian Risorgimento movement in Italy. (In hindsight, for such a time of enlightenment, the huge rise in slave labour needed to work on the coffee plantations in Brazil and the Dutch East Indies, is an uncomfortable parallel development.) However, public meetings, harangues, resolutions and "the rest of the machinery of agitation" were not part of the culture. Coffee houses became the chief outlet through which public opinion could vent itself.

Thirdly, developing alongside these changes was a growing criticism of the unwelcome effects of wine and beer. Coffee was obviously the perfect alternative since it provided a means of socializing without fear of intoxication.

In Europe, as in Turkey, the coffee house attracted clientele from all walks of life; professional and political mingled with commercial, creative and commoner. New forms of social interaction developed. Merchants

Above: "Blowing a cloud at Offley's", Interior of Offley's coffee house, c. 1820, scene of much animated discussion.

seeking an alternative to the ale-house needed a place where they could transact their business, as did the emerging financial and insurance communities. The coffee houses were also the type of place where artists and writers working in isolation could make contact with each other and the world.

When the coffee houses first opened, communication and information services – newspapers, telephones, directories and street maps, for example – were non-existent. The owner or head waiter of a coffee house therefore fulfilled yet another need by taking on the multifarious role of social arbiter, diplomat, matchmaker and message-taker. As George Mikes says in *Coffee Houses of Europe*: "(the head waiter) shared your secrets and knew them if you didn't want to share them, lent you money and lied for you when pursued by persistent creditor, kept letters for you especially those not meant for wife's eyes. Not everyone knew your private address but everyone knew which coffee house you went to".

Taxation and Duty

Aware of the potential income from mass consumption, revenue-hungry governments tried to stimulate demand by abandoning their former policy of prohibition and concentrating on taxation instead.

The English government in 1663 was quick to license coffee houses and levy an excise duty on coffee sold. Even so, compared to alcohol, coffee remained a bargain. The English coffee houses enticed huge numbers of working men from the ale-houses – a trend deemed beneficial by both wives, in the early days at least, and Government, though not by the breweries. Realizing that further taxation would reverse the trend, the Government progressively reduced the duty – each reduction marked by huge increase in consumption.

In complete contrast, Frederick the Great of Prussia, in support of the barley growers and breweries, banned the working classes from drinking coffee and insisted they revert to drinking beer.

Coffee consumption

The figures demonstrate the rapid growth of coffee consumption in the 19th century particularly in the United States where no import duty was charged.

weight in millions of pounds	1832	1849
Holland and Netherlands	90.7	125.0
Germany and North of Europe	71.7	100.0
France and South of Europe	78.4	95.0
Great Britain	23.5	40.0
United States and British North American Provinces	45.9	120.0 (US) and 15.0 (BNAP)

THE COFFEE CONSUMERS

Coffee is universally popular, but there are some countries where it seems much more than just a drink. How coffee is drunk, and by whom, is part of its continuing appeal and mystique.

ITALY

Italy was the first country in Europe to import coffee commercially. The first shipments arrived in Venice in the 1600s just after citrus fruits had been introduced from the East. Vendors roamed the streets selling beverages such as lemonade, orangeade, chocolate and herbal infusions. Once coffee was available in reasonable quantities, the vendors added it to their wares, though they were still referred to as *limonáji* (lemonade sellers) rather than *caffetiéri* (coffee sellers). Coffee was immediately accepted by the Italians and became a familiar and widely used beverage.

As coffee flourished as a drink, so did the coffee houses. One of the earliest on record, situated in Leghorn (Livorno), dates back to 1651. It was mentioned by an English traveller who was intrigued by the roasting of coffee beans. He surmised "that roasting was by chance or perhaps from a debauch'd palate, as some with us love the burnt parts of broil'd meat", which also indicates that the barbecue may have had its devotees from very early on.

By the end of the century, Venice boasted several coffee houses situated around the Piazza di San Marco. Florian's, said to be Europe's most celebrated coffee house, was opened in 1720. Venetians and the international elite flocked there to enjoy the gossip and the music from the orchestra playing on the terrace. It was patronized by famous artists and writers including Byron, Goethe and Rousseau. Perhaps because Florian's was the first coffee house to admit women, Casanova was a regular patron too.

In Padua, a former lemonade seller opened Pedrocchi's – one of the most beautiful and flamboyantly kitsch coffee houses ever to be seen. Caffè Greco in Rome, named after its Greek owner, was patronized by the international music set – Mendelssohn, Rosetti, Liszt and Toscanini were regular visitors.

Above: "Cafe Greco in Rome", painting by Ludwig Passini, 1832-1903.

Above: Drinking coffee on the steps of the Cafe Florian, early 19th century drawing.

Though not all the coffee houses were as elegant as Florian's – some were little more than dimly lit back rooms – they were a melting pot of intellectual, creative and political ideas. Throughout the 18th and early 19th centuries, coffee houses opened one after the other in most major cities. By the end of the century the *bottega del caffè* had become an indispensable part of life. They were the centre of information, conversation, entertainment, and even education, for all levels of society – professional, artisan, trades-people, ladies and gentlemen of the leisured classes, intellectuals and political activists.

Coffee and the Spanish

The 17th-century Spaniards were committed chocolate drinkers since it was their conquistadors who had 'discovered' the cocoa bean in Central America. It was not until as late as the 19th century that coffee house culture began to take hold. By the early 20th century, artists and writers were frequenting coffee houses in Barcelona, Granada and Madrid. Even so, for many years chocolate still remained the drink of the traditionalists.

FRANCE

Coffee was reputedly brought to France in 1644, but it was almost fifteen years later before the beverage became popular. Consumption was at first centred around Marseilles, where it was introduced by traders who had grown used to drinking it in the Middle East.

Meanwhile, in Paris, in 1669, the Turkish ambassador Suleiman Aga brought coffee to the court of Louis XIV. The most extravagant coffee parties were held in opulent castles hired especially for the purpose. Isaac D'Israeli gives a graphic description: "On bended knee, the black slaves of the Ambassador, arrayed in the most gorgeous costumes, served the choicest Mocha coffee in tiny cups of eggshell porcelain, hot, strong and fragrant, poured out into saucers of gold and silver, placed on embroidered silk doylies, fringed with gold bullion, to the grand dames, who fluttered their fans with many grimaces, bending their piquant faces – berouged, bepowdered and bepatched – over the new and steaming beverage."

Though many of the aristocracy were quick to adopt coffee, there were some who found it distasteful. The German wife of Louis XIV's brother compared it to the Archbishop of Paris's breath; Madame de Sévigné, after an initial flirtation, rejected it as violently as she had chocolate; another nobleman would use it only as an enema, though he remarked that it did the job very well.

The Rise of the Café

The first coffee house opened in 1672 but it was little more than a bar in which sales of cognac exceeded those of coffee. Coffee houses really came into their own in 1686 when an Italian, Francisco Procopio dei Coltelli, an ambitious and astute waiter, opened Procope's. Wisely marketing itself a lemonade shop, Procope's sumptuous decor and air of sophistication attracted a clientele keen to distance itself from the more loutish elements of the day. It was only when coffee began to outsell other beverages that the name *café* was given to the whole establishment.

Procope's quickly became a literary salon frequented by eminent poets, playrights, actors and musicians. Rousseau, Diderot and Voltaire, among others, drank excessive amounts of coffee there. Later, during the French Revolution, the young Napoleon Bonaparte was also a patron.

The opening of Procope's marked the beginning of serious coffee drinking in Paris. Other coffee houses soon opened and they were not short of customers. Aux Deux Magots was another favourite haunt of the literary set; Verlaine and Rimbaud were among its patrons. Artists and intellectuals flocked to the Café de Flore nearby. The Café de la Paix was a monument to ostentatious display, attracting clientele which included royalty and poets. It was a competitive business, just as it had been for Turkish proprietors a century earlier. The owners of the newer establishments had to be resourceful in attracting customers. Entertainment was laid on – poetry reading, plays, songs and dances – and eventually food was served too.

The objectors naturally started to make themselves heard. Feeling threatened, the wine makers, in a burst of patriotism, claimed that coffee was an enemy of France. They were joined by doctors, who up until then had shown neither misgivings nor enthusiasm about coffee. They argued that it was the fruit of a tree desired only by goats and animals, and that drinking it burned the blood, weakened

Above: French breakfast coffee, in its traditional large bowl, and croissant.

Above: Entertainment and coffee at the Café de la Paix, engraving from Parisian Life by David Carey, 1822.

the spleen and produced leanness, palsies, impotence, quiverings and distempers. Needless to say, their warnings fell mostly on deaf ears.

At home, the French were somewhat avant-garde in their coffee-drinking. They were probably unique in serving coffee not only in large bowls in which the breakfast baguette was dipped, but also *au lait* (with milk). They were the first to initiate the after-dinner coffee, which they served strong and black in tiny cups (*demi-tasse*), usually with a liqueur to aid digestion. Mrs Anne Roe, an English traveller and author, wrote around 1777: "Coffee is so much the fashion in France, especially in genteel houses, that one can scarcely finish their dinner before coffee is introduced, and they drink it scalding hot; all which conspire utterly to destroy the coats of the stomach".

Coffee and the French are beautifully summed up in this esoteric description by a 19th-century English journalist: "Coffee is to the Frenchman what tea is to the Englishman, beer to the German, *eau de vie* to the Russian, opium to the Turk, or chocolate to the Spaniard... The *garçon*, at your call for *demi-tasse*, has placed before you a snowy cup and saucer, three lumps of sugar, and a *petit verre*. He ventured the *petit verre*, inferring, from your ruddy English face, that you liked liqueur. Another *garçon* now appears; in his right hand is a huge silver pot, and in his left, another of the same material, uncovered: the former contains coffee – the latter, cream. You reject cream, and thereupon the *garçon* pours out the former until your cup – aye, and almost the saucer – actually overflows. There is hardly space for the three lumps, and yet you must contrive, somehow, to insert them...*Café noir*... pleases all the gustatory nerves, its savour ascends to rejoice the olfactory, and even your eye is delighted with those dark, transparent, and sparkling hues, through which your silver spoon perpetually shines. You pronounce French coffee the only coffee."

Above: Still an institution, the Café de la Paix as seen by night, 1938.

Impressions of coffee

"Black as the devil, hot as hell, pure as an angel, sweet as love." Prince Talleyrand (1754-1839), French diplomat and wit, on the ideal cup of coffee.

"The history of coffee houses, ere the invention of clubs, was that of manners, the morals and the politics of a people." Isaac D'Israeli.

"Strong coffee, and plenty, awakens me. It gives me warmth, an unusual force, a pain that is not without pleasure. I would rather suffer than be senseless." Napoleon Bonaparte, French emperor. *Painting, left, by Gérard von François, 1770-1837.*

AUSTRIA

Records show that the Viennese were drinking coffee at home in the mid-1660s, though the coffee houses themselves did not open until the 1680s. The Viennese predilection for coffee was undoubtedly inspired by the Ottoman Ambassador, who set up residence for several months, bringing with him a vast retinue of servants and, of course, coffee. Coffee was served to Viennese guests, who took to the strange new drink with enthusiasm – so much so that a formal complaint was lodged by the city treasurer about the amount of wood being used for the fires needed to prepare the brew. By the time the Ambassador came to leave, the Viennese were buying beans from a trading company in the Orient and brewing coffee for themselves.

About 20 years later, in 1683, Vienna was under siege by the Turks. A Polish immigrant, Franz Kolschitzky, having something of a Turkish appearance, bravely slipped through enemy lines to carry messages between a waiting Austrian relief army and the besieged Viennese. Thanks to his heroism, the Turks were defeated and they fled in confusion, leaving behind a variety of exotic equipment. Amongst the loot were sacks of green beans which Kolschitzky claimed for himself.

In recognition of his bravery, the city elders awarded Kolschitzky a house in which he is reputed to have opened the first of the city's many coffee houses. According to some versions of the tale he first started selling coffee beans door-to-door and then demanded the house; still other variations indicate that the honour of opening the first coffee house went to an Armenian. Whatever the truth, coffee had arrived in Vienna.

The city's coffee houses were an institution – not just a place but more a way of life. They served excellent coffee (a legendary twenty-eight different types) and provided newspapers and journals in abundance. Unique to the Viennese style were the wooden newspaper poles, marble-topped tables and bentwood chairs that later became the hallmark of coffee houses throughout Europe.

Above: Cafe Sperl, Vienna, 1910.

Viennese patrons – male, naturally – were as unique as the coffee houses. As one writer put it, they shared a *Weltanschauung* – a way of looking at the world by those who do not want to look at the world at all. Another wrote

Above: Karlsplatz – the café booth built by Otto Wagner during his Secessionist period in Vienna.

Right: "The coffee boiler" Viennese coffee house scene with chess players, a smoking Armenian, and a newspaper reader, c. 1840.

that a hatred of fresh air and exercise was an almost universal trait, and that they were no great lovers of home life either. Many dropped by their favourite coffee house several times a day – in the morning and afternoon for a quiet read of the papers, in the evening for games or intellectual discussion.

The most famous coffee houses, such as the Griensteidl, and the Sperl, had an erudite clientele of writers, political activists and artists. Many became a stronghold of extreme views – the Griensteidl, for example, was opposed to women's emancipation. But there were also other establishments for "textile merchants, dentists, horse dealers, politicians and pickpockets".

Chicory

Although the Dutch had access to some of the best coffee in the world, they were curiously partial to chicory – the roasted and ground root of the wild endive. An English coffee planter complained it had "no other virtue than that of colouring...the water in which it is boiled or infused". Since good quality coffee was cheap, a possible reason for its use was that it tamed the effect of caffeine. Chicory later became popular in northern France, Germany and Scandinavia.

Coffee houses continued to proliferate not just in Vienna, but all over the Austrian Habsburg dominions. Those in Prague, Krakow and Budapest were as popular as any in Vienna. However, Vienna remained the "mother of coffee houses". By 1840 there were over 80 in the city, and by the end of the century the total came to an unbelievable 600.

THE NETHERLANDS

As one of the major coffee-trading nations, it is hardly surprising that the Dutch were free of the usual conflict surrounding the use of coffee. Consumption began in the home at the turn of the 16th century. By the time the first coffee houses opened in the mid-1660s, there was "hardly a house of standing where coffee is not drunk every morning". Not only the middle and upper classes, but even their servants had acquired a taste for coffee.

The coffee houses had their own unique style. Though elaborately furnished, their dark panelled walls and gleaming copperware gave them a particularly cosy atmosphere. Many were located in the financial areas, where merchants and administrators gathered to conduct business.

In some Dutch cities the coffee houses were situated in beautiful gardens. Here, patrons could enjoy a coffee under the shade of a tree while looking out onto a magnificent view. The garden cafés were particularly popular in spring when the gardens were ablaze with fruit blossoms and tulips.

SCANDINAVIA

Although the Finns now hold the world record for coffee consumption, paradoxically, Scandinavia was slow to take it up. Introduced in the 1680s, probably by the Dutch, coffee aroused hostility from early on. By 1746, a royal edict had been issued against coffee- and tea-drinking. The following year, those who continued to indulge had to pay a hefty tax, or suffer the indignity of having their crockery confiscated. Coffee-drinking was completely prohibited in 1756, though the ban was eventually lifted and huge taxes imposed instead. Sporadic attempts at suppression continued until the 1820s when the government simply gave up.

Not much has been written about the early coffee houses, but it seems they lacked the opulence of their southern counterparts. In Oslo, they were Spartan single-room establishments, popular with students, serving not only coffee but food to go with it – bowls of porridge, for example.

Middle-class Finns did better at home, holding large and elaborate coffee parties at which guests would drink up to five cups.

Individual preferences

Frederick the Great of Prussia was said to take "only seven or eight cups in the morning, and a pot of coffee in the afternoon". Made with champagne, the coffee was occasionally flavoured with a spoonful of mustard.

Above: Drinking coffee in a German café, for female patrons only. Illustration 1880.

GERMANY

Coffee was introduced in 1675 to the court at Brandenburg in northern Germany by a Dutch physician. He was encouraged by Frederick William, a ruler known for his Calvinistic attitudes and temperate habits. Around the same time, the first coffee houses opened in Bremen, Hanover and Hamburg. Other cities rapidly followed suit and by the early 18th century, there were eight in Leipzig and ten or more in Berlin alone.

Coffee remained a drink of the aristocratic classes for some time. The middle and lower classes did not take to it until the early 18th century and it was even later before coffee was drunk at home.

Above: A coffee house for the European wealthy classes. Print by Von August Hermann Knopp, 1856.

Since the coffee houses were a male stronghold, middle-class women set up *Kaffeekränzschen* (coffee clubs) – referred to by their uneasy husbands as *Kaffeeklatch* (coffee gossip).

In 1777, in an ill-concealed attempt to protect the breweries and to stem the flow of income to foreign dealers, Frederick the Great, rather hypocritically, issued a manifesto, part of which reads: "It is disgusting to notice the increase in the quantity of coffee used by my subjects...My people must drink beer...Many battles have been fought and won by soldiers nourished on beer; and the King does not believe that coffee-drinking soldiers can be depended upon to endure hardship or to beat his enemies..."

Coffee was prohibited from the working classes on the grounds that it caused sterility, but this simply gave rise to a lively black market trade. The king finally outlawed the roasting of beans in private homes, even appointing "coffee sniffers" to track down illicit aromas to their source. This ludicrous state of affairs was short-lived, though, and by the beginning of the 19th century, coffee had been reinstated.

Germany now took the lead in European coffee consumption. Coffee was served at mealtimes, at the *Kaffeekränzschen*, and at family get-togethers on Sunday afternoons. Coffee houses nevertheless remained no-go areas to respectable women. However, in public parks there were pavilions and special tents (*Zelte*) to which families could bring their own pre-ground coffee, and the patron simply provided hot water. The turn of the century saw the rise of another family-style institution – the Café – which sold cakes as well as hot drinks. At first these *Konditorein* were used as an alternative to the coffee houses, but eventually they took over and the old-style coffee house gradually disappeared.

Coffee and music

Bach's *Coffee Cantata* (1734) was a satirical operetta which provides an insight into bourgeois attitudes. It tells of the efforts of a stern father to check his daughter's propensity for coffee-drinking by threatening to make her choose between a husband and coffee. Unperturbed, the daughter sings an aria beginning, "Ah, how sweet coffee tastes – lovelier than a thousand kisses, sweeter far than muscatel wine".

GREAT BRITAIN

The early history of coffee in Britain is substantially different from that of mainland Europe and North America. Firstly, the coffee house era in Britain was intense but short-lived. Secondly, coffee-drinking at home was not a common feature. The majority of the British public, it seems, found the intricacies of roasting, grinding and brewing beyond them; pouring boiling water on tea leaves was more to their liking. That said, Britain was one of the first countries to start importing coffee.

John Evelyn's diary provides the first reliable reference in 1637, when a Turkish refugee brought coffee to

Right: English coffee party relaxing after parade at military station in India, c. 1850.

Above: English coffee house, anonymous artist, 1668.

Oxford. The beverage became popular with students and dons, who sooner or later discovered that its stimulating properties were beneficial to prolonged or nocturnal study. The Oxford Coffee Club was eventually formed – later to become the Royal Society. Around 1650, a Jew named Jacob opened the first coffee house, called the Angel. Another soon appeared in London, in St Michael's Alley, Cornhill, set up by a Greek named Pasqua Rosée.

The new beverage had its opponents as well as advocates. A disgusted 17th-century commentator complained that it was "made of Old Crusts, and shreds of Leather burnt and beaten to a Powder"; another described it as "Syrup of soot and essence of old shoes". William Cobbett (1762–1835), politician, reformer and economist, was one of the few within his peer group to denounce coffee as "slops".

Coffee Houses Become Established

Nevertheless, by 1660 the London coffee houses were a deeply entrenched institution and were to remain so for the next fifty years. Even disasters such as the Great Plague (1665) and the Great Fire (1666) failed to stop their rapid spread across the city. Coffee houses became vital to the lives of anyone involved in business – meetings took place in them, deals were done, contracts signed and information exchanged. They were the birthplace of modern institutional monoliths such as The Stock Exchange, the Baltic and Lloyds Insurance. The coffee houses also provided a watering hole for artists, poets and writers, lawyers and politicians, philosophers and sages, who all had their favourite haunts. In his diary, Samuel Pepys (1633–1703) makes countless references to visits paid to this or that coffee house throughout London.

Some establishments charged an admission fee of one penny and, in return, visitors were offered the opportunity to debate current issues. These became known as "penny universities" and were centres of political and literary influence.

The coffee houses were also the strongholds of the gossipmongers, as this extract from a verbal attack on "Newsmongers' Hall" shows:

"There they can tell you what the Turk
Last Sunday had to dinner;
Who last did cut De Ruyter's corns,
Amongst his jovial crew...
You shall know there what fashions are,
How periwigs are curled;
And for a penny you shall hear
All novells in the world..."

Above: Rowdy behaviour in an English coffee house, c. late 17th century.

The Prohibition of Coffee Drinking

In 1675, fearing potential political unrest, Charles II issued a proclamation closing down the coffee houses. He already had the support of the women of London who, in a strongly worded and somewhat lewd petition, expressed their concern about the "Excessive Use of that Drying, Enfeebling LIQUOR". Claiming that it made men sexually inactive, the women, who were not allowed in the coffee houses, complained that their husbands spent idle time and money away from the home, as a result of which the "entire race was in danger of extinction". The men responded with equal vigour, stating that it was not the coffee that made them "less active in the Sports of Venus", but the "insufferable Din of your ever active Tongues".

Despite the women's support, prohibition of the coffee houses was short-lived. After vigorous petitioning by merchants and retailers, they were reopened on condition that the proprietors should prevent the "reading of all scandalous papers and books and libels; and hinder every person

Above: The Great Subscription Room at Brook's Club, St James's Street, London. Painting by Rowlandson and Pugin, 1809.

Above: An English outdoor coffee stall, c. 1860. Painting by C. Hunt, 1881.

from declaring, uttering or divulging all manner of false and scandalous reports against government or ministers". The absurdity of the stipulation was obvious, and it was soon withdrawn. Coffee houses continued to operate as usual and no more was heard of suppression.

Along with the rise in coffee's popularity, the temperance movement was starting to gain hold. Under its influence, many of the working class were starting to exchange the fireside of the ale house for that of the coffee house. Since coffee houses were now frequented by all levels of society, there was anxiety – in some circles at least – about improper or unwelcome behaviour. Printed regulations were hung in conspicuous places (*see box*).

The Decline of Coffee Drinking

By the early 18th century, no matter how conspicuous the regulations, the atmosphere of the coffee houses changed. Many of them started to serve alcohol and attracted a different sort of clientele. As a result, the intelligentsia moved on to form literary clubs, while "gentlemen" retreated to the safety of their own exclusive clubs in Pall Mall and St James's. Commercial and financial groups found it more practical and convenient to operate from offices or from new types of premises set up for professional associations. Another factor was the growth of circulating libraries in the latter half of the 18th century. Up until then, the coffee houses had been the sole supplier of newspapers and pamphlets, but now the libraries not only made available literature of all types, but also supplied English and foreign newspapers. Patrons who had once enjoyed a quiet read of the papers in the coffee house, now preferred to do it elsewhere.

Although the upper and middle classes had adopted coffee-drinking, tea was rapidly gaining in popularity. Other cafés emerged, selling other types of non-alcoholic drink, and food. By the end of the century, coffee was on the way out. Coffee's popularity would not soar again until the late 20th century.

Above: A group of people enjoying cups of coffee and tea from a late-night stall at Blackfriars, London, England, 1923.

The rules and orders of the coffee house

"First, gentry, tradesman, all are welcome thither,
And may without affront sit down together:
Pre-eminence of place none here should mind,
But take the next fit seat that he can find...
Let noise of loud disputes be quite forborne,
Nor maudlin lovers here in corners mourn,
But all be brisk, and talk, but not too much;
Of sacred things, let none presume to touch...
To keep the house more quiet and from blame,
We banish then cards, dice and every game..."

Below: The sumptuous interior of the Army and Navy Club House, London. Painting by R. K. Thomas.

NORTH AMERICA

Coffee was probably drunk from early on by the Dutch colonists in New Amsterdam (renamed New York in 1664), but the first reliable reference to its entry into North America occurs in 1668. Two years later, a license to sell coffee was issued to Dorothy Jones in Boston, and coffee houses soon opened throughout the eastern colonies.

In those hard-working days, coffee house management was looked on as women's work, though respectable women would not actually have been patrons. In complete contrast to European attitudes, the concept of whiling away idle hours in the coffee house was anathema. The coffee houses themselves lacked the clubby atmosphere of their European counterparts – the majority were closer to taverns which offered rooms to travelling workers and soldiers, and they attracted a correspondingly rowdy clientele. One of the more respectable was Boston's celebrated Green Dragon, headquarters of Revolution-plotting colonists, and in that sense did not differ greatly from coffee houses the world over.

The Boston Tea Party

Symbol of protest at the British tax on tea, the Boston Tea Party (1773), marked the acceptance of coffee as America's national beverage. Thereafter, coffee houses continued to spring up in major cities, some playing a vital role in the shaping of American history. Merchants Coffee House in New York was the scene of endless political discussion, declarations and strategic planning. Its famous rival, the Tontine, jointly owned by over 150 New York businessmen, served as a Stock Exchange, as well as occasional banqueting rooms and a record office for the arrival and departure of ships.

Like their English counterparts, habitués of the American coffee house eventually took their custom elsewhere as other social institutions evolved: business associations, gentlemen's clubs, banks and stock exchanges. The coffee house itself started to merge with taverns, hotels and restaurants.

Though the coffee house failed to maintain a stronghold, coffee itself became increasingly popular. The influx of European immigrants undoubtedly helped. The annexation of territories such as Florida and the French-speaking regions along the Mississippi, further expanded the market.

Coffee kept the pioneering spirit going – when the covered wagons set out for the west, coffee went too. It was even drunk by Native Americans, and legend has it that land was swopped for tools, rifles and bags of Java beans.

For the soldiers fighting the Mexican War and the Civil War, coffee was an essential part of their rations. They liked their coffee "hot, black and strong enough to walk by itself". It was so highly prized that the soldiers went to amazing lengths to make sure it was shared out equally. Identical piles of coffee were apparently spread out on a mat and the sergeant, with his back turned on the soldiers, would call out names at random.

By the mid-19th century coffee was firmly embedded in the lives of Americans. They were consuming a staggering 8½ pounds of coffee per head every year, compared to a European intake of 1½ pounds. Coffee was drunk in town and country, by all, regardless of social standing. Coffee had become the national beverage.

Above: Colonials dressed as Indians throw British tea into Boston Harbour, heralding a rise in coffee drinking lithograph, 1846.

COFFEE SOCIETY TODAY

By the 1900s, coffee was still the beverage of choice in Europe and coffee house culture was firmly entrenched. Intellectuals and artists frequented the cafés in large numbers, particularly in Germany and Eastern Europe.

Coffee Drinking in Europe

In Germany, Berlin, for example, was rapidly becoming an international metropolis. Coffee houses such as the *Nollendortplatz* were regular meeting places for droves of enthusiastic young Germans, Scandinavians, Russian and Jewish émigrés who flocked there to read their plays and poems out loud. The scene attracted more and more people who simply wanted to be part of what was going on – including "young girls who style themselves as sculptresses and art experts", as one scathing male author wrote.

The coffee house scene in Vienna was equally cosmopolitan. By 1910, the city was home to countless immigrants from neighbouring Danube countries and beyond. With the exception of Paris, few European cities formed the cultural focal point for such a wide area. The coffee houses were allowed to stay open for as long as they had customers. For writers or students living in cramped and noisy lodgings, the coffee house became a second home. For the price of a cup of coffee, they could sit and read or write all day in comfort and warmth. There was no shortage of reading matter. Even in the 1900s, a licence was needed to sell newspapers in the street, so they were not so easy to come by. The coffee house, however, had most newspapers and magazines delivered directly, and thus provided a service similar to the modern public library reading room.

Budapest and Prague also boasted countless coffee houses which, in one way or another, were key to the development and growth of important artistic and literary movements. In Budapest, the Café Vigadó – though some say it was the New York – was the meeting place for the editorial board of a now-famous magazine *Nyugat* (West); Café Gresham was the haunt of a famous group of artists, dealers and experts, known in art history as the Gresham Circle. The reading of the first draft of Kafka's *Metamorphoses* took place in a back room of the Café Central in Prague.

Changes to coffee houses Though they fulfilled a vital social and cultural function, the economics of city life made it impossible for the coffee houses to continue in this way. Rising rents are not paid by allowing a person to "occupy a whole table by himself, stay there for hours for the price of a cup of coffee, insist on getting glasses of water and all the newspapers and magazines of Europe". Many of these delightful places became café-restaurants where the unique atmosphere became a thing of the past. In those that remain, the price of a cup of coffee reflects economic reality.

Above: A coffee house between the two World Wars.

Coffee in Britain

By the 1900s, the British taste for coffee had all but disappeared and tea-drinking had taken its place. Encouraged by the government, the British East India Company was importing more and more tea from Asia, and as a result, tea had become fashionable among all levels of society.

There was something of a revival of coffee house culture with the advent of grand establishments such as the Café Royal in London. Run by French proprietors, the Café Royal attracted a sophisticated clique of artists, poets and writers, including Oscar Wilde and Aubrey Beardsley, but it was a mockery of café life in Paris. People were thrown out for not being smartly dressed, and the "art" promoted was "homogenized for Mayfair drawing rooms".

With these magnificent cafés came the phenomenon of "café society" with its overtones of glamour and wealth. As American comedian Bob Hope said: "Café society is where they have mink for breakfast".

In complete contrast, coffee – if it can be called that – was also sold in dreary railway refreshment rooms and "cafés", along with sandwiches curling at the edges and ageing, stale cakes.

The Festival of Britain, in 1951, marked the end of post-war parsimony, and the start of a celebration of the bright new world of contemporary British culture. In keeping with the spirit of the times, The Coffee House opened near London's Trafalgar Square with the aim of providing not only a meeting place where coffee and light meals could be had in pleasant surroundings, but also lending wall-space to up-and-coming young artists. The Coffee House was soon followed by another establishment in nearby Haymarket. This was a gleaming shrine to contemporary design, notable for its striking ceiling-high edifice of coloured glass panels over which trickled a stream of water. Though both establishments in their intent and purpose attempted to replicate the early coffee houses, they differed wildly from their prototypes in terms of atmosphere and decor.

Above: Though the inspiration behind the revival of coffee drinking in Britain was the traditional Parisian pavement café, below, most of the new coffee bars, such as this one in Coventry Street, London, above, soon developed their own particular style.

Above: The 1950s in Britain saw the rise of coffee bars open to men and women.

Gone was the warm fug of wood-panelled rooms; the modern coffee house was a "shining thing of chromium and plated glass; brilliant colour and contemporary design". This was to set the style for the years to come.

The coffee bar The end of the 1950s saw the emergence of the coffee bar, with its hissing espresso machine and youthful clientele. The first to open in London's Soho included The Moka Bar, Act One Scene One, The Two I's, Heaven and Hell and the Macabre – the latter painted entirely in black with coffins as tables. The names of these places went down in history for people growing up in the early 1960s, for they were the birthplace of the music industry as we know it today. Music singers and groups such as Lonnie Donegan played live, and pop singer Tommy Steele began his show business career in The Two I's. Juke boxes were installed playing the latest hits. Just like their 17th-century counterparts, these establishments provoked the same vociferous debate.

It was the era of the teenager and teenage gangs, and there were invariably some caffeine-induced disturbances. While reviled by some critics, the music played was looked on by others as an "emotional stabilizer". A rather patronizing article in a contemporary catering magazine stated: "Juke boxes have proven their worth by keeping young people off the streets and out of the pubs, drinking coffee and soft drinks instead of spirits. Most coffee bars have found the younger customers well behaved...more often than not they are content with talking, listening, humming or tapping their fingers...rather than getting up and 'jiving' about."

Coffee bars spread rapidly to the provinces. By 1960 there were over 2,000 of them, and at least 200 in London's West End. They were not only popular with teenagers, but also with patrons wanting light refreshment while shopping, or before and after the theatre, and, unlike their 17th-century predecessors, they were popular with most women.

Despite their lively atmosphere, the coffee bars of the 1950s and 60s gradually faded from view. Again, many became restaurants and others started selling alcohol. Eventually they had also to compete with the wine bars of the 1970s.

The 90s revival The 1990s saw something of a coffee house revival, though. The ubiquitous spread of the Internet brought with it the cybercafé, equipped with computers and coffee, where those so inclined may sit and surf the web. These places fulfil a need by providing a meeting place for like-minded souls and for those who might otherwise spend their days in isolation in front of a computer screen.

The 1990s also saw the development of speciality coffee shops, selling fine single-estate beans, often equal in quality to the finest of wines, and treated as seriously. Developing alongside came a rash of modern coffee houses – the antithesis of the 50s' coffee bar – styled on minimalist lines and selling a bewildering choice of coffee from around the world.

Coffee in 21st-century Britain The popularity of cafés specializing in coffee continued to rapidly increase at the beginning of this century. From a vast choice of small privately run cafés or one of the ever-expanding chains such as Costa and Starbucks, which can be found all over the world, coffee has never been so widely available. Cities and towns have an endless choice of coffee-drinking establishments for socializing and working. With the advent of free wi-fi, luring in customers of all ages, both work and screen-based leisure activities can be enjoyed with a cup of your favourite beverage.

The choice of coffee on the menu is seemingly endless too – gone are the simple black or white days – type, size and flavour, as well as an array of options of milk (or not) all need to be considered before making a choice.

Above: Breakfast USA-style – coffee and a fruit juice while reading the paper at a roadside coffee stall, c. 1949.

Coffee Drinking in the United States

The habits of coffee drinkers in America developed quite differently from those in Europe and Britain, and the tastes and coffee drinking establishments often differed, too. For Americans travelling abroad in the late 19th and early 20th centuries, European coffee simply did not measure up to their home-brewed coffee. In *A Tramp Abroad*, Mark Twain declares: "You can get what the European hotel keeper thinks is coffee, but it resembles the real thing as hypocrisy resembles holiness. It is a feeble, characterless, uninspiring sort of stuff, and almost as undrinkable as if it had been made in an American hotel."

Conversely, Europeans travelling in North America bemoaned the lack of congenial coffee houses in which to while away the hours.

By the early 20th century, coffee imports to the United States had tripled, and annual consumption was up to 5kg/11lb per head. Consumption peaked after World War II in 1946 at 9kg/20lb a head.

The 1920s saw a number of coffee houses established in New York's Greenwich Village, the artists' traditional quarter. They became known as "Java spots" and were popular with American writers, film-makers, singers and actors, and with the many new emigrant writers and artists.

During the 1960s these coffee houses had become popular with the young. The legendary musician Bob Dylan is said to have arrived from the West at the Café Wha in Greenwich Village, and asked the manager if he could sing a few songs.

Since these decades, coffee consumption in the US has dropped from 60–70 per cent of the population to around 50 per cent. This is partly due to increased competition from other beverages and partly due to increased health consciousness, particularly among women.

Coffee in the 1990s Though the majority of Americans do their coffee drinking at home, the 90s saw the rise in popularity of outlets such as Starbucks, selling speciality coffees. These include gourmet or single-estate coffees as well as various kinds of cappuccino, espressos and flavoured coffees. As in the United Kingdom, there is also an increasing number of cybercafés and drive-throughs, as well as coffee shops in upmarket fast-food outlets, convenience stores and bookshops.

Coffee in 21st-century America Coffee drinking as a social event or over a work meeting has become even more popular in the 21st century. The choice of coffee-based drinks is increasing, and coffee establishments are enjoyed by a wide range of ages. The introduction of free wi-fi has led to more people frequenting cafés for both work and pleasure.

THE ART OF BREWING COFFEE

From the moment coffee-drinking took hold, an enormous amount of ingenuity and effort went into perfecting the art of brewing. Not content with the simple act of pouring hot water over grounds and letting it sit, inventive minds in Europe and the United States managed to produce an astonishing variety of equipment – drips, filters, percolators and pressure machines, to name but a few. Edward Bramah states in his classic *Tea and Coffee*: "Between 1789 and 1921 the United States Patent Office alone recorded more than 800 devices for brewing coffee, not to mention 185 for grinders, 312 for roasters and 175 miscellaneous inventions with some bearing on coffee". Automatic vending machines were later added to the list.

The Cafetière

One of the earliest devices was the cafetière, which made its debut in France around 1685. Its use became widespread throughout the reign of Louis XV. It was no more than a simple jug (carafe) with a heating plate warmed by a spirit lamp below. It was superseded in about 1800 by the first percolator, invented by Jean Baptiste de Belloy, the Archbishop of Paris. In Belloy's cafetière, the ground coffee was held in a perforated container at the top of the pot and hot water was poured over it. The water passed through the small holes in the container and into the pot below.

Unusual Early Inventions

A few years later after the invention of the cafetière, a formidable American named Benjamin Thompson, also known as Count Rumford, moved to Britain. Dissatisfied with the standard of coffee served – in those days it was subjected to lengthy boiling – he set about inventing a coffee-maker and eventually came up with the ominous-sounding Rumford Percolator. It was a great success, instantly finding a place in the annals of coffee-making history.

Just before 1820, the coffee biggin – the predecessor of the filter – became popular in England. In this device, ground coffee was placed in a flannel or muslin bag suspended from the rim of an earthenware pot. Hot water was poured over but, because of the bag, the water remained in contact with the coffee for longer, producing a different type of brew.

Brewing Coffee on a Large Scale

Up until the Industrial Revolution, there was no real need to make coffee in large quantities. However, with the growth of workshops and factories, combined with long working hours, some form of liquid refreshment was needed. Rail travel was becoming established, and with it, the evolution

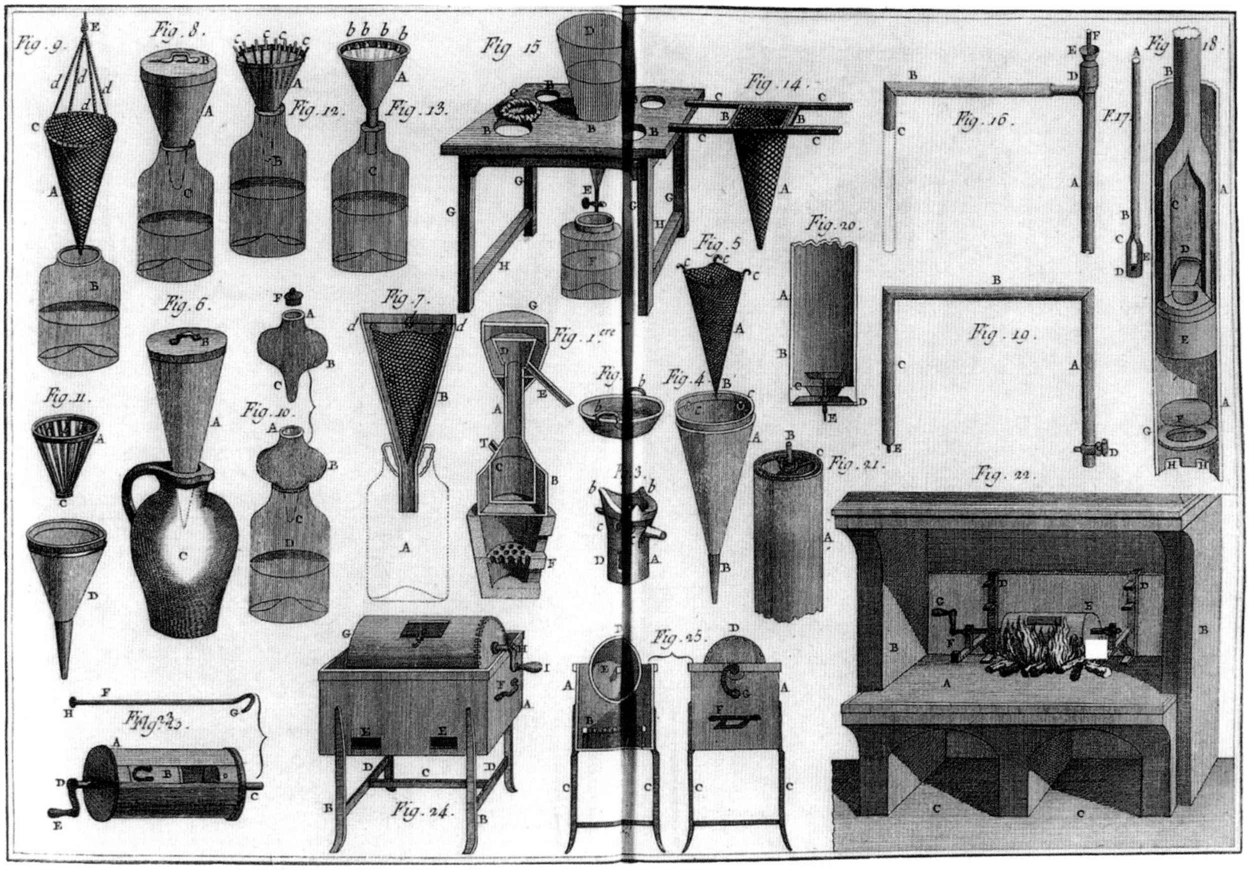

Above: Early inventions in the development of coffee brewing techniques, from the late 18th century.

Above: The Parisian Grill, London, with an Italian espresso machine, instrumental in the transformation of British drinking habits.

of the station buffet. At the same time, coffee houses, and later on hotels and restaurants, needed to find a way of producing a continuous supply of the beverage in a quick and efficient manner. We thus have the start of the development of catering equipment.

Around 1840, a Heath Robinson-like piece of apparatus appeared in Britain, invented by Robert Napier, a well-known Scottish marine engineer. The machine worked on a vacuum principle in which coffee was siphoned from a heated container through a filter and into a receiving vessel. Though not very efficient, it was to provide inspiration for later inventions capable of producing coffee in industrial quantities.

Coffee was made on a larger scale in France in a monstrous contraption which Isabella Beeton in *Modern Household Cookery* refers to as "Loysel's hydrostatic urn". Invented in 1843 by Edward Loysel de Santais, the device worked on the principle of hydrostatic pressure in which the build-up of steam forces hot water through a valve and then down through the coffee grounds. It was a sensation at the Paris Exposition of 1855, where it supposedly produced two thousand cups of coffee an hour – presumably in small cups.

The Cona

The Cona (vacuum pot) was a rather unique system that became widespread in the late 1930s. This consisted of two interconnecting toughened glass containers placed on top of each other and heated by a spirit lamp or gas or electric heater. The water in the lower container was forced into the top and drained through the coffee grounds back into the lower container.

The Espresso Machine

Perfecting Loysel's system from the previous century, the Italians went on to produce the revolutionary espresso machine which was to become so integral to Italian life. It was invented in 1948 by Achille Gaggia from Milan. These shiny hissing monsters were feared for their temperamental natures and billowing clouds of steam, but the dark, rich espresso coffee they produced was worth the time and trouble. The machines were also unique in producing a steaming hot foam of milk which transformed an espresso into a cappuccino – so called because its colour was reminiscent of the pale brown robes of the Capuchin monks. The classic cappuccino is traditionally a double espresso crowned with frothed milk and sometimes sprinkled with a powdering of rich, dark chocolate.

IN SEARCH OF THE IDEAL BREW

The majority of early coffee-drinkers in Europe made the beverage in much the same way as the Turks. Boiling water was poured on to finely ground coffee in the cup, resulting in a thick and potent brew. As coffee-brewing equipment proliferated, however, so did the nuances of national styles. Various individuals, too, had their own somewhat eccentric methods.

French Perfection

Coffee as perfected by the French was generally acknowledged among connoisseurs to be the best. Cast-iron coffee roasters and wooden coffee grinders were *de rigueur* in every household. Instead of boiling the beverage for hours, the French generally favoured the infusion method at first, before moving on to the drip-filter coffee pot and, later, the more sophisticated percolator.

Napoleon Bonaparte had his own way of brewing the perfect cup, and favoured the use of cold water. A connoisseur at the time wrote: "Put about two ounces of ground coffee for each person into a Percolator Coffee-Pot, pressing down with a ramrod, withdraw this and put on the tin covering for spreading the water over the coffee. Pour on the coffee clear cold water, and when a sufficient quantity has filtered through, plunge the jug containing the liquor into boiling water just before taking it to the table."

Some of the 19th-century coffee houses served specialities such as *mazagran*, an Algerian-style coffee extract diluted with cold water and served in a special stemmed glass. The practice of spiking coffee with alcohol also developed. William Ukers describes a unique iced coffee served in Normandy: "The man...takes half a cup of coffee, and fills the cup with Calvados, sweetened with sugar, and drinks it with seeming relish. Ice-cold coffee will almost sizzle when Calvados is poured into it. It tastes like a corkscrew, and one drink has the same effect as a crack on the head with a hammer".

Left: A classic combination – coffee with a dash of liqueur.

Above: Coffee and cream, which was a speciality of Austrian coffee houses.

Cream Lovers

Austrian coffee-drinkers favoured the French-style drip method or a pumping percolator device called the Vienna coffee machine. They were among the first to serve coffee with a cloud-like topping of whipped cream.

On entering an Austrian coffee house, it was an absurd request to simply ask for a coffee. As George Mikes points out, there was a rich choice to be had: "strong, weak, short, long, large, medium, small, in a glass, copper pot, light brown, with milk, whipped cream, espresso...Turkish – gold, nut gold, nut brown, Kapuziner (dark) or Franciscans (lighter), with rum, whisky, with egg".

Northern Europe and Scandinavia shared the Austrian weakness for cream, though the Danes preferred their coffee black. The Dutch were particularly civilized in their manner of serving – good quality coffee was served in a pot on a tray accompanied by a pitcher of cream, a glass of water and a tiny plate with three sugar cubes.

In Scandinavia, the more sophisticated European brewing methods and manner of serving did not catch on. Coffee was generally boiled or stewed in a kettle and then brought to the table in a pot, or even poured straight from the kettle. The Finns were reputed to use fish skins to settle coffee grounds and clarify the brew.

Unusual Brewing Methods

British coffee in the 19th century was not always universally recommended. Despairing of procuring a good cup of coffee in Britain, one former planter concluded: "coffee is spoiled in the burning, and sufficient care is not taken in preparing it for the table". He goes on to deplore the "antediluvian method" of frying coffee beans with butter, declaring: "In private families, where this beverage is taken once a day, a coffee-roaster must be provided...Those who have not the facilities for roasting the berries themselves, should employ one or other of the leading coffee-roasters...who may be safely entrusted with the...berry".

Slow and steady Dr William Gregory of Aberdeen, Scotland, swore by lengthy cold water percolation requiring a laboratory-like arrangement of glass cylinders, funnels and bottles. The process took three or four days which, as he himself acknowledged, was a little tedious, stating: "it is necessary, as soon as the first portion is exhausted, to see a second in operation. In this way a supply is always to hand".

American eccentricities The Americans were particularly esoteric in their coffee-brewing habits. Boiling was the preferred technique, for ten minutes or even up to several hours. Some early recipes advised adding the white, yolk and even the crushed shell of an egg to provide richness of colour when milk was added. If fresh eggs were in short supply, an uncooked square of codfish skin was sometimes recommended. These curious techniques were reputedly popular with many American coffee lovers as late as 1880.

"Why do they always put mud in the coffee on paddle steamers?" *William Thackeray, writer and traveller, 1850.*

Advice from a 19th-century epicure
"Beat up an egg – two for a large pot – and mix it well with the coffee, till you have formed it into a ball; fill the pot with cold water, allowing room enough to put in the ingredients; let it simmer very gently for an hour, but do not think of stirring it, on any account; just before it is required, put the pot on the fire and warm it well; but as you value the true aroma, take care that it does not boil. Pour it off gently, and you will have as pure and strong an extract of the Indian berry as you desire. Use white sugar-candy in powder in preference to sugar; cream, if attainable; if not, boiled milk." Benson Hill writing in *Epicure's Almanac.*

Left: Despite the basic simplicity of the coffee-brewing procedure, variations on coffee-brewing technique are endless and ingenious. Everyone has a particular method which works best for them, as this 19th-century method for brewing coffee with eggs demonstrates.

Gone was the warm fug of dark wood-panelled rooms; the modern coffee house was a "shining thing of chromium and plated glass; brilliant colour and contemporary design". This was to set the style for the years to come.

The coffee bar The end of the 1950s saw the emergence of the coffee bar, with its hissing espresso machine and youthful clientele. The first to open in London's Soho included The Moka Bar, Act One Scene One, The Two I's, Heaven and Hell and the Macabre – the latter painted entirely in black with coffins as tables. The names of these places went down in history for people growing up in the early 1960s, for they were the birthplace of the music industry as we know it today. Music singers and groups such as Lonnie Donegan played live, and pop singer Tommy Steele began his show business career in The Two I's. Juke boxes were installed playing the latest hits.

Just like their 17th-century counterparts, these establishments provoked the same vociferous debate. It was the era of the teenager and teenage gangs, and there were invariably some caffeine-induced disturbances. While reviled by some critics, the music played was looked on by others as an "emotional stabilizer". A rather patronizing article in a contemporary catering magazine stated: "Juke boxes have proven their worth by keeping young people off the streets and out of the pubs, drinking coffee and soft drinks instead of spirits. Most coffee bars have found the younger customers well behaved...more often than not they are content with talking, listening, humming or tapping their fingers...rather than getting up and 'jiving' about."

Coffee bars spread rapidly to the provinces. By 1960 there were over 2,000 of them, and at least 200 in London's West End. They were not only popular with teenagers, but also with patrons wanting light refreshment while shopping, or before and after the theatre, and, unlike their 17th-century predecessors, they were popular with most women. Despite their lively atmosphere, the coffee bars of the 1950s and 60s gradually faded from view. Many became restaurants and eventually they had also to compete with the wine bars of the 1970s.

Above: Advertisement for Paterson's "Camp Coffee", 1890.

Below: Just some of the many syrups, essences and flavourings, such as vanilla and cinnamon, that are available today for adding to coffee.

The 90s revival The 1990s saw something of a coffee house revival, though. The ubiquitous spread of the Internet brought with it the cybercafé, equipped with computers and coffee, where those so inclined may sit and surf the web. These places attract a particular clientele, but, just like their forebears, they fulfil a need by providing a meeting place for like-minded souls and for those who might otherwise spend their days in isolation in front of a computer screen.

Below: Coffee in a can from Japan.

Coffee Around the World

The tropical belt girding the earth is studded with coffee plantations. People cultivate coffee, or at least pick the fruit from untended trees, in more than seventy countries. In many of these countries, the fortune and well-being of the citizens hangs in the little red cherries of the fragile coffee tree. In a comprehensive country-by-country analysis, the different coffees produced around the world are discussed and described. This section also covers all the stages, from harvesting, processing, sorting, grading through to roasting, that are involved in transforming the unripe green bean into the aromatic roasted coffee bean appreciated the world over.

WHAT IS COFFEE?

Above: Clumps of green fruit form on the branches of the coffee tree.

The *coffea* plant is a genus of the *Rubiaceae* family. Classification of coffee plants is complicated, as there are many species, varieties and strains. The two species from which most commercial coffee comes are the *coffea arabica*, a very complex species with numerous varieties, and the *coffea canephora* species, usually called *robusta*, which is the name of its most productive variety. Other species of coffee trees include *coffea liberica*, discovered in Liberia in 1843, and *coffea dewevrei*, better known as excelsa, both of which have robusta-like qualities and are generally rather unsavoury, to say the least. Much effort has gone into the development of hybrid coffee trees, but the general consensus is that although the new strains add productivity, hardy resistance and perhaps longer life to coffee trees, the hybrid flavours are simply not as good as the old ones.

All coffee is grown in the wide tropical belt surrounding the Equator between the Tropics of Cancer and Capricorn, but depending on their species and variety, the plants vary enormously in appearance. The evergreen foliage may be practically any shade in a range from yellowy-green to deep green or even bronze, and the shiny leaves are corrugated, more so for robusta than arabica. Some plants remain small shrubs, while others would tower at 18 m/60 ft if they were not kept pruned for ease of harvesting.

Above: One of nature's most beautiful plants: the lush foliage of the coffee tree.

The Coffee Tree

A coffee plant, if not propagated from a cutting, begins life as a sprout issuing from a "parchment" bean which has been planted in shallow, sandy soil. As the sprout takes root, it pushes the bean out of the soil. In a few days' time the first two leaves emerge from the bean, now at the top of the tiny sprout. The old bean husk, hollow, soon falls to the ground. Next, the tiny seedling is transferred to its individual container in a nursery. For about a year, it is tended carefully and introduced to open weather as the nursery "roof" of logs or other protective covering, is gradually removed; at most, a few hours per day of direct sun is all the rather temperamental coffee tree will ever want. The small plant will then be set out in the field, possibly under the protection of a banana tree's broad leaves, particularly if the plantation is located on flat terrain nearer the Equator, where the sun's rays are more direct. If the tree is

Above: Lovely white coffee blossoms are similar to jasmine in looks and smell.

Above: Early morning watering at a coffee nursery in Indonesia.

planted on a mountain slope it may need no protection, as mountainsides receive direct sun for only part of a day, and coffee trees on high plateaux often enjoy the humidity and sun-screen resulting from high altitude cloud-cover.

For several years the tree will not produce any fruit, although it may require irrigation, pruning, weeding, spraying, fertilization and mulching. The latter two help if the soil is not the best for coffee, which thrives in the rich loam formed from volcanic ash, full of nitrogen, potash and phosphoric acid. Finally, when the tree is four to five years old, it bears its first crop. It quickly reaches its productive peak within a couple of years, but will yield fruit for a total of about twenty to twenty-five years, during which time it must be constantly tended.

All coffee trees are capable of bearing blossom, green fruit and ripe fruit simultaneously on the same branch, thus almost certainly necessitating harvesting by hand. There are one or two main harvests, and possibly several secondary harvests, as the growing seasons vary depending on the species and the location. A coffee plantation, therefore, is seldom without some blossoms. The flowers, which develop in clusters, are creamy-white and produce a fragrance reminiscent of jasmine. The flowers last only a few days; they are soon replaced by clusters of small green berries, which take several months to become ripe red cherries, ready for picking.

Above: Young coffee seedlings.

Coffee Species

Numerous factors affecting coffee cultivation depend very much on the species and vary considerably from country to country.

Arabica The oldest-known species of coffee tree, arabica is the high-grown species, cultivated on mountainous plateaux or volcanic slopes at optimum altitudes of 1000–2000m/3,280–6,561ft, where the annual rainfall ranges from 150–200cm/59–78in, and where mild days alternate with cool nights in a yearly average temperature range of about 15–24°C/59-75°F. Arabica trees flower after a rainy season, and then require up to nine months for the fruit to mature. In one year a typical arabica tree may produce less than 5kg/11lb of fruit, which processes down to about 1kg/2.2lb of actual coffee beans. Much of the arabica harvest around the world is "washed", or wet-processed, and the beans, which are generally larger, longer and flatter than those of robusta, and which contain less caffeine, produce a more delicate, acidic flavour.

Arabica coffee accounts for about 70 per cent of the world's coffee, but it is more difficult to grow, being more susceptible to disease, pests and frost, and is, not surprisingly, more expensive. Of the many varieties of arabica, the *typica* and *bourbon* are the most distinct and the best known, and from these have come other strains, such as *tico*, *Kent*, *mokka*, *Blue Mountain*, the Brazilian hybrid *mondo nuevo* (or *mundo novo*), *garnica*, and *mibirizi*, to name only a few. Cultivars from the mondo nuevo variety include *villa Sarchi*, *Geisha*, and *Villalobos*, and *catuai* is a hybrid of mondo nuevo and *caturra* (a large-beaned bourbon mutant). Catuai's fruit may be yellow (*amarelo*) or red (*vermelho*). *San Ramon* is another large-beaned typica mutant.

Below: The Nicaraguan version of Maragogype beans is the world's largest coffee bean.

Maragogype The most famous typica mutation was first discovered in the Maragogype region of Brazil's state of Bahia. *Maragogype* trees produce the world's largest coffee beans, sometimes called "elephant" beans (not to be confused with a certain bean defect, called an "elephant ear"). Maragogype beans are grown in several countries and are a sought-after coffee for their smooth flavour as well as attractive appearance. Unfortunately, because their yield is low, maragogype trees are expensive to maintain, and at the end of their productive lives, many of the trees are being replaced with more "normal" growths.

Canephora or robusta The canephora species of coffee is very different from the arabica; it is as robust in taste as it is in its resistance to diseases and pests; unfortunately, in this case strong is not best, and its flavour is not as desirable as that of arabica. Consequently, robusta accounts for less than 30 per cent of world coffee production, in spite of being cheaper in price.

Robusta's commercial use is primarily in blends, where its full body is appreciated, and in soluble, or instant coffee, where the processing reduces its more obtrusive flavour. Although robusta trees must be pollinated or grown from cuttings, they are far easier to grow, and when many arabica plantations were destroyed by rust disease in the second half of the 19th century, many estates were replanted with robusta trees. It is now grown throughout the tropical zone, but most of the world's robusta comes from West and Central Africa, South-east Asia, and Brazil, where it grows in altitudes from sea-level up to 700m/2,296ft.

Robusta can withstand heavier tropical rainfalls of 300cm/118in or more, although, as with all coffee, the trees should never stand in water. Conversely, the shallow roots of robusta enable it to live successfully where rainfall is unpredictable or even scanty. Similarly, it survives when equatorial temperatures soar, although it's happiest at an average temperature somewhere between 24–30°C/75–86°F.

Robusta trees flower rather irregularly, and take 10–11 months to go from blossom to mature cherry. The ripe cherries are generally picked by hand, except in Brazil where the flat terrain and vast spaces allow machine harvesting. Robusta is processed mostly by the "unwashed", or dry method, and the beans are smaller and more hump-backed than those of arabica; they are also often distinguished by small points at either end of the central "crack" on the bean. Robusta trees produce a slightly higher yield per hectare than do arabica trees. The most common varieties of robusta are *conilon* from Brazil, the *Java-Ineac, Nana, Kouilou* and *congensis*.

Other cultivars Hybridization has produced other cultivars which are propagated from cuttings rather than seeds, such as the more successful *arabusta*, developed by the French Coffee and Cocoa Institute in the 1960s and exported to many parts of the world from the Ivory Coast. The goal of most hybridization is to combine the best qualities of arabica, robusta, and perhaps of some of the better natural mutants, with the hope of possibly improving all. The natural *hibrido de Timor*, the dwarf *Ruiru Eleven* from Kenya, the rust-resistant *catimor*, and the *icatu* hybrids are names of some strains involved in, or resulting from, experiments in hybridization.

There are many reasons why the development of new coffee hybrids is the object of so much activity around the globe. In various cases, these efforts have pursued higher crop yields, larger beans or uniformity in bean size, better cup flavours, drought-resistant trees, adaptability to specific soil, and variants in caffeine content, to name but a few sought-after results. Almost no factors, however, present a greater challenge to coffee researchers than the two biggest enemies of the coffee plant: insects and diseases.

Above: A Javanese woman searches for the ripe fruit among the coffee tree leaves.

PESTS AND PROBLEMS

There are countless pests and diseases that regularly wreak great damage on coffee crops every year around the world. Perhaps one of the most surprising things about the fact that coffee production is the second largest in the world after oil, is that it is an industry subject to such a great number of natural disasters, in the form of pests, diseases and weather patterns.

Above: It may look harmless, but the grasshopper is a prey on the coffee tree.

Pests

It has been estimated that there are at least 850 species of insects that regularly book tables at their favourite coffee plantations. There are those who enjoy a salad of tender green leaves, such as various leaf-miners; leaf-cutting ants; leaf-skeletonizers; thrips; countless caterpillars; and nutrition-sucking scale, which come in shades of green, white and brown, and are such messy eaters that the mucus they leave behind breeds a fungus disease called "soot". There are many mealy bugs and numerous nematodes, whose secret binges on coffee roots go unnoticed until the plants appear to suffer from nutritional problems, while stem and twig borers prefer a liquid lunch straight from the tap. The antestia bug, whose first choice is green cherries, but who will settle for buds or even twigs, is like an elegant vampire; no one knows he has supped until the pulping process exposes the darkly stained zebra-striped parchment coatings, and the beans within, shrivelled and black, decayed with the fungus which often accompanies him. The Mediterranean fruit fly does her damage by laying her eggs in the pulp of the coffee fruit, which then becomes an all-you-can-eat buffet for the young maggots. The yellow tea mite may find itself in the wrong venue, but it stays nevertheless.

By far the most serious coffee pest is the dreaded coffee berry borer, the *broca del cafeto*, a tiny black female beetle that bores into a coffee cherry, going through the fruit pulp and penetrating the coffee bean itself, where she lays her eggs. If the bean is not totally destroyed by the voracious tunnel-making larvae, it will succumb to the secondary rot fungus carried by the borer. Coffee berry borers were first noted in Africa in 1867, since which time they have infested every coffee-growing continent around the world, causing billions of dollars' worth of damage and devastation.

Global trends in pest control management are attempting to reduce, and hopefully ultimately replace, the use of chemical pesticides by the introduction and encouragement of natural predators and parasites of the coffee-preying pests. For example, a current International Coffee Organization project, funded by the United Nations' Common Fund for Commodities, hopes to control the coffee berry borer in at least seven member coffee-producing countries, by releasing certain wasps which prey on the borer beetles.

Diseases

Unfortunately, coffee diseases have no natural predators, and although fewer in number than the hordes of coffee pests, coffee diseases are still largely chemically controlled. Although fungicides are not as ecologically harmful as pesticides and herbicides, all chemical treatments are expensive. The best control of coffee plant diseases is careful quarantine, but that is not easy to enforce, especially given the extent of international travel. One of the worst coffee plant diseases is leaf rust (*Hemileia vastatrix*). First reported in 1861 in Africa, by 1870 it had completely wiped out the coffee industry of Ceylon, which resorted to tea-growing. The virulent leaf rust quickly spread to every continent in the

Above: Leaf rust.

coffee-growing world, although some countries have thus far been spared. It is thought that leaf rust is spread by spores being carried on the clothes of travellers from one country to another, particularly by people working in the coffee trade. It is lethal for arabica trees, but robusta is resistant to it.

A soil-inhabiting fungus causes another devastating coffee disease, tracheomycosis, also known as vascular fungus, or coffee wilt disease, to which robusta is more susceptible than arabica. In fact, it was this disease that almost totally destroyed the Ivory Coast's original coffee plantations of liberica trees in the 1940s, after which time the Ivory Coast became a large grower of robusta and the developer of arabusta. In the Democratic Republic of Congo, coffee production has fallen consistently since 1994, due to this disease and internal tribal warfare affecting the same regions.

Another very serious disease affecting arabica trees is coffee berry disease (*colletotrichum coffeanum*). Also called brown blight and red blister, coffee berry disease is a fungus, first identified in Kenya in the 1920s, which may attack a coffee tree in the wake of its carrier, the antestia bug. Rain splashes can also spread residues of the disease, even those from a previous crop. The disease attacks the coffee cherries, causing maximum damage to green cherries, turning them dark with decay. Fungicidal sprays are successful in controlling coffee berry disease only to some extent, and therefore this disease is the subject of much hybridization research.

Hybridization can certainly offer hope for conquering many coffee enemies, as one variety, susceptible to a particular pest or disease, is crossed with another variety which is naturally resistant. Although crossbreeding may eventually see the disappearance of some coffee diseases (thus far what is seen is more the disappearance of flavour), there is a category of coffee enemy to which all varieties are vulnerable: these are the natural disasters that plague many coffee-growing regions.

Natural Disasters

Because of the particular climate and soil required for growing coffee, plantations are sometimes located in rather precarious positions on the slopes of volcanoes. Active or not, volcanoes exist in areas of seismic instability, as evidenced by the terrible earthquake of January 1999, which struck the Colombian coffee-growing centre of Armenia, a victim of similar devastation in only 1988. Indeed, since 1972, Mexico, the Philippines, Panama, Costa Rica, Guatemala and Nicaragua have all suffered earthquake damage.

Hurricanes are endemic to the tropics, and although little coffee is grown in coastal areas, almost all tropical islands and the countries of the narrow isthmus of Central America are subject to serious tropical storms. Out of Nicaragua's 30 per cent crop loss due to Hurricane Mitch in 1998, only ten per cent consisted of destroyed trees, mostly by mudslides; the rest was cherries going rotten because the roads to processing mills were impassable. Tidal waves are more infrequent than hurricanes, but can be equally devastating, as witnessed by the massive force of the wave that hit Papua New Guinea in 1998.

Less dramatic, but seemingly always present *somewhere* in countries heavily dependent on coffee crops, are more universal disasters such as droughts, famine, bad weather (such as the freak hailstorm of October 1998, in the Brazilian state of São Paulo, which went largely unnoticed by the rest of world because it destroyed *only* an estimated 100,000 bags of coffee), political disturbances if not actual revolutions, and of course, the coffee enemy that causes chaos in coffee prices for the entire world: frost.

Frost is the bane of the Brazilian coffee crop, but it can occur in any country where the best coffee is grown in higher altitudes near the extremities of the tropical belt. Although a mild frost can sometimes be alleviated slightly with hot air machines, even one night of freezing temperatures can certainly do enormous damage to a coffee crop; a truly hard frost will completely kill the trees. Considering the years of labour and cost invested in a plantation of mature coffee trees, it must be heartbreaking to see it all come to nothing in just a few hours of cold weather.

Below: Frost destroys a Brazilian crop.

HARVESTING AND PROCESSING

Far more is done on a coffee plantation than just growing and harvesting the fruit. When coffee cherries ripen, they must be picked almost immediately, not an easy thing to time when a single tree's fruit is in various stages of maturity simultaneously. In most arabica-growing areas the ripe cherries will be carefully hand-picked and dropped into the picker's basket, the weight of which determines the picker's pay and, in areas of smoother terrain and shorter trees, can be as heavy as 100kg/220lb by the end of the day. The same tree will be visited on several different days as more cherries ripen.

A harvester will "strip-pick" the entire tree when the majority of its cherries are ripe, by sliding his or her fingers down the branches, causing all the cherries, ripe or not, to fall to the ground. Alternatively, a large vehicle will be driven slowly down the row of coffee trees, and its revolving arms will knock the looser, and hopefully riper, fruit to

Below: Hand-pickers head out for a day's work in the mountainous regions of Java, where they use ladders to reach the tops of the trees.

Above: The process of winnowing requires the use of a large sieve-like hoop for tossing everything into the air and retaining only the cherries.

Left: A Brazilian winnower tossing the machine harvest into the air, hoping to lose all but the coffee cherries.

the ground. Harvesting machines are used primarily in Brazil, where the immense, flat terrain of the large *fazendas* (estates) allows the trees to be planted in even, widely spaced rows.

If the fruit is on the ground, it must be raked up and "winnowed" by workers who, using large meshed hoops, fling the sweepings into the air several times; twigs, leaves, cherries and dust are tossed up high, and the worker, like a juggler, catches the cherries as the lighter weight materials are blown aside. A major problem with the hand-stripping and machine methods of harvesting is that many cherries are included which are not at a point of perfect ripeness; these under- or overripe cherries must be removed by extra sorting or else they will lower the grading quality. All quality arabicas will be sorted several times, beginning with hand-sorting the cherries. This initial task of hand-sorting is often done by women and children.

The Coffee Cherry

The coffee fruit is called a cherry primarily because it is about the same size, shape and colour as an actual cherry. Beneath the bright red skin is the pulp, a sweet, sticky yellow substance, which becomes slimy mucilage towards the centre of the fruit, where it surrounds the coffee beans, which are actually the seeds. There are normally two beans per cherry, facing each other's flat side, like peanut halves. On the surface of the beans is a very thin, diaphanous membrane, called the silver skin. Each bean (and its silver skin) is encased in a tough, cream-coloured, protective bean-shaped shell, or jacket, called parchment, or pergamino, which serves to keep the bean separate from the mucilage. Beans destined to be seed beans for growing new coffee plants must remain in their parchment if they are to sprout.

Left: Hand-sorting in Indonesia.

Above: Coffee cherries set out in the Kenyan sun to dry.

Normal coffee trees sometimes produce a few smaller-than-average cherries in which only one bean forms. This single bean, called variously a peaberry, perla or caracol, will not have a flat side; rather, it will be small and almost completely round. Sorted out and collected together, peaberries sell at a slightly higher price than do normal coffee beans from the same trees. Many people swear that the peaberry flavour is better, although it may just be that, because of the special sorting, few, if any, defective beans are able to slip through.

Processing the Cherry

The next step after harvesting is to remove the beans from the surrounding fruit pulp, which is done by either the washed (wet process), or the unwashed (dry process). The latter, dry processing, is the separation method, used where there is a shortage of water or equipment, or both. Because most robusta and much low-quality arabica coffee is dry-processed, many people, experts included, wrongly assume that any dry-processed or "natural" coffee, must be inferior. On the contrary, most of Ethiopia's wonderful varied arabicas are dry-processed, and some of these are world class coffees; almost all Brazilian arabicas are naturals, or unwashed, and there are some superbly smooth, sweet and full-bodied Santos beans.

Dry processing In spite of its description, dry processing begins with the washing of the newly harvested cherries, not only to clean the cherries but to implement another sorting procedure, as the floaters – defective beans due primarily to insect infestation or over-ripeness – are easily picked out at this stage. The cherries are then spread out to sun-dry; if on patios they are raked, and if they have been placed on matting stretched across trestles, or on some other raised platform, they are hand-turned, for about three weeks. They are protectively covered from any night condensation or rain – the unwashed process tends to be used in drier regions anyway – and the drying process may be finished with hot-air machines. When only about 12 per cent of their moisture content remains, they are either stored in silos or are sent on for final processing at a mill or factory, which may be under government control. Here they undergo hulling, which in one operation removes all of the dried skin, pulp, and parchment from the beans.

From this point the procedures are the same for both washed and unwashed beans: they are polished, screened and sorted, processes usually done with more sophisticated equipment, including electronic sorting machines; and then graded and bagged. After this the bags of green (still unroasted) beans may go into storage or they may be exported.

Wet processing This system is much more expensive, due to far greater requirements of equipment, labour, time and water. Before any fermentation can begin in the freshly picked cherries, they are immediately washed in large

Right: Pushing the pulped beans through the system of channels, which sorts them by size and weight.

tanks from which the water carries them into a system of channels. Staying in contact with the fresh-flowing water helps to loosen the outer skin, while the cherries are carried towards a depulping machine. Here they lose their skin and some of the pulp, but the flowing water takes the beans, still wearing their parchment covering and a lot of the sticky mucilage, through various screens, sieves and sluices, which further sort the beans by size and weight.

At last the beans arrive in a fermentation tank, where any remaining mucilage is broken down by natural enzymes during a 36-hour soak. The fermentation is monitored and controlled, as it must only remove the mucilage and not develop off-flavours in the beans themselves. The parchment beans, once clear of mucilage, are rinsed, drained and spread out on patios or wire-mesh platforms, and left to dry in the sun.

As in the dry method, the parchment beans are turned and raked for between one and two weeks, or they may go into low-temperature drying machines, until their moisture content is about 11–12 percent: the last stages are critical because over-drying makes them brittle and they can lose quality; under-drying means vulnerability to unwanted fermentation, fungi and bacteria or bruising during subsequent hulling. Parchment beans are stored for about a month, and can be stored for several months in a controlled atmosphere. When exportation is imminent, the beans are taken to the curing mill where the parchment is removed by hulling, and the washed beans undergo the same processes as do the dry-processed beans.

Right: Once through the various stages of soaking and pulping, parchment beans are rinsed, drained and spread out to dry on large, flat patios or wire-mesh platforms.

SORTING AND GRADING

Governments of countries which export coffee usually operate or advise a department or agency which establishes a standard, regulates and monitors the coffee trade, and assesses bean quality through quality control inspectors. In many countries the administrator is a coffee board authority; in others it is an institute, possibly under the control of the ministry of agriculture or of trade and industry.

Above: The task of sorting through the wet-processed beans is a methodical one.

Grading Coffee

Unfortunately, there is no international standardization of coffee quality, as coffee is graded by a set of characteristics peculiar to each producing country. A sample of beans is taken from a bag, judged according to that country's standards, and the sack of beans from which the sample was taken is given a quality rating, good or bad, depending on the outcome of the assessment. The characteristics by which most coffee is graded are appearance (bean size, uniformity, colour); number of defective beans per sample; cup quality, which of course includes flavour and body; and whether the beans roast well and evenly. Because the classifications of grades and the descriptive terminology differ from country to country, and the standards of quality are only relevant within that country's range of coffees, it is not easy to interpret a coffee's true quality without some familiarization of the particular country of origin's grading system. There is at least one constant, uniform reference from country to country: all countries determine bean size with standardized screens, so the buyer doesn't have to guess how large is large or how small is small from the producer's relative point of view.

A coffee may bear an exotic regional name, and/or may be classified by the processing (washed or unwashed). It may have a descriptive title, or just an alphabetical letter or two, possibly followed by a number. For example, in certain countries where the coffee industry has been nationalized, the grading system may seem to be rather uninspiring, as in Kenya, where a bag of coffee may be a washed "AA", with a number to denote one of ten cup-quality classes; yet this ordinary-sounding coffee is acknowledged by most experts to be consistently one of the world's best coffees. In India, however, a Plantation A – assume "washed" because an unwashed is designated "cherry" – was one of the highest qualities available, but was not in the same league as the Kenyan. India, however, has recently changed to a free market, so it remains to be seen what grading system will be used.

Most Caribbean and Central American countries indicate quality by words denoting altitude: Costa Rica's eastern regions produce LGA (low grown Atlantic), MGA (medium grown Atlantic), and HGA (high grown Atlantic), while the western slopes grow HB (hard bean), MHB (medium hard bean), GHB (good hard bean) and SHB (strictly hard bean); the harder the bean, the higher the altitude and the price! The best plantations of Costa Rica can label their own bags as well as denote the altitude, and both Costa Rica and Nicaragua also use exotic regional names. Nicaragua also indicates classifications of quality and altitude with titles like Central Bueno Lavado (MG), Central Altura for high grown, and Central Estrictamente Altura (SHG). Guatemala is a bit more obscure with its altitude designations, since the adjectives, which sound purely descriptive, indicate altitudes beginning at 700m/2,296ft and rising to 1,700m/ 5,577ft: Good Washed, Extra Good Washed, Prime Washed, Extra Prime Washed, Semi Hard Bean (SH), Hard Bean (HB), Fancy Hard Bean and Strictly Hard Bean (SHB).

National systems for grading Countries that have unique ways of designating different qualities of coffee include Brazil, which classifies each bag by the species of coffee, the port from which the coffee is exported (Santos, Parana, etc), and then by a defective bean qualification, for example: NY (meaning "we are counting the defective beans the way the Americans understand it") and Standard 3 (which means an average sample of 300 grams would have 12 defective beans). The defects also include points for stones and twigs. Brazil's grading also includes bean size, colour, density, shape, roast potential, cup quality, processing method, crop year and lot number.

Modest Ethiopia, with some truly aristocratic world-class coffees, is content to denote simply the processing, the name of the region of production, and a grade number between 1 and 8, each of which indicates a certain number of defects. Colombia's grading is even simpler: each bag has the name of the region, and sorts by size, e.g. Excelso beans are smaller versions of the Supremo.

Indonesia has recently changed from its old Dutch system of grading. Now, R=Robusta, A=Arabica, WP=wet processed, DP=dry processed; six quality grade numbers, with 1&2 High, 3&4 Medium, 5&6 Lower grades; AP after the grade number means After Polished, and L, M and S stand for bean sizes large, medium and small. For example, R/DP Grade 2L would be a dry processed large-bean robusta of very high quality; A/WP Grade 3/AP would denote a medium-quality polished washed arabica.

The glossary overleaf lists some terms used by the coffee trade to describe particular coffee beans and their attributes. In some cases several explanations are given because, in general, there is no standardization of terms; interpretations may therefore vary or even seem to be contradictory.

Above: Professional sorters grade coffee beans by size, by painstakingly putting the beans into corresponding holes.

Grading Terminology

While the following terms may vary slightly from country to country, these are the generally accepted definitions and will give you an excellent idea of how one sample of coffee beans is differentiated from another.

Above: Black bean.

Black bean Insect-damaged; dead cherry fallen from tree pre-harvest; decomposed bean; overripe; metal contamination.
Bold bean The size falling between medium and large.
Broken Over-dried brittle beans, easily broken into pieces during hulling.
Brown bean In arabica, a colour denoting overripeness; over-fermentation; under-fermentation (brownish tinge); or soiled, lack of pre-washing.
Discoloured bean Any bean outside the range of normal (green/blue in arabica, khaki/brownish/yellowish in robusta) colour, indicating poor processing, with possible defective flavour.
Elephant ear Malformed cherry containing one large bean partly encircling a smaller; the two interlocking parts can separate in roast, but flavour is not impaired (East Africa).

Elephant bean Slang name for Maragogype variety, world's largest coffee beans; generally prized for appearance, good roast, smooth flavour; gradually dying out as financially unprofitable. Not to be confused with the malformed elephant/elephant ear bean.
Floater Under-ripe, or overripe bean, or brown bean that surfaces in washing – lacks density.
Foxy Off-flavour from beans either with red tinge, perhaps overripe; over-fermented (delay in pulping); yellow cherry; frost.
Hard bean Fairly mediocre arabica beans, indicates lower altitudes in countries where "strictly hard bean" is the best quality; not to be confused, however, with "hard" flavour.
Hull coffee Dry-processed beans before hulling has removed the surrounding dried cherries.
M'buni East African word for dry-processed (sun-dried) cherry. Also over-fruity, tart, sour flavour.
Natural bean Denotes dry-processed coffee bean.

Above: Insect-damaged beans.

Pale Yellow in colour, from immature cherries or drought-affected; will not darken satisfactorily in roast; unpleasant nutty flavour of several can spoil batch (*see* Quaker).
Parchment Protective covering or jacket (endocarp) encasing bean within the cherry, which must be intact if bean is to germinate; also "pergamino".

Left: Over-fermented beans.

Parchment coffee Wet-processed beans before hulling has removed their parchment coverings.
Peaberry Also, perle, perla, caracol; small rounded bean (malformation) produced singly in a small cherry; sorted together they command a higher price than normal beans, even ones from the same trees.
Pod Beans still encased in the dried cherry after hulling, constitutes defect in sample.

Above: Pulper-nipped beans.

Pulper-nipped Bean damaged during pulping; subsequent appearance can lower quality assessment.
Quaker Similar to Pale, but not caused by immaturity, although terms are sometimes used interchangeably (*see* Pale).
Ragged Bean not fully developed due to drought.
Stinker Overripe cherry; or over-fermentation; insect- or microbe-damaged bean; bean flavour is powerfully pervasive and rotten, sour odour when crushed; undetectable by human eye, glows under ultraviolet light of electric sorting machines; contaminates entire batch.
Strictly hard bean (SHB) Quality arabicas grown at highest altitudes, where density of bean concentrates flavour.
Strictly high grown (SHG) Different grading terminology for basically the same conditions as strictly hard bean.
Triage Lowest grade of coffee, never exported; left-overs; figurative factory floor sweepings.
Unwashed Dry-processed beans.
Washed Wet-processed beans.
Yellow bean In arabica, bean colour caused by over-drying.

COFFEE TASTING

Coffee tasting, also called "cupping", is the sensory evaluation of coffee, which assesses more than just taste; the senses of smell, taste and "feel" are all involved. Smell and taste are very dependent on each other, and difficult to separate in assessment; of course, there are some coffees that will not taste as they smell, but in general the attribute of flavour can be interpreted almost as much an aroma as a taste, and an aroma is a very good indication of the taste to follow. There are four basic tastes – salt, sweet, acid and bitter – and most specific tastes fall into one of these categories. The sense of feel involved in assessing coffee evaluates the coffee's body – its weight, fullness and texture in the mouth.

Coffee beans are regularly tasted all along the market route, though the really serious tasting is done when the coffee is graded, in its country of origin, and at a second stage when it is sold to the importing country.

Evaluating the Flavour

First, prepare the samples and equipment needed: identical cups (ideally) for each coffee to be tasted; the coffee samples and a coffee measure; another empty cup; a spoon (silver is traditional) about the size and shape of a soup spoon, or shallower; a glass of water in which to rinse the spoon between coffees; a glass of room-temperature water (or a water biscuit or cracker) for clearing the palate; a jug (pitcher) or spittoon (garboon is the specialist term); and a kettle of very hot water, just under boiling point.

- Plan to taste at least two coffees, as a frame of reference.
- Grind should be medium ("cafetière/percolator" grind). If the coffees are ground in succession in the same grinder, start with a clean grinder and wipe out the grinder between samples.
- If the tasting is a true comparison, the degree of roast should be as much the same for all samples as possible; if tasting is simply to choose a preferred coffee, taste every coffee in whatever style or roast it comes supplied. The lighter the roast, the more the true unique flavour of the coffee is exposed; the darker the roast, the more all coffees begin to taste the same, and the easier it is to hide the flaws. In a darker roast, the coffee tastes less acidic, but since acidity is the main indicator of altitude, quality and price, it is a shame if the expensive acidity disappears in the roaster.
- Measure out the same amount of dry coffee into each cup, about 8g/1 heaped tbsp to 150ml/5fl oz/⅔ cup of water. Sniff the dry coffees. Write down any noteworthy observation about the dry smell. It is always advisable to arrange the coffees in an orderly row for tasting, placing those which may be the strongest – particularly if any robustas are to be tasted – at the end.
- Pour water just off the boil to the same level in each cup. Do not stir. Wait a couple of minutes, then bend over each cup and smell the surface, which is a mass of floating grounds.
- Break the crust (the grounds floating on the surface of the cup), by inserting the tasting spoon through the surface flotsam, again while bending over the cup and inhaling the aroma at very close range. You could spoon up and smell some of the grounds and liquid from the bottom of the cup – this action will probably help to settle the grounds as much as anything.
- With the spoon, lightly skim any remaining grounds off the coffee's surface, and sling them into the extra empty cup. (Dipping the tasting spoon into the glass of rinsing water will get rid of any grounds left on it.)
- Get a medium-full spoonful of coffee, place it against the lips and virtually inhale it, with plenty of air and into the mouth, slurping noisily, attempting to get some of it all the way to the back of the mouth immediately. Swish it around the mouth, and after a few seconds, spit the liquid out. Make some notes for later comparison, rinse the spoon and go on to the next coffee.
- Try to taste all the coffees at the same temperature and in close conjunction with each other. As the coffees cool, go back and taste them again, as the flavours may change slightly.

Below: A professional coffee taster with the samples of brewed coffee.

Above: The basic taste of coffee is made up of body, aroma and flavour.

Coffee Tasters' Terminology

This list may seem a little daunting, but remember that what you are looking for in a good cup of coffee is essentially body, aroma and flavour. Choose a coffee that you like and see what you can detect. Alternatively, try coffee where the taste is not as it should be, and compare it with a good brew to try to see where the differences lie.

Acidic Very desirable coffee quality, sharpness detected towards front of mouth; denotes quality and altitude; can be fruity (citrusy, lemony, berry-like, etc) or a pure tongue-tip numbing sensation (Costa Rica, Kenya, Mexico offer good examples).

Aftertaste/finish Flavour/mouthfeel remaining after coffee has left the mouth, sometimes surprisingly different from actual coffee taste.

Aromatic Coffee with intensive pleasant fragrance (for example Hawaii, Colombia, Jamaica, Sumatra).

Ashy Coffee with flavour/aroma of cold fireplace ashes.

Astringent Mouthfeel characteristic that "draws" the tongue and tissues, often apparent as after-taste.

Bitter Basic flavour sensation detected at the back of the mouth and soft-palate, often as after-taste, sometimes desirable to a limited degree (as in dark-roast, espresso). Not to be confused with acidity.

Right: Where it all starts – with the whole roasted coffee beans.

Blackcurrant Flavour reminiscent of blackcurrant or berries; some acidity but with stronger undertones not found in citrusy, highly acidic coffees; not a negative term.

Body Signifies the perception of texture or weight of liquid in the mouth; thin or light body can feel watery (a few high-grown arabicas); full-bodied means heavy liquor, as in Sumatra, Java, and most robustas.

Broth-like Pleasant flavour in some lighter East African coffees similar to clear soup, like bouillon, often accompanies slightly citrusy flavour.

Burnt Carbon-type flavour and aroma, as in burnt toast; over-roasted.

Caramel Sweet flavour reminiscent of caramelized sugar, or, slightly different: candy floss (cotton candy).

Cerealy Flavour like unsweetened grain or oatmeal, sometimes found in under-roasted robusta coffee, bland and not particularly pleasant.

Cheesy Rather pungent flavour/ aroma of slightly sour, curdled milk or cheese.

Chemical/medicinal Coffee with unnatural off-flavours, real or reminiscent of tainting.

Chocolatey Flavour reminiscent of chocolate which can be found in various crops (some Australian, New Guinean and Ethiopian, for example).

Citrus Flavour reminiscent of citrus fruits due to high acidity; very desirable, denotes quality and high-altitude growth.

Clean Pure coffee flavour, no twists or changes in the mouth, no different after-taste (Costa Rica sometimes provides good examples).

Dirty Coffee tasting as if the beans have been rolled in dirt or soiled.

Dry A certain type of acidity and/or mouthfeel, but not, as in wine, the opposite of sweet; often accompanies light, or even delicate coffees, such as Mexican, Ethiopian and Yemeni.

Dusty Dry-earth taste and smell, exactly like dust, though not the same as dirty or earthy.

Earthy Aroma/flavour reminiscent of damp black earth, organic, mushroomy, cellar-like (can be found, for example, in some Javan or Sumatran coffees "gone wrong").

Floral Coffee beans having a very fresh, floral, heady aroma, like that of floral-scented perfume.

Fruity Flavour/aroma often found in good arabica coffees, reminiscent of a wide range of fruits: citrus, berries, currants, etc, always accompanied by some degree of acidity; this is usually positive, but can indicate overripeness or over-fermentation.

Gamey Unusual and interesting flavour, often found in dry-processed East African coffees (such as Ethiopian Djimmah), reminiscent of cheesy, but not sour or negative.

Grassy Green and astringent aroma with an accompanying taste like a new-mown lawn, sometimes found in coffees from Malawi and Rwanda.

Green Aroma/taste of unripe fruit or plants, as when green stems or leaves are crushed or broken; can denote under-roasting.

Hard Flavour, not to be confused with hard bean. In terms of flavour, hard signifies a brew lacking sweetness and softness.

Harsh Strong, unpleasant, sharp or "edgy" flavour; also used to describe Rio-y, iodine-like flavour.
Hidey Aroma/taste like animal hides, uncured leather, or, at best, new leather shoes.
Lemony Flavour very like mild lemon found in very acidic coffee, such as that from Kenya.
Light, mild Light-bodied coffee, pleasant low-to-medium acidity. Some Mexican, Honduran and Santo Domingan coffees exhibit these characteristics.
Malty Coffee flavour very like malted barley, sometimes in combination with chocolatey, sometimes alone.
Mellow Soft, with pleasant low-acidity.
Metallic Sharpness, acidity slightly gone wrong. Some Nicaraguan coffee, for example, can be overly metallic.
Mocha, mokka Arabica coffee originally named for the old port of Yemen, now also associated with Ethiopian Harrar coffee. Nothing to do with chocolate, although coffee drinks with mocha imply chocolate with coffee.
Musty Flavour of improper drying, mildew, generally undesirable.
Neutral Bland coffee, very low acidity, not derogatory, as implies no off-tastes; good for blending (often describes many ordinary Brazilian arabicas).
Nutty Pleasant flavour reminiscent of nuts, often peanuts (some Jamaican).
Papery A taste/aroma exactly like dry paper, slightly similar to dusty.
Phenolic Flavour/aroma so medicinal as to cause olfactory sensation reminiscent of phenol.
Rancid/rotten The flavour of a spoiled oily product, as in rancid nuts or rancid olive oil; fairly disgusting; can cause involuntary gagging.
Rio-y Iodine, inky flavour from microbe-tainted beans. Prized for traditional brewing in Turkey, Greece, Middle East.
Rounded Cup balance with no overpowering characteristic, well-balanced; can also mean pleasantly smooth, without being sharp.
Rubber Aroma/taste reminiscent of tyres, garages, often detected in certain robustas, for example.
Sacky Coffee tainted by improper storage, flavour/aroma of hemp, possibly damp.
Salty One of four basic tasting categories, occurs occasionally in coffee; also can denote presence of chicory in coffee blend.
Smoky Aromatic flavour of woodsmoke, very pleasant attribute sometimes found in certain coffees such as some from Guatemala and also occasionally some Indonesian arabicas.
Smooth Mouthfeel not sharp or astringent, pleasant, sometimes combines with winey flavour.
Soft/strictly soft Coffee with low acidity, mellow sweetness, pleasant roof-of-the-mouth easiness (possibly similar to the feel of Italian red Lambrusco wine); some Brazilian Santos for example.
Sour Undesirable "dirty socks" flavour of over-fermentation.
Spicy Aroma/taste of spice, perhaps sweetish or peppery, found in certain coffees, such as those from Java, Zimbabwe, Guatemala; or the more erratic Yemen and Ethiopian coffees.
Stalky This gives a flavour reminiscent of dry vegetable matter or other plant material stalks.
Stinky Rotten flavour indicating possible contamination by "stinker" bean.
Sweet Pleasant, mellow, agreeable; sometimes used to describe soft coffees, but also can be found in highly acidic coffees.
Thin Term when coffee's body does not equal acidity or flavour; out-of-balance, watery, wishy-washy in mouthfeel.
Tobacco-y Aroma/flavour characteristic of unsmoked plug (chewing) tobacco.
Turpentine-y Smell or taste reminiscent of chemical, possibly phenolic-like substance.
Well-rounded, well-balanced Cup giving impression of good mix of flavour, acidity, body, and perhaps aroma.
Wild Term describing certain Ethiopian/Yemeni coffees – suggesting unusual, inconsistent, and interesting; sometimes used with spicy; also exotic, tangy, complex.
Winey Combination of slightly fruity flavour, very smooth mouthfeel and texture reminiscent of wine. Term should not be used indiscriminately to denote acidity; better reserved for coffees with genuine feel (more than taste) of wine, slightly rare but unmistakable (in some Kenyan as after-taste; found in some Ethiopian Harrars, Yemeni, and various others).
Woody Flavour peculiar to either dead (indicating old crop, coffee stored too long) or green wood flavour found in certain coffees, like fresh saw-dust; neither very pleasant.
Yeasty/toasty Flavour reminiscent of either yeasty (unbaked) bread, or bread lightly toasted.

Left: Roasting coffee darker can hide the less desirable characteristics of a coffee sample which may not be of the highest quality.

COFFEE-PRODUCING COUNTRIES

Today, because of increased communication and improved transportation, the world now appears very small, and almost anything is accessible to those who want it. It is, therefore, remarkable how much the coffee trade seems still to follow the old colonial routes. The explanation for this is to be found in the national coffee taste preferences established during periods when European powers supported, or exploited, their own colonies, either by using the plants indigenous to the colony, or by introducing certain crops desirable or profitable for the mother country.

If coffee, an extremely lucrative and sought-after commodity, was not native to a colony, its cultivation was often quickly encouraged and nurtured. For example, much of the coffee consumed in France today contains a surprisingly large amount of robusta, the coffee variety produced in those West African countries which made up much of France's empire and were, geographically, – important in the days of shipping – France's nearest colonies.

Because of the activities of the British East India Company, which traded coffee among Eastern countries, but introduced tea to India and Britain, Britain drank far more tea than coffee from the mid-1700s. The British colonial acquisitions during the late 1800s and after World War I were primarily concentrated in East Africa, all arabica-growing regions; and, along with that from Jamaica, the coffee Britain consumed was primarily arabica. Even today, although many British coffee companies import robusta, they will seldom admit to doing so, as the overall preferred taste in Britain is for arabica.

Portugal, the great power in early exploration and colonization, did not retain many of its early colonies, although today it is still the main buyer for its last coffee-growing colonies, Angola and Cape Verde, which it gave up in 1975; Mozambique, also lost that year, basically stopped growing coffee when the Portuguese colonists pulled out. Portugal lost Brazil quite early on when the colony became independent in 1822, as an indirect result of Napoleon's invasion of Portugal.

North America, made up of colonies itself and a melting pot of all nations, is also a melting pot of coffee, with a wide range of coffee preferences, and accommodating virtually all tastes.

Production figures used in the following coffee-producing country profiles are based on information received at the time of publication.

Right: One of the best ways to familiarize yourself with the many different types of coffee available is to think about the countries that grow coffee, and to sort them into a few main coffee-growing regions. This book has grouped coffee growers into four principal regions: Africa; Central America and the Caribbean; South America; and the South Pacific and South-east Asia.

The map opposite shows all of the countries covered in the following pages, highlighting the main types of coffee grown there: arabica, robusta, a combination of these two, and the new hybridizations.

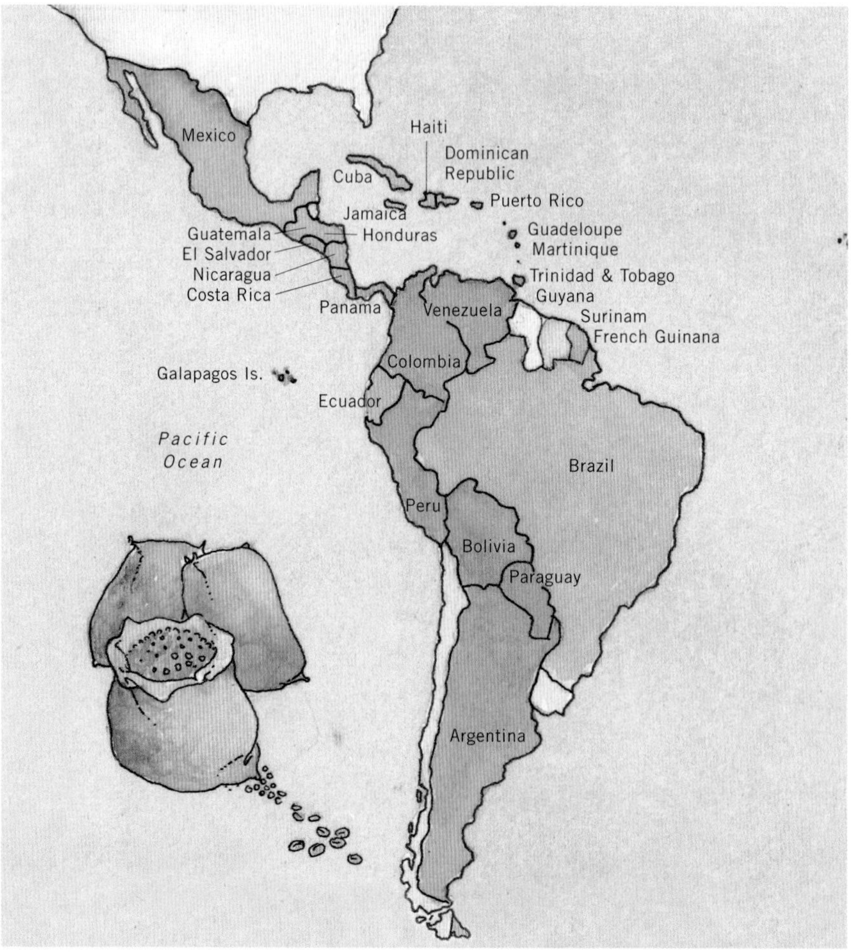

The estimated statistics given in the country profiles can differ from year to year depending on the variables of climatic changes. Coffee bag figures represent a unit of 60kg/132lb of green coffee, no matter what size bag is actually used in any particular country. Also, exportable production figures may differ from those of actual exports, as green coffee can be stored for some time before shipment.

The ICO reports that the 2019/20 global coffee crop was a very good harvest of about 165,053,000 bags. The statistics of coffee-producing countries who are not members of the International Coffee Organization, are not included in this figure.

Right: Every year nearly 126 million bags of coffee are exported around the world.

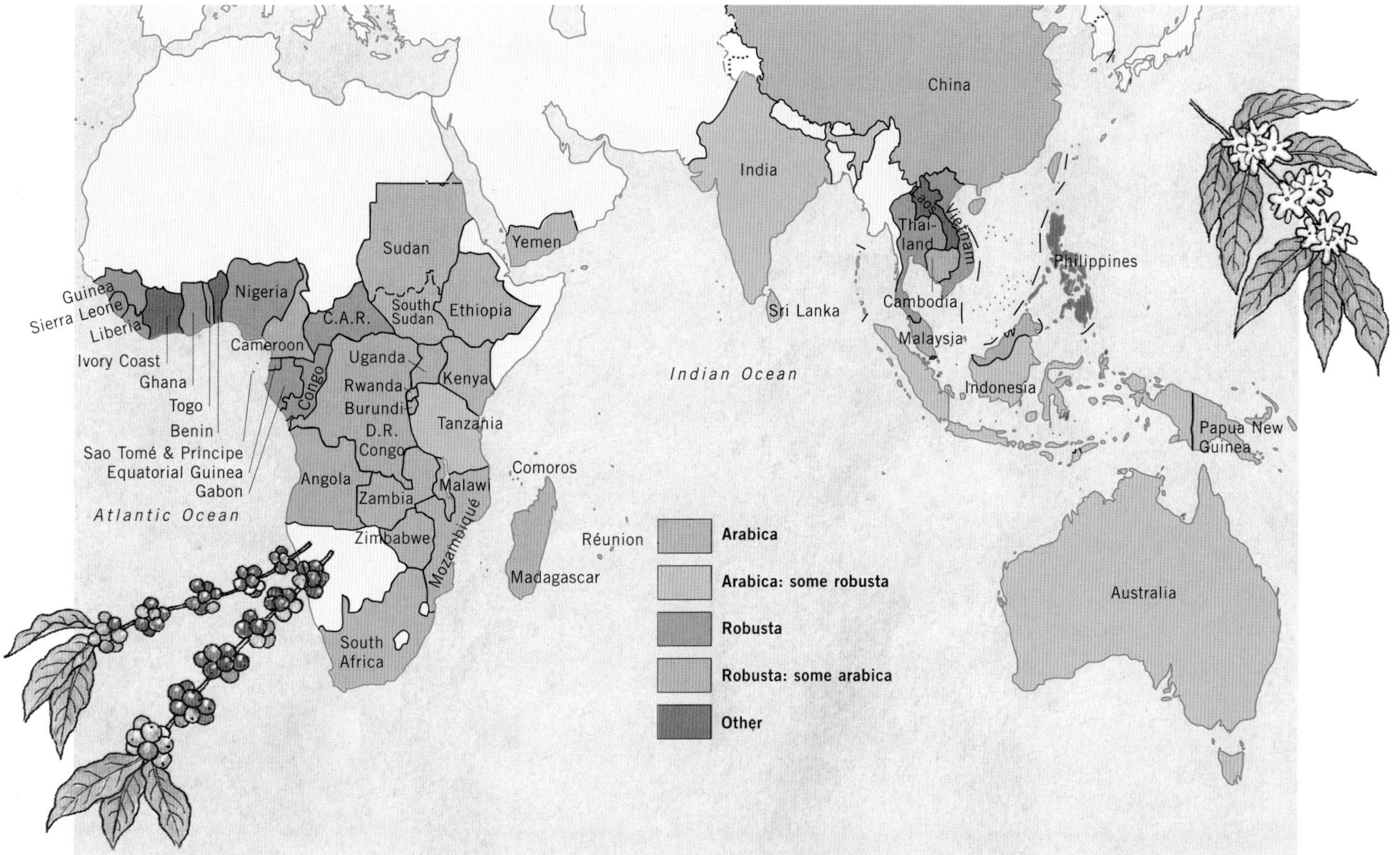

AFRICA

As the birth place of coffee, it is fitting that the continent of Africa produces some of the world's finest coffees. In many countries, however, social, political and economic problems make the production of coffee a difficult task.

Angola

In the 18th century Portuguese colonists began coffee cultivation in what is now the People's Republic of Angola. Although robusta is not generally a word associated with high quality, that is exactly what differentiates the best of Angola's robusta (Ambriz and Amboin) from that of other countries. The beans are uniform in size and colour, cleanly processed (mostly by the dry method), sorted and carefully graded. The robusta is grown on shaded trees in the northern plains, approaching the delta of the Congo River. Angola's inland plateau has a far more temperate climate than the plains, and an altitude of 1,800m/5,905ft allows some cultivation of arabica coffee, which is mild, unassumingly neutral, and in blending could easily substitute for an average-quality Brazilian Santos. Since the devastation of the civil war, however, it is very scarce; before the 1994 peace treaty, production sank to 33,000 bags, compared to 3.5 million bags in 1973.

Benin (formerly Dahomey)

Shaped a bit like a vertical house key, Benin can really only grow coffee in the south, its least arid zone, where many small-holders intersperse the coffee trees with palms. Although Benin's coffee – robusta and some arabusta – is too small a crop to list as a percentage of world production, it still probably exports more coffee than it grows, due to smuggling activities with Nigeria.

Burundi

Coffee brings far more income to this small land-locked African country than any other commodity. Indeed, its citizens, while appreciating the very good washed arabica, of which Burundi grows more than robusta, will consume less than one per cent, preferring the earnings from exporting the rest, which is good quality, clean, well-graded, and has both good acidic flavour and body. However, there is some concern over future production of coffee due to tribal unrest.

Above: Burundi superior full wash, top quality green beans.

Cameroon

Cameroon is known as a producer of robusta coffee, although about one-third of its crop is the Blue Mountain variety of arabica, which is grown in the western volcanic regions. Primarily wet-processed, at one time the arabica coffees produced on the European plantations equalled the high-quality coffees of Central America. The robusta growths, first brought from Zaire, are grown now in all the provinces except in the extreme north.

Cape Verde

Cape Verde, the Windward and Leeward Islands off the extreme west coast of Africa, is not a member of the International Coffee Organization, so no statistics are available on its current coffee production. The Portuguese, who dominated these islands from the 15th century until 1975, first planted arabica trees in 1790. The gradual transformation of the islands to desert, due to severe droughts, has reduced coffee growing in the volcanic soil from various heights to only the higher mountainsides, at altitudes between 500–900m/1,500–2,700ft.

There is no hydroelectric power, and no irrigation is possible, so water is precious and scarce, but the humidity from the fog generated by the north-west trade winds sustains the few remaining coffee trees, which also serve as windbreaks and soil-erosion deterrents. In a good year the dry-processed coffee yield may be sufficient to export, mostly to Portugal, but the islanders, coffee-drinkers themselves, actually have to resort to importing coffee, mostly from Angola, to satisfy local demand.

Central African Republic

The Central African Republic, which used to be part of French Equatorial Africa, still sells most of its coffee, a very important cash crop for the country, to France. Italy is its other main buyer. The robusta varieties are the usual canephora and the more interesting Nana robusta, first discovered growing wild on the banks of the Nana River in the extreme western region. The coffee is carefully classified, and consistent in quality and

Above: Cameroon robusta green beans.

roast, but because the country is land-locked, any problems in steady availability are due to transportation difficulties. The debilitating coffee disease tracheomycosis originated here.

Comoros

Between the Mozambique coast and the island of Madagascar lie four small islands which were under French control for many years. Today they make up the Federal and Islamic Republic of the Comoros, although one of them, Mayotte, opted to remain under French territorial administration. Coffee, mostly robusta, is grown on Mayotte and Mohéli islands, shaded by banana and coconut trees. The quality of the hand-picked dry-processed beans is not bad, and about two-thirds of the small crop (often less than 1,000 bags) is exported. The remainder satisfies the high consumption demands of the local population, about 700,000 people.

Congo

This country of nine provinces includes a small section of Atlantic coastline, and was once the middle part of French Equatorial Africa. The equator runs across the top third of the country, and its climate is basically the non-varying heat and humidity of equatorial regions. The all-robusta crop produced by the republic seems to be increasing. Unusually, the average-to-good coffee is not graded by size, as the beans are generally uniform, but rather by number of defective beans, of which the top grade Extra Prima has none. The cup quality is that of an average-to-good robusta, neutral and clean.

Democratic Republic of Congo

The former country of Zaire grows robusta, mostly of the Marchand type, but far more interesting to the specialist coffee trade is the arabica crop, which makes up less than 20 per cent of the harvest. These trees are grown at a very high altitude in the mountainous plateau regions of Kivu province, where the land rises towards the volcanic mountains marking the edge of the Great Rift Valley, and the lake-studded borders shared with Tanzania, Burundi, Rwanda and Uganda.

Most of the wet-processed arabicas, of good, bright blue or blue-green colour and consistent appearance, have remarkably few defects. At best the Kivu arabicas can be described as a fine,

Left: Cash cropping. In many countries the exportation of coffee provides most of the income from foreign sources.

perfect balance of good body and acidity, and the Maragogype is an extremely pleasant soft coffee.

Unfortunately, the coffee crop of the Democratic Republic of Congo has been decreasing gradually over the past decade. The larger plantations are poorly maintained, and the finest coffees, grown in a region rife with tribal warfare and tracheomycosis, must be transported through other countries on the land-locked eastern border before exportation from the Indian Ocean ports The Kivu arabicas are thus extremely rare to find. The new Kabila regime intends to rebuild a free market economy, hopefully supportive of greater coffee production.

Right: Kivu arabica beans from the Democratic Republic of Congo.

Equatorial Guinea

Coffee is second only to cocoa in importance for this beautiful country, which consists of five islands and a bit of continental West Africa. The coffee is mostly robusta and liberica, but arabica is grown. Independence in 1968 after 190 years of Spanish rule led only to disastrous dictatorships, and today, in spite of its fertile, rich soil, Equatorial Guinea's reduced production of coffee (and cocoa) has not recovered. The country has resumed relations with Spain, buyer of almost its entire crop.

Ethiopia

The earliest accounts of coffee all refer to its being a native of this region of old Abyssinia; indeed, the coffee processed today by many Ethiopian villagers is simply picked off untended, wild bushes. Although an extremely poor country, suffering from an infrastructure destroyed by civil war, and racked by periodic serious droughts, Ethiopia is a significant producer of coffee, both in quantity and quality, still managing to export some of the world's finest and most individual coffees, some of which have a very low natural caffeine content. The regions growing the best coffees are generally the Sidamo, Kaffa, Harrar and Wellega, but within each region some coffees are traditionally unwashed (naturals) and some are washed. In general, the unwashed coffees may be described as wild or gamey in flavour, not a taste to everyone's liking, but extremely interesting, if variable. At times, other terms, such as lemony, delicate, winey, floral and soft may be applied to certain Ethiopian coffees. In appearance, the beans are not only unimpressive, but may be downright off-putting, and in some cases the processing is a bit haphazard, if not careless, resulting in a maddening unpredictability. Nevertheless, these coffees are not run-of-the-mill, and may represent the epitome – in other words, as good as it gets – of coffee-tasting. Some of the best-known Ethiopian coffees are Djimmah, Ghimbi, Lekempti, Harrar (both long berry and short berry, known for their soft, winey Mocha flavour – a name stolen from the old Yemeni port of Mokka), Limu, and Yergacheffe.

Due to the unique, wonderfully delicate flavours, it is never a wise thing to dark-roast Ethiopian beans. In fact, to come across these beans dark-roasted might suggest an inferior crop for that year's production.

Above: Ethiopian Sidamo grade 2 washed medium-roasted beans.

Gabon

The former French colony still sells much of its crop of decent, neutral robusta to France, and the rest to the Netherlands. Interestingly, much of Gabon's coffee is grown in the north, and as it occasionally seems to export more than it grows, there is a strong possibility that the more enterprising Equatorial Guineans, on the north-west border, smuggle beans into Gabon, where the small, mostly urban population enjoys relative prosperity due to oil-rich natural resources.

Below: Ethiopian Djimmah roasted beans.

Ghana

Formerly the "Gold Coast" British colony, Ghana provides 15 per cent of the world's cocoa, which is cheaper to grow than coffee. In areas where the soil is not favourable for cocoa, however, the government encourages coffee cultivation. Although the coffee is rather nondescript robusta, it is bought mainly by Britain, Germany and the Netherlands.

Above: Ghanaian robusta medium roast.

Guinea

In 1895, the French introduced arabica from Tonkin to their colony, but the yield was poor; the climate and soil of this republic (since 1958) however, grows good "neutral" robusta in its forest shades. Unfortunately, 25 years of Marxist dictatorial rule broke many trade connections between Guinea and Western countries, and today rivalry between ethnic groups, questionable legislative elections, as well as crippling world debts, have not been conducive to re-establishing the stable trade needed to improve coffee quality or quantity. Some Guinean coffee finds its way into the Ivory Coast, its neighbour to the east.

Ivory Coast (Côte d'Ivoire)

The Ivory Coast is usually Africa's second-largest coffee producer. Thirty three years of a stable one-man presidency, with a relatively smooth transition to another seemingly stable leader, plus monetary and defence aid from its former ruler, France, have helped to provide the stability that a long-term, labour-intensive industry such as coffee requires. The rather average quality and its consistent and reliable supply, make Ivory Coast robusta attractive to many coffee blenders throughout the world, although France and Italy buy much of the crop (which may include beans smuggled in from its neighbours, poor, land-locked Mali to the north, and Guinea to the west). An agricultural research centre near Abidjan recently developed arabusta, the most successful coffee hybrid yet produced.

Kenya

For quality rather than quantity, Kenya's high-grown, wet-processed arabica is one of the world's great growths. The fairly narrow range of flavours is good and consistent, probably because the Kenyan industry is strictly regulated by the Coffee Board of Kenya (Nairobi), which determines the grading of each bag of green beans, at times even blending together green beans from different plantations under the House Blend label. Those bags marked "AA" are the top quality and are sought-after by the gourmet coffee trade. Kenyan coffee is noted for its sharp, fruity, sometimes even lemony or citrus flavours, due to high acidity, and for the consistent (small, round and deep greeny-blue) appearance of the beans, be they AA, the more commonly exported "AB", or the celebrated and expensive Kenyan peaberries.

Above: Ivory Coast robusta grade 2.

Above: Kenyan peaberry green beans.

Liberia

What can be said about a country that in 1980 had 165,000 bags – though not all of it traceable to its own coffee plantations – of exportable coffee, and now produces less than 5,000? Though the quality was never particularly good, the robusta was usable – the USA bought most of it – which is more than could be said for the native liberica. There were high hopes for the arabusta possibilities, and a soluble-coffee factory was planned. Unfortunately, warring factions and corruption of power have led to a total economic collapse in recent years.

Madagascar

Coffee is Madagascar's most important export, although the island is the leading world producer of vanilla. A French colony until 1960, Madagascar, after 18 years of radical socialism, is now a multi-party democracy trying to re-establish its ties with Western trade and rebuild its agricultural programmes. The larger robusta growth is ranged along the slopes of the long eastern coastline, while the arabica regions are on the central plateau. Generally, the coffee, much of which is bought by France, is excellent, and there are plans to develop more plantations, especially as the more-than-14-million residents are enthusiastic drinkers. Part of any future plans for coffee expansion, however, is the desire to preserve the forests, home to unique species of flora and fauna.

Above: Malawian medium-roast beans.

Malawi

When Malawi (formerly Nyasaland) became independent from British rule in 1964, it spent nearly thirty years under the rule of one despot, Banda. Now, under stable multi-party rule, poverty is still endemic, but human rights, education and literacy are increasing; all conducive to the labour-intensive business of growing coffee. The arabica coffee is grown mostly on small-holdings and processed locally in the mountainous plateaux at the extreme ends of this long, narrow country. Drought eclipses all other problems, but it is hoped that more of this excellent coffee, reminiscent of an average Kenyan, will be available for world consumption in the near future.

Mozambique

Portugal used this colony to grow tea, while its coffee-growing colony was Angola. Consequently, the arabica (Blue Mountain variety) grown here, supplemented by the wild *racemosa*, meets only local demands. After independence in 1975 and a 15-year civil war, Mozambique is one of the poorest countries in the world. Now, with a fragile democracy and many millions in aid pledges, there is a remote possibility that someday Mozambique could be an exporter of good coffee once again, as it has not only the climate and soil, but also the second-largest harbour in Africa.

Above: Freshly picked cherries show a mix of both ripe and immature fruit.

Nigeria

Unfortunately, there is little positive to say about this country's coffee. The mostly robusta crop is of poor and inconsistent quality, although Britain is one of the main buyers of its former colony's crop. Smuggling, corruption, crime, debt, pollution, and aid-stopping human rights violations have helped to shrink the economy since the oil-rich boom of the 1970s, which the various military regimes sadly allowed to totally eclipse the more long-term government agricultural support.

La Réunion

Today, the main crop of this small volcanic island 805km/500 miles east of Madagascar is sugar cane. How very different from the days when coffee planting was mandatory of all free citizens, when destroying a tree exacted the death penalty, and when the monetary currency was backed by coffee! The island of Bourbon, as the French colony was then named, gave its name to the oldest, and still best, variety of arabica coffee, and it was from two trees brought here from Yemen in 1715 that many of the world's coffee plantations originated.

Rwanda

German and Belgian colonizers reinforced Tutsi domination here, and since a Hutu government achieved independence in 1962, there has been violent, if at times intermittent, tribal warfare. The arabica coffee quality is generally good, although it could be said it almost suffers from excess; the extremely rich soil, abundant rainfall, strong sun and quick growth may be the collective cause of a peculiar grassy taste sometimes found in all but the superior grade. Coffee is still very much Rwanda's primary source of income, and in spite of the warfare and pest infestations, its production is increasing. The Rwanda Coffee Board currently plans to rehabilitate 76 of the 140 coffee-growing communes by providing fertilisers, pesticides and new high-yielding plants.

St. Helena

This South Atlantic island, the only dependency still receiving British budgetary aid, was annexed by the East India Company in 1659 and began growing coffee when seeds were brought from Yemen in 1732. At some point the cultivation was abandoned, and the only remaining trees were wild.

Although at present the island's main economic activities cannot support the population, an enterprising coffee roaster in the 1980s began the revitalization of a tiny coffee industry which may soon become noted for hand-produced, totally organic, good-acidity and balanced, quality coffee.

São Tomé & Príncipe

Although cocoa brings in 90 per cent of São Tomé's export earnings, it still produces coffee, most of which is a reputedly lovely arabica, grown in the rich soil sloping up to the island's volcano. Since the Marxist regime, which greatly reduced coffee-growing, was replaced by a democratic constitution in 1990, the islands are seeking closer relations with various Western countries, in particular their old colonizer, Portugal, and the United States, so perhaps more of this coffee will become available on world markets.

Sierra Leone

Another sad story of a country decimated by military coups and civil war. Until as late as 1985, the robusta grown in this former British colony of freed slaves was some of the best of African blending coffee – FAQ (Fair Average Quality) and neutral (an important term for robusta) in the cup.

South Africa

For a long time South Africa has grown some good quality arabica coffee, cultivated from plants of the Bourbon and Blue Mountain variety, originally brought from Kenya. The region of growth is mostly that of Kwa-Zulu Natal, which, with Southern Brazil, is one of the few regions which dares to grow coffee outside of the tropical zone. There are many reasons, however to doubt that much of the coffee grown here will ever reach the world market; the 1996 constitution is decidedly fragile, and racial tensions and personal dangers run high; the country is heavily populated and, indeed has to import much of the coffee it consumes; and because much of the international trading is based on lucrative mineral and mining resources. The labour-intensive coffee production and accompanying slow profit turnover do not seem encouraging to those lovers of good coffee around the world.

Above: Picked coffee cherries lose skin and pulp in wet-process pulping machines.

Above: Drying coffee cherries must be raked and turned to dry evenly and thoroughly before hulling.

Sudan

This country is blessed with high altitudes, and wild coffee, probably spread by bird and beast from Ethiopia, already grows there. Ambitious plans, however, of a few years past to grow more of this excellent arabica, have sadly come to little. A series of problems, from civil wars, droughts, disease and starvation, through to international isolation due to concerns for human rights and terrorism have resulted in the decimation of any coffee industry whatsoever.

Tanzania

Although Tanzania is still a very poor country, in almost every area of activity it is improving. An economic reform programme has helped to cut inflation and the budget deficit, and IMF-backed aid is helping to reorganise the agricultural sector. Coffee is Tanzania's number one crop, but where previously most of the arabica coffee was produced on large estates, leaving robusta production to the small-holders, today many small-holders with access to the equipment of a co-operative are able to grow arabica coffee. The washed coffee is excellent, reminiscent of Kenyan coffee, but the acidity is less intense and the overall feel slightly milder and lighter; also the quality is not quite as consistent as that of Kenyan beans. The older bourbon variety still produces the best flavour, aroma and body. Moshi, near Mount Kilimanjaro, is a main coffee-marketing centre in an area where many small-holders grow a combined crop of coffee shaded by banana trees.

Togo

Togo's coffee story is happily different from many other former colonies in Africa. The democratic government and efficient civil service encourage and help the cultivation of the rather ordinary, but well-graded, dry-processed neutral robusta. It produces a fairly large harvest, considering that Togo is a very small country. Its own domestic coffee consumption is low, so it can export most of what it grows and it is happy to diversify its market, selling its coffee to various European buyers, including its former colonizer France, although the Dutch often take the bulk of the crop.

Togo maintains a good road system, and its capital is a coastal port, which can make a real difference to the success of a coffee crop. Although the country has few natural resources, its citizens, particularly the market-women of Lomé, who basically control the country's retail trade, are enterprising.

Right: Tanzanian Chagga.

Uganda

Since 1986, President Museveni's "no-party democracy" has thus far saved Uganda from the ethnic tensions which have destroyed the economies of neighbours Rwanda and Sudan, from which thousands of refugees have poured into Uganda. Economic liberalizations have attracted aid receipts and private sector investments; the road system is under repair, and coffee production, mostly robusta, is high. Financial experts know that one crop providing 93 per cent of a country's export earnings is not always healthy. However, it is great news for coffee lovers, as a small percentage of tea-drinking Uganda's coffee is very good washed arabica, grown mostly in the Bugisu region adjoining the border with Kenya (whose coffee is very similar). Indeed, before privatization, some arabica beans were smuggled into Kenya for its better, unregulated prices; since privatisation some arabica is now smuggled to avoid the Ugandan government's tax.

Above: Uganda arabica Bugisu AA green beans.

Yemen

As Arabia (Arabia Felix to the Romans), this small country gave its name to arabica coffee, which was introduced to the world through its ports. Lying on the eastern shores of the Red Sea, geographically it is Asian, but in reality the general coffee character is closer to those of its nearest coffee-growing neighbour, Ethiopia.

Mocha coffee Yemeni coffees are the original Mocha, taken from the name of the old port, today's Al Mukha. "Mocha"

Above: Yemeni roasted mocha "31".

coffees grown in Ethiopia (notably Harrar and Djimmah), are the impostors, although the tastes, like those of unwashed arabicas, may be similar to the Yemeni flavours: wild, gamey, winey, dry, delicate, varied and unpredictable, possibly with some chocolate overtones. They are, however different coffees; the Ethiopian mochas will be cheaper, as the true Yemeni beans, even the most common (Sanani, from San`a, and Matari, from the province of Bany Matar) are quite scarce.

After Yemen sided with Iraq in the Gulf War, Saudi Arabia expelled a million Yemeni workers, whose return so burdened the government that it stopped many farm subsidies, and farmers began growing the more profitable narcotic *qat* plants. Also, the political instability which resulted in a civil war in 1994 was disruptive to the Yemen economy for years afterwards.

Zambia

Unlike some other African countries, Zambia's problems do not seem to be political (other than the one of bureaucratic corruption) or racial; its weakness is the fact that it is dependent

Above: Zambia green beans.

on copper for 90 per cent of its export earnings, and copper prices have fallen and Zambia's reserves are declining. Perhaps because it is land-locked and lacks a good road network, Zambia's arable land is under-utilized. At any rate, the government seems committed to market reforms, and certainly its encouragement of more cultivation of the excellent Zambian coffees is resulting in greater crops. Zambian coffee is similar in flavour to other East African arabicas; its lightness is particularly reminiscent of coffee from Tanzania, with whom it shares its Northern border near the coffee-growing Muchinga Mountains.

Above: Zimbabwe dark-roasted beans.

Zimbabwe

Although much of land-locked Zimbabwe is a high-altitude country, rainfall is erratic and drought common, except in the mountains of the eastern region near the Mozambique border, where most of its fine washed arabica coffee is grown. Coffee from Zimbabwe, the best of which is found near the town of Chipinge, may not be as famous as Kenyan, but it shares many of the same cup characteristics: it is generally free from off-tastes, and has fruity acidity and good aroma; it may also have a slightly peppery flavour not found in coffee from Kenya.

Like Malawian coffee, it is sometimes recognised as a gourmet coffee by the speciality coffee trade, depending on the particular crop. Whether the government's repeated declarations to nationalise farms and plantations will ultimately affect coffee production, remains to be seen.

CENTRAL AMERICA AND CARIBBEAN

The coffees from Central America are justly renowned for their completeness in terms of body, flavour and aroma.

Costa Rica

Many people hope to go to Heaven when they die; coffee lovers hope to go to Costa Rica. This little Central American republic enjoys the best possible conditions for growing superb coffee: a high-altitude central plateau (the Meseta Central) basking in a mild, temperate climate with good moisture and cool nights, and covering about 2,000 square miles; rich volcanic-based soil; ports on two oceans; and a stable, organized, commercially-oriented government. Of course, Costa Rica is not problem-free: the inaccessibility of the highest altitudes makes coffee transportation difficult and expensive, and there is always the worry of volcanic activity and the devastating tropical storms which plague Central American existence. Costa Rica, unlike its neighbours, lost only about 90,000 bags of coffee to Hurricane Mitch.

The coffee, Costa Rica's agricultural mainstay, is all washed arabica – it is socially unacceptable even to mention the word robusta – and natives enjoy a high standard of consumption; in fact, Costa Ricans drink more than twice the amount of coffee consumed in Italy.

Quality coffee The best coffees are generally those from around the capital city of San José, and the nearby towns of Heredia and Alajuela. The Tarrazu region to the south of San José produces some superb coffees of exquisite acidity and "clean" cup liquor. Bags of beans may be labelled by the area, such as Tarrazu's Tres Rios, Dota, and San Marcos, or by owner/estate names, such as FJO Sarchi company, located on the slopes of the Poas volcano. La Minita, Windmill, Henri Tournon (HT) – whose green beans are really turquoise – are names indicative of high altitude and a sharp, tangy acidity, perhaps the most desirable attribute in a cup of coffee. Some experts shriek at the idea of drinking Costa Rican coffee any way but black; however, the sharpest acidity gives a wonderful mild flavour when the coffee is drunk with a little milk or cream.

Costa Rican coffee is almost always very fragrant, and the cup flavour is "clean" and pure. Occasionally, the body in a cup of Costa Rican coffee may err to the thin side, but the flavour is so exquisite, that a thinner liquor can be excused. Sometimes one hears of Costa Rican coffee being dark-roasted. Unless the coffee is below the usual standards or somehow defective, such a practice should be avoided at all costs, as a darker roast destroys the lovely acidity, and the flavour loses the desired distinctive (and expensive-tasting) qualities.

Above: A traditional Costa Rican painted cart carries the fruit picked on the plateau.

Above: Tuj San Marcos de Tarrazu green beans.

Right: A dark roast spoils the acidity of Costa Rican beans.

Below: Cuban Extra Turquino.

Cuba

Since the collapse of the USSR, Cuba's mainstay in export trade, Cuba's economy has been in recession. Desperate to attract foreign capital, Cuba is allowing some outside investments in the hotel and tourist industry, a showplace for its arabica coffees, which are increasing in production, although sugar, of course, is still the main export crop. Cuban coffee, which has been grown since the mid-1700s, is clean and flavourful, and carefully processed and graded; it is marketed under exotic names, which in reality indicate only particular bean-size averages, the largest being Extra Turquino. Cuban coffee is lower in acidity than that of most other Caribbean coffees due to Cuba's lack of high altitudes. It is, however, pleasant in the cup and is best dark-roasted.

Dominican Republic

When Hispaniola was partitioned in 1697 between France and Spain, Spain's share was the eastern two-thirds of the island. Coffee, which has been grown here since the early 1700s, and is still traded under the Santo Domingo name, is not a major crop, but the washed arabicas are good. The best coffee, grown in the south western Barahona region, is known for its acidity and full body. Slightly less acidic but very satisfying in the cup are the soft, full-bodied Bani and Ocoa coffees, from the slopes of the southern end of the central *cordillera*. Cibao are the rather average beans. Dark-roasting accents the lovely, mellow sweetness of the Cibao, Bani and Ocoa coffee beans.

El Salvador

This poor country, small and densely populated, precariously nested on top of a seismic zone with 20 volcanoes, possesses no natural resources. Its infrastructure (roads, bridges and electricity), destroyed by eleven years of civil war, hangs on to its fragile existence by two thin strings: coffee and international aid. With little chance to diversify, the country has relied on its wet-processed arabica to bring in 90 per cent of its export earnings in spite of serious attacks of rust and pests.

In October 1998, Hurricane Mitch's torrential rains figuratively washed away at least 150,000 bags of coffee, and probably more was ruined by humidity-induced fungus after the floods abated. Salvador coffee (its trade name) is grown at various levels of altitude, all of it rather high, and is graded accordingly; the blue-green SHG is the best, with its acidy flavour, medium-to-full body and sweet overtones. "Pipil" is the brand name of a reputedly excellent organic coffee.

Guadeloupe

This little island at the northern end of the Caribbean Windward Islands is caught between wanting complete autonomy from France's Overseas Department while being almost completely dependent on French aid. In 1995, its unemployment was 26 per cent. Because banana prices are extremely unstable, it is now seeking to expand sugar production. Yet, it still grows tiny amounts of what must have been a world-class coffee, described by Philippe Jobin as "one of the best 'crus' of the world...hard to replace for lovers of high class coffee". The climate, soil, workforce, expertise and resources are available, so perhaps the gourmet coffee trade could encourage Guadeloupe to bring this coffee back from virtual extinction.

Guatemala

Coffee is the first crop of Central America's largest economy, where 90 per cent of the population still live below the poverty line. The extreme inequalities in wealth and land distribution limit modernization. Coffee is grown on very large, wealthy *haciendas* (estates), and on a few thousand *fincas*, or farms, all owned mostly by *ladinos* (non-Indians), as well as on many thousand subsistence small-holdings worked by poor Indians, mostly in the highlands. Guatemala has not yet

Left: Salvador high-grown coffee, classified according to superior European Preparation standards.

Right: Guatemalan Huehuetenango green beans.

succumbed to the temptation to replace old varieties of trees, such as Bourbon, with high-yield, low-taste varieties, although the low yield per hectare is costly. There are sponsored programmes to help small-holders to minimise their costs, enabling them to continue with high-quality, low-yield trees for the gourmet market.

Above: Guatemalan genuine Antigua green beans.

Types of coffee Guatemalan coffee is rated by many experts as one of the best growths in the world. Unlike the Costa Rican coffees, Guatemalans vary more from region to region, although the general flavour profile of "medium-to-full-bodied liquor, perfectly balanced with good acidity and complex smoky, spicy and chocolate tones" would fit many, if not most. Near the capital city is the famous Guatemala Antigua, the old city founded by the conquistadors and destroyed by an earthquake in 1773, which gives its name to one of Guatemala's finest coffees. Towards the north is Cobán, another city whose name represents high altitude resulting in high-quality acidity. There are numerous other regions of superb Guatemalan coffees, but Huehuetenango, in an isolated western area, is a name increasingly noted for fine acidity and unique flavours in coffees grown mostly on small-holdings.

Haiti

In the 1697 partition of Hispaniola, France received Haiti, the western third of the island. Aided by Toussaint L'Ouverture's rebellion, Haiti was free by 1804, and thus began what will soon be two hundred years of political instability. This poorest of countries, where many houses are windowless earthen huts, depends very much on coffee for much of its income. Unfortunately, the coffee grading and classification is a confused process, and the simplest explanation is that coffee samples are graded by size of bean, altitude, cup quality, defective beans and number of stones included. The old trees, growing nearly wild, still produce lovely large bluish beans of the typica variety, heavy with humidity, which are often dry-processed, mostly by peasants. Sweet and mellow, these full-bodied coffees with lowish acidity – particularly the rich, winey, washed SHG beans – can be excellent, but not reliably so; they are perhaps at their best roasted medium-dark.

Most Haitian coffee is biologically pure simply because fertilizers, pesticides and fungicides are too expensive for the average Haitian grower.

Honduras

Like most other Central American countries, Honduras markets its coffees by designation of altitude. Honduras produces washed arabicas, clean with good acidity and flavour, possibly lacking only slightly in body – overall, a high-quality coffee, perhaps not in a gourmet class, but a worthy contributor to a blend. Hurricane Mitch caused direct losses of nearly 500,000 bags of Honduran coffee, but future production may also be affected, depending on transportation, infrastructure damage and time required for repair.

Jamaica

Few coffee-drinkers realize that Jamaica earns most of its money from, and is the world's third-largest producer of, bauxite, and that, in fact, its famous Blue Mountain coffee grows only on the eastern tip of the island, in a small area extending no further west than Kingston. The production is shared by only three parishes: St. Andrew, where coffee was originally planted in 1728 by Sir Nicholas Lawes; Portland, on the northern slopes of the mountains; and the parish of St. Thomas on the south side. Other coffee-growing parts of Jamaica, which collectively would occupy an area twice the size of the Blue Mountain coffee estates and farms, actually grow about 75 per cent of Jamaica's coffee.

These other regions sell coffee bags labelled High Mountain Supreme and Prime Washed Jamaica, names

Left: Honduran green beans.

Right: Jamaica Blue Mountain roasted beans.

perfectly innocent on their own, but dangerously close to Jamaica Blue Mountain in all but quality. In fact, although we speak in "bags", the real Jamaica Blue Mountain comes in barrels, and anyway, all exported Jamaican coffee is certified by the Coffee Industry Board. Even so, the unwary would-be JBM consumer is seldom safe, as when buying 200 grams of roasted beans (which is about all anybody can afford), they might not actually see the container the beans were shipped in. Also there are many countries who grow the Blue Mountain variety of arabica, and a few even have a Blue Mountain range of hills.

As more Jamaica Blue Mountain coffee is sold than that small area could possibly produce, remember Davy Crockett's motto, "Be sure you're right, then go ahead": buy 100 per cent pure Jamaica Blue Mountain Coffee only from a reputable source.

Aroma and balance Jamaica Blue Mountain is only a high-quality Caribbean coffee, and as such, is subject to much the same vagaries that Mother Nature inflicts on other Caribbean coffees. A good crop will produce a cup that is an exquisite balance of nutty aroma; bright, but not overwhelming acidity; delicate sweetness; and a clean but nectar-like finish. The body may be slightly lacking in fullness, and someone who likes a hearty cup of coffee may need to use more than normal to brew a satisfying cup – another consideration when getting out your wallet at the cash till. An inferior crop, especially possible with recent years of over-production leading to possibly less careful processing, may be disappointingly mediocre, and could be easily outclassed by a Costa Rican, Guatamalan, or even Cuban.

One possibility for change in the Jamaican Blue Mountain market is that while Japan has for nearly thirty years been its major purchaser, with the rest of the world scrambling to pay princely sums for the remnants, Asia's economic crisis has plunged Japan into a terrible recession, and this could alter somewhat the distribution of the world's most expensive coffee.

Martinique

This tiny island in the middle of the Lesser Antilles, described by Columbus as "the most beautiful country in the world", was where Capt. Gabriel Mathieu de Clieu, in the 1720s, decided to plant the coffee tree "stolen" from Louis XIV's royal greenhouse. The first coffee specimen to enter the Western Hemisphere, it flourished in the rich volcanic soil of Mt. Pelée's slopes, and became the progenitor of the millions of coffee trees grown throughout the New World in the early colonial period.

After a hundred years of success, Martinique's coffee plantations declined, greatly hindered by the natural disasters that seem to strike Martinique, situated in "Hurricane Alley", about every five years. Today, Martinique's citizens, like those of

Above: Jamaica Blue Mountain green beans.

Above: The first stage of processing the cherries is rinsing in water.

Right: Mexican roasted beans.

Guadeloupe, receive French subsidies for their high levels of unemployment. Coffee production seems a thing of the past. The few remaining ageing trees are sporadically attended to, but as Martinique has the climate, the soil, workforce, etc., one can only hope the situation will improve.

Mexico

Mexico, which grows some fairly average, mostly washed arabica coffees, classifies its crop by altitude-denoting terms similar to those of Nicaragua. Although many regions of southern Mexico grow coffee, there are some coffees which rise above the average, not only literally in altitude, but in interesting, hard-to-describe and sometimes unpredictable flavours.

In the state of Veracruz on the Gulf of Mexico, the mountainous region near Coatepec produces an excellent "altura", characterized by a light body, but with a slightly sharp, dry acidity, which sometimes has nutty or chocolate hints. The alturas of nearby Huatusco and further inland Orizaba are also fine coffees. Oaxaca, the more remote south-western state, gives its name to good coffees, including Oaxaca Pluma. Chiapas, adjoining the southern border with Guatemala, grows large amounts of arabica marketed under the name of Tapachula. Flavourful and particularly aromatic, and occasionally bordering on the "sour", Mexico's alturas and SHG's are not to everybody's taste, but they are very individual and never boring.

Like many Central American countries, Mexico is subject to earthquakes, particularly in the mountainous regions where the better coffees are grown. Due to its size and location, however, Mexico is not always affected simultaneously by the same problems as other Central American producers. While Honduras, El Salvador, Nicaragua, Guatemala, and Panama were all plagued by floods, rain, or heavy humidity caused by Hurricane Mitch, Mexico was in the throes of a severe six-month drought, that eventually caused the loss of about 400,000 bags.

Nicaragua

The very poor country of Nicaragua, for which coffee is the main export crop, reported crop losses of up to 30 per cent of its more than 1-million-bag-average crop after it was hit by Hurricane Mitch in October 1998. Thankfully, 20 per cent of the devastation was due to impassable roads preventing the crop reaching the processing mills, and therefore was not permanent damage. The remaining 10 per cent of the loss was direct damage when a massive mudslide from the Casita volcano destroyed entire coffee fields in the region of Matagalpa. All Nicaraguan coffees are wet-processed arabicas grown in fertile volcanic-based soil.

Under normal conditions, Matagalpa and the neighbouring town of Jinotega produce the best Nicaraguan coffee, of which the SHG is known for its large beans, slightly salty acidity, and medium-to-full body and good aroma. The Nicaraguan version of the Maragogype variety represents the world's largest coffee beans, although the flavour is generally not quite as universally appreciated as that of the Guatemalan Maragogype.

Above: Nicaraguan SHG medium roast.

Panama

Panama's main coffees grow in the far western region nearest the Costa Rican border in the high-altitude slopes around the Barú volcano, where the regional names are Davíd and Boquete; the district of Chiriquí, and slightly to the east, Tole, produce notable high-grown washed arabicas. Café Volcán Barú is a newer gourmet coffee from the same region. The SHB Panamanian

Below: Nicaraguan Maravilla roasted coffee beans.

Above: Medium-roasted beans from Boquete, in north-western Panama.

coffees are known for their deep green colour, light body, bright but not sharp acidity, and pleasant, sweet taste; major buyers of Panama coffee are the French and the Scandinavians. The damage sustained by Panama's coffee crop from the heavy rains brought by Hurricane Mitch was about one-fifth of the 1998/1999 crop, or about 45,000 bags.

Puerto Rico

What a nice change to read about a Caribbean island revitalizing a dying coffee trade, which is exactly what Puerto Rico has been doing. Always reckoned to have been one of the world's best growths, Puerto Rico is supplier to the Vatican. A few years ago it grew less coffee as it drank more, and in 1968 stopped exporting coffee completely, as it was importing far more than it grew.

At the same time, the US minimum wage law, effective in the Associate State of Puerto Rico, ensured the Puerto Rican workforce a far higher standard of living than that enjoyed by any other Caribbean population, while attracting US industry to its "cheap" labour. As almost no struggling coffee plantations could afford to pay US minimum wages, coffee-growing was nearly a thing of the past, except for a few thousand small-holders, grouped into local cooperatives. Now, at least two of these cooperatives, Yauco, (whose "Yauco Selecto" is simply superb) and Lares, have revived coffee production by producing, in the wake of the US's demand for "specialty" (sic) coffees, high-quality beans of the grand old varieties, carefully picked and graded. The gourmet coffees are expensive to produce, but they exact high prices, which quality-seeking buyers from several foreign countries are willing to pay.

The Puerto Rican *crus*, which could be called the world's most "powerful" coffees, were always known for their intense aroma and deep, rich, and amazingly sweet flavours, fully balanced by a heavy liquor; how wonderful to have them back again.

Trinidad & Tobago

These two islands, 14km/9 miles off the coast of Venezuela, grow what is called "small amounts" of robusta coffee, mostly for instant coffee processing; in fact, these "small amounts" make up a crop that annually exceeds the combined harvests of Liberia, Gabon, Equatorial Guinea and Benin. But "small" is relative to the matter of income: after gaining independence from Britain in 1962, the oil-rich islands enjoyed a high level of prosperity – Trinidadians for several years had the reputation of importing more Scotch whiskey per capita than any other country – while constantly increasing its oil production and refinery.

In recent years, however, world oil price movements have highlighted a need to diversify. Tobago is finally developing its tourism, as not only its beaches but also its butterfly species attract tourists. Behind the all-is-well façade, the interior of Trinidad is home to dissatisfied poverty-stricken farmers; unemployment, crime, drugs-related problems, and oil-spills are a constant threat. The day may yet come when the demanding, but satisfying, business of growing more coffee may offer an alternative to the tourist trade.

Above: Coffee tree with ripe cherries ready for picking.

SOUTH AMERICA

Brazil, as the world's largest coffee producer dominates this region, but there are a number of countries producing superb beans worth trying.

Argentina

Argentina grows so little coffee that its production figures are difficult to obtain. The Tropic of Capricorn runs across the extreme north of the country, and the two general areas where coffee can be grown are the moderately humid and tropical north-east, where it was introduced by the Jesuits in 1729 in Misiones, and the north-west Andean provinces around Tucumán. Because of their exclusion from the tropical zone, the Argentine coffee trees, which are arabica, are subject to the periodic ravages of frost.

Bolivia

The Bolivian coffee crop is hand-picked, mainly washed arabica. Although most of it is of exportable quality, Bolivia is land-locked, and the problem is one of supply. Coffee is cultivated on about 30,000 acres, many in areas so remote that there is practically no way to transport the beans out during certain seasons. Also, as is the case with several South American countries, the temptation to produce coca is often too much for the inhabitants of poorer regions to resist.

Bolivian coffees tend to be slightly bitter, but, based on figures of the last several years, the coffee crop is improving in both quantity and quality, as older trees are being replaced. Perhaps Bolivia will soon be able to provide more accessible, available beans for the world market.

Brazil

Just how much is "an awful lot"? Although the quantity may vary from year to year, there is simply no other way to describe the Brazilian coffee crop, which can usually claim one-third of total global production. Unlike many other coffee-producing countries, however, who may export all of the good coffee and drink very little at home, Brazilians in one year will consume about 12 million bags, much of it in the form of the much-beloved *cafèzinho,* the tiny cup of usually good-quality black coffee drunk by most Brazilians several times a day.

It is interesting to note that in Brazil the word for "breakfast" is *café da manhã* (morning coffee), whereas in Portugal, which in theory speaks the same language, "breakfast" is the rather less descriptive *primeiro almoço* or *pequeno almoço* (as in the French "little lunch" definition of breakfast).

Types of coffee Brazil grows both arabica and robusta, but the crop is primarily arabica, mostly dry-processed. With both the Equator and the Tropic of Capricorn passing through it, the bulk of Brazil lies in the tropical zone, and around eight million acres of Brazilian land is dedicated to coffee-growing. Towards the northern part of the country, where the climate is hotter and the terrain flatter, is where the robusta (conilon variety) is grown, shaded from the more direct rays of the sun.

The coffee improves towards the south of the country, where the best arabica is grown in higher terrain, but these plateau regions are very close to the bottom edge of the tropical zone, and frost is frequently a problem, if not a major disaster. When frost warnings are reported in southern Brazil,

Above: Each bag in this Brazilian warehouse contains the annual harvest of 60 trees.

Above: Aerial view of one of the many large coffee-growing plantations in Brazil. The flat terrain suggests robusta cultivation.

Above: Brazilian Santos green beans.

international trade coffee prices immediately jump in anticipation of a possible shortage.

Seventeen Brazilian states grow many varieties of coffee, but there are four or five regions which dominate the exportable coffee cultivation. Brazilian beans are identified, categorized and graded by many different criteria, the first of which is the port of export. The more northerly state of Bahia, which produces some good washed arabica among its generally average dry-processed coffees, and small amounts of Maragogype, exports its coffee through the port of Salvador de Bahia. The smaller state of Espírito Santo ships its rather average beans from Vitória; the large state of Minas Gerais (Sul de Minas is an excellent coffee), uses both the ports of Rio de Janeiro and the more southerly port of Santos, which is also the port for the various coffees produced in the state of São Paulo. Santos exports the "flat bean" Santos and the superior Bourbon Santos. The southern-most Brazilian coffee port is Paranagua, from which the state of Paraná ships its coffees.

Quantity or quality Brazilian arabicas are not usually included in the ranks of gourmet or speciality coffees. Indeed, pushed to a general description of these enormously-varying growths, most experts would say that Brazil coffee is poor-to-average quality, low-to-moderate acidity and neutral or bland in flavour, a fairly accurate profile of most of the millions of bags exported by Brazil. Part of the problem with the quality is the fact that the sheer space in Brazil allows the operations of huge plantations, where the picking is not picking at all; it may be "stripping" or even machine-harvesting. In either case, the mix of fruit will include coffee cherries at wide ranges of maturation, and the odds are that no amount of later sorting will

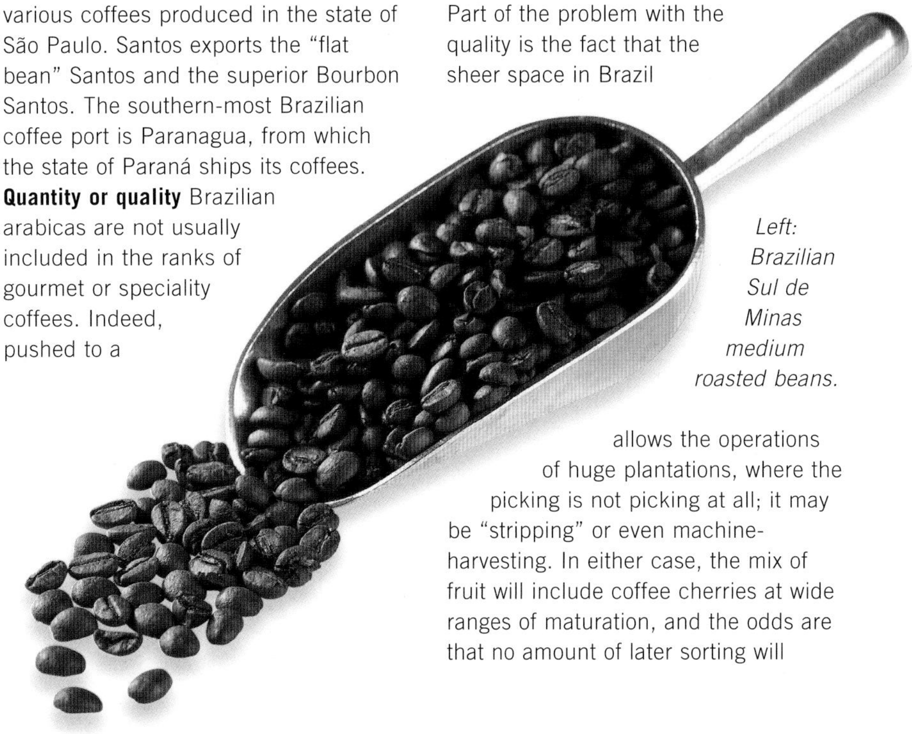

Left: Brazilian Sul de Minas medium roasted beans.

Above: Graded and sorted coffee beans are bagged, to be made ready for export.

produce a truly homogeneous yield. Hypothetically, even the most meticulous harvesting could not make up for the lack of any really high altitudes in Brazil's topography; without the altitude there is little acidity, and the result is the bland character attributed to most of Brazil's coffees.

Of course, there are exceptions to every rule, and those who automatically dismiss Brazil from the list of the world's "gourmet" coffee producers probably have never been privy to some of the best Brazilian Santos coffees, which may not be common or easily obtainable, but do exist.

There are estates in southern Brazil where high quality is pursued intensely, and careful tending and detailed experimentation in processing have led to the production of some truly wonderful coffee – smooth, well-balanced and mellow. The best Brazilian coffee comes from young trees of the bourbon variety, whose small, rounded beans produce excellent cup qualities, fine acidity and sweetness. After the Brazilian bourbon trees have produced a few crops, the beans become larger and lose a bit of their flavour; the coffee is then described as "flat bean Santos".

The cup quality classifications can be mystifying, since, besides rather obvious terms such as "full body", "bad cup", "fair cup", and "fine cup" among others, there are more elusive terms used to describe Brazilian coffees, such as "strictly soft" and "Rio-y" (pronounced with a long "i", despite the fact that it comes from the state of Rio).

The term "hard" in Brazilian coffee means, as might be expected, the opposite of "soft". "Rio-y" coffee is easier to explain: this is the coffee which gives Middle Eastern coffee blends their distinctive flavour. On its own, "rio-y" coffee tastes medicinal, harsh, inky or iodine-y. The flavour is thought to be the result of certain micro-organisms and is not always present every year in crops from the same soil, although the geographic areas in which it is found have increased considerably. Shunned by most countries for being strongly defective, rio-y coffee is avidly sought by Turkey, Greece, Cyprus and most Middle Eastern countries, as well as by Denmark. Blended with Ethiopian coffee, the rio-y flavour seems to benefit from the Middle Eastern practice of boiling the coffee with sugar.

There was a time when Brazilian coffees made up 60 per cent of the world crop, and they were the standard "extenders" for almost every blend in the world; their unobtrusive character, generally good body and plenteous supply ensured that Brazilian coffee was the basis for most of the world's blended brands. It is interesting to note that the International Coffee Organization's preliminary statistics for the 1998 crop list the average "unit value" of Brazilian exports at 110.95 US cents per pound, which is extremely close to the prices of all the world's coffees averaged together: 110.05 US cents per pound. These figures mean that if a blender, when considering what beans to buy in order to produce a decent flavour in an average-priced blend, must bulk out his blend with something cheaper than the average Brazilian coffee, to offset the higher prices of coffees used for better flavour.

Left: Of the millions of bags of coffee exported by Brazil, the quality is generally only average.

Colombia

Unfortunately, the rich soil which produces Colombia's best coffees is the result of past volcanic activity in an area of continuing subterranean instability. Although the massive earthquake which tore through the heart of Colombia's largest coffee-growing region in January 1999 miraculously did little damage to the trees themselves, farming infrastructure suffered 65 per cent damage, which could cause a drop in quality as farmers economize for necessary repairs. Whatever the outcome, Colombia will still hold its position at second place in the global statistics for coffee-growing, as its nearest rival is Vietnam, whose production of robusta, though increasing, is less than half Colombia's.

Coffee-growing areas Colombia's three mountain ranges, or *cordilleras*, are really lines of Andean foothills which run from north to south, and it is on their slopes that the arabica coffee of Colombia is grown in altitudes ranging from 800–1900m/2,624–6,233 ft. The coffee is all hand-picked – it would be extremely difficult to harvest it any other way, given that the slopes are steep in the mountainous terrain – and the trees are usually shaded by interspersed banana trees. The climate provides plenty of moisture, so there is no irrigation or mulching required.

Above: Colombian "supremo" medium-roast beans.

Above: Colombian Popayán excelso dark-roasted beans.

The central *cordillera* is the most productive region both in quantity and quality, particularly as it contains the well-known name of Medellín, one of the best-balanced coffees of Colombia, combining full-bodied heaviness with good flavour and medium acidity. Manizales, another town of the central zone, and Armenia, whose coffees are less acidic, but winey in texture with excellent aroma, in the western *cordillera*, together with Medellín, form the MAM acronym under which the majority of bags from Colombia are exported. Another central zone favourite is coffee from Libano, which in the "supremo" form is a visual delight, as its large beans roast smoothly and evenly. Popayán and San Agustín are notable coffees from the southern part of the central *cordillera*, as is coffee from the district of Nariño, very near the Ecuador border. Nariño has the reputation of producing the cup preferred by the Vatican, (a distinction claimed equally by the island of Puerto Rico), and Starbucks, the chain of coffee speciality shops, also allegedly holds exclusive rights to the supremo beans from Nariño.

Colombia's eastern coffee region produces another half-dozen or so commercial coffees, of which two are better known for excellent quality: Bogotá, from the area around the capital city, is a fine coffee with a slightly lower acidity than those of the central zone. Bucamaranga, from the more northerly part of the eastern *cordillera*, has the low acid and mellow, rounded flavour of a "soft" coffee.

Flavour and aroma The old arabica cultivars are gradually being replaced with other more productive varieties, such as the cost-efficient "variedad Colombia", as the aged trees are removed. Developed in Colombia, this arabica strain is also being planted in other countries, much to the dismay of discerning tasters, who find the flavour of the new variety disappointing, especially in comparison to the bourbon beans, which can be a felicitous combination of flavour, aroma, body and a golden colour when milk or cream is added. The acidity of Colombian coffees seldom matches that of certain Kenyans and Costa Ricans, but in general Colombia produces a more balanced cup, particularly in coffees of slightly heavier body.

Above: Colombian San Agustín medium-roasted beans.

Colombia enjoys one advantage over all other South American countries: it can export coffee through ports on either ocean. The export crop is fairly evenly divided between the ports of Buenaventura on the Pacific, and Cartagena, Barranquilla, and Santa Marta on the Atlantic. Such easy access from the plantations to international trade routes, coupled with the world-wide promotional work done by the Federation Nacional de Cafeteros de Colombia, has ensured a strong market for Colombian coffee in both North America and Europe.

Colombia also exports the highest volume of soluble (instant) coffee in the world, the expected 1998/99 figure of which is a whopping 659,000 bags' worth, mostly freeze-dried.

Above: Hand-picking coffee in Colombia: not an easy job in mountainous terrain.

Ecuador

Ecuador, like Brazil, grows arabica as well as robusta; the robustas are unwashed, and the arabicas are wet- or dry-processed. The large (gigante or Galapagos classifications) arabica beans are heavy with humidity, but produce a thin-bodied liquor, and a slightly woody and mediocre flavour, although the aroma is good. The trees are interspersed with banana and cocoa trees for shading.

French Guiana

South America's last "colony" – a French Overseas Department – once famous for the notorious offshore penal colony of Devil's Island, is composed mostly of equatorial jungle and species-rich rainforest. The only coffee grown here now is from robusta trees in domestic gardens, but French Guiana had its moment of coffee glory when, through a romance of illicit passion and deception in the early 18th century, the little colony was the gateway through which the all-conquering bean first reached Brazil.

Left: Peru exports most of its washed arabicas, keeping the unwashed for internal consumption.

Galapagos Islands

Gourmet coffee lovers might want to keep a look out for a coffee grown in very high altitudes on the small island of San Cristóbal. The coffee estate was established long before the islands became a national park, which banned any further agricultural development and any use of chemicals. The organically-produced coffee is said to be superb, and there is scope for the production on this family-run plantation to increase.

Guyana

The Dutch founded three colonies here, Berbice, Demerara and Essequibo, which passed to Britain in 1814 and became British Guiana. Independent since 1966, Guyana produces bauxite, gold, rice, sugar and diamonds, but it still grows some coffee, primarily low-quality liberica, most of which is consumed locally, but may be shipped to the US for instant processing before re-importation into Guyana.

Paraguay

This country has been attempting to increase its arabica coffee crop for some time. As a country with no minerals, land-locked and remote, it must depend on its own agriculture for general subsistence, and hope that its neighbours stay financially healthy, as its biggest exports are electricity (for which Brazil's "standing charges" sometimes represent 25 per cent of the total Paraguayan national budget), and contraband. The coffees are unwashed arabicas, cultivated mostly towards the eastern border where the altitude is highest, and the cup quality is unsurprisingly similar to the rather nondescript arabicas grown in Paraná, across the Brazilian border. All of the coffee must be taken overland through seasonally impassable terrain for shipping from the ports of Brazil, Argentina and Chile.

Peru

Coffee is one of Peru's main crops, and it provides a living for many poor families who work small-holdings in the Andean foothills. Punto, on Lake Titicaca, Cuzco and the Urubamba and Chanchamayo Valleys, and the northern provinces of Piura, San Martin, Cajamarca and Lambayeque, are producing some good quality coffees, certified as organically grown and are all areas where quality is important and improving. In general, Peruvian coffees are excellent blending coffees, as they are mild, pleasant and sweet, and occasionally some really top quality Peruvians are beginning to appear.

Suriname

Suriname was Dutch-owned from 1667, when the British swapped it for New Amsterdam (New York), until its independence in 1975. It was through Dutch Guiana, as it was called in 1714, that coffee-growing came to South America. Today it grows only small amounts of wild-tasting liberica, sold to Norway.

Venezuela

The best coffees produced in this oil-rich country are those grown practically on the spine of the Andean *cordillera de Mérida*, which collectively are known as Maracaibos, as they are shipped from the port of that name. Several names of good Maracaibos include the word Táchira, the far western state; and the regions of Mérida, Trujillo and the town of Cúcuta (which is so far west it appears to be in Colombia!) also give their names to fine coffees. Other coffees are shipped under the names of the *haciendas* where they are grown. Coffee from the eastern mountains is designated as Caracas, for the proximity to the capital.

The coffee industry, having lapsed into mediocrity under government nationalization in the 1970s, is now pulling itself out of the decline, no doubt encouraged by the growing gourmet coffee market. Some of the old haciendas are once more the source of some lovely, if slightly unusual coffees. Venezuelan coffees, unlike other South American growths, tend to be delicately light, if not actually thin; slightly winey, and of only moderate acidity, with a rather appealing individual aroma and flavour.

Above: Venezuela has been producing beans like these since 1730.

SOUTH PACIFIC AND SOUTH-EAST ASIA

This area contains some of the most enterprising coffee producing countries.

Left: Australian "Skybury" green beans.

Australia

Nearly 40 per cent of Australia lies above the Tropic of Capricorn, but much of the area in this tropical zone is not suitable for coffee cultivation: the rainfall, if adequate at all, is very variable, and the altitude conducive to producing good arabica is limited. Even so, at least since the 1970s arabica coffee has been grown in Queensland, some on a rather experimental basis; one in particular, "Skybury", hit the world stage in the early 1980s and has not looked back. Grown from the same Blue Mountain variety as the celebrated New Guinea Sigri, Skybury has received great commendations by many experts. At least its price will ensure that it doesn't suffer the same fate as that of other well-meaning Australian coffees of the 1980s: because Australians consume far more coffee than the farmers can hope to grow, any average Australian product that acquires favour with the home market will probably at some point have to be extended with imported coffee, particularly that from Papua New Guinea.

Cambodia

About forty years ago, commercial coffee plantation in Cambodia began. Soon coffee, mostly robusta, but a little arabica as well, was grown in at least five different regions of Cambodia. After the terrible events that befell Cambodia in successive years, it is difficult now to guess the state of the plantations. It is worth hoping, however, that Cambodia, like Vietnam, may have a future as a coffee-producing country once again.

China

It is known that arabica coffee is grown and processed in China's south-west province of Yunnan, where a mountainous region is crossed by the Tropic of Cancer, the northern edge of the tropical belt. Here the summer temperatures are modified by higher altitudes and good rainfall, and the mild, dry winters enjoy a temperature range of 8-20°C/46-68°F. The Chinese government releases no figures on its coffee production, however, and because certain countries, especially Tanzania, repay debts to China in coffee beans, there is no assurance that any coffee exported from China was actually grown there. The International Coffee Organization is actively encouraging more coffee consumption in China, of which a by-product could be greater production of coffee, as the necessary growing conditions are present.

Fiji

After twenty-seven years of independence from Britain, Fiji has just rejoined the Commonwealth, having replaced its constitution with one more acceptable to the international community. At one time Fiji grew a small crop of robusta, which it processed by the washed method, and which was sold primarily to New Zealand. It also imported coffee for its own consumption.

The island of Vitu Levu consists of mainly mountainous terrain, including Mount Victoria (1,324m/4,344ft) and some higher places on the other smaller islands. As Fiji is attempting to further diversify its income perhaps it will be encouraged to grow more coffee.

French Polynesia

This French Overseas Territory is really a combination of 130 islands spread out over a Pacific area the size of Europe. The bourbon arabica is grown on various islands, each of which carries out its own wet processing, and the coffee is then sent to Papeete, Tahiti, for hulling and grading. The islands tend to consume all that they grow and process. The large-bean coffee has been described as pleasantly mild rather than acidic, with good strength and aroma, and is therefore a well-rounded satisfying cup. Tahiti Arabica is the commercial name, but it is seldom found outside the islands which grow it.

Hawaii

Hawaii has been growing coffee since 1818, and today both the island of Kauai and the big island of Hawaii grow it, although it is the latter's coffee from the slopes of the Mauna Loa volcano in the western Kona zone that gives its name to the only coffee grown in the United States. Expert opinions on Kona coffee vary; certainly in several ways it can be compared to Jamaica Blue Mountain: although the climate and soil are ideal, the growing area is limited, the processing is extremely careful and the appearance of the beans impeccable; it is a natural product and some crops are better than others. It is scarce and expensive, and many blends

Above: Hawaiian Kona medium-roast coffee beans.

Above: A coffee plantation in the flat terrain of Kauai, Hawaii.

are sold as "Kona" which may contain five per cent of the genuine coffee. (The blends may, of course, be excellent, depending on the other coffees, which are likely to be superior, but more affordable, Latin Americans.) The Hawaiian coffee industry must compete with the tourist trade for its workers, and therefore wages are extremely high, compared to those of other countries.

Flavour and aroma Hawaiian Kona differs from Jamaica Blue Mountain in many ways, although both are known for a mild, "fair" acidity, medium body and fine aroma; also, the descriptor "nutty" is sometimes applied to the flavour profiles of both. Some experts detect in Kona a spicy, cinnamon-like flavour, a quality not found in Jamaican coffee, while other experts have difficulty detecting much flavour at all.

In sheer bountiful yield, no other coffee trees on earth can vie with the volume of fruit taken from Kona trees. The best, and surest, way to drink Hawaiian Kona is to sip it with the locals, as the best quality is kept at home. Tourists are willing to pay the normal "high dollar" price, which really is at a premium, as there are none of the normal shipping costs involved.

India

The entire economy of India is undergoing a radical change, as the government is shifting from a position of protectionism to the encouragement of totally free, global marketing. The coffee industry, which had been nationalized some time back, did little to encourage growers to improve their quality or produce coffee with individual character; same-grade beans from all regions were "blended" by the Indian Coffee Board under a uniform grading system, producing simply "Plantation A", "Plantation B", etc. As of December 16, 1998, the Indian parliament finalised a decision to allow coffee growers to sell 100 per cent of the produce on the open market. It can only be assumed that the old romantic coffee names will have true significance once more, particularly for the 40 per cent of India's crop that is arabica.

Above: Indian Plantation A medium-roast beans.

Coffee growing areas The arabica coffee-growing region of India is basically three states in the Southwest. Mysore, which accounts for most of the arabica, is that grown in what is now the state of Karnataka. Mysore can be described very generally as having good body, low acidity, mellow sweetness and a well-balanced strong flavour; however, it sometimes can be described as neutral, which probably reflects on those Kent-variety arabicas, which generally have less distinctive flavour than the older classics like bourbon. The state of Tamil Nadu produces good arabica; one in particular is grown in the high altitude of the Nilgiri region in the state's west.

Above: Green beans from Mysore, India.

The most interesting arabica of India in both name and taste is the unwashed "Monsooned Malabar". The Malabar coast is the western shore of the entire state of Kerala. In the days of sailing, when coffee took months to reach Europe, it developed a particular taste during the voyage because of exposure to sea-air and humidity; the colour also changed from green to a rather strange yellow. European consumers became fond of the enhanced body and enriched, if slightly peculiar, flavour, so when steamers shortened the sailing time, India began to "artificially" reproduce the flavour by exposing coffee for about six weeks to the humid south-west monsoon winds that begin in May or June.

These unusual coffees are not dissimilar to other "aged" coffees, such as those of Sulawesi, Java and Sumatra, and they are generally cheaper and easier to obtain.

Above: Indian Monsooned Malabar medium-roast beans.

Above: Sumatran Lintong Grade 2 roasted beans.

Indonesia

The coffee industry provides a livelihood for around five million people in Indonesia, and currently vies with Vietnam as the third most prolific coffee producer, and 90 per cent of its crop is ordinary robusta. The arabicas, however, are another story, and the word "ordinary" doesn't come into it; Indonesia, as the world's largest archipelago, sprawls across 5,000km/ 3,107 miles, and its 13,677 islands lie in three different time zones. It is therefore not surprising that its arabicas, which have far more scope for individuality than robustas, cover an amazing range of sometimes quirky but always interesting differences. A general description of most of the Indonesian arabicas would contain the words rich, full-bodied, lowish-acidity, and a prolonged aftertaste, in addition to terms more specific to the individual coffees.

Sumatra There are three main islands and one or two smaller ones which together produce very nearly 100 per cent of all Indonesian coffees, arabica and robusta; Sumatra, the western-most large island, grows 68 per cent. Much of the arabica is sold simply as Sumatran or Blue Sumatran; many of the Sumatran trees are newly planted in virgin, highly organic, volcanic soil, which is very fertile, and the coffees, which are only partly wet-processed, are strong and assertive.

Above: Sumatran Mandheling grade 2 green beans.

One of the few washed coffees is the gourmet-quality Gayo Mountain, sweetly spicy and exotically herbal in character, named for its area of origin in the extreme north-western province of Aceh. Linthong, or Lintong, from North Sumatra, is similar to, but generally not quite as consistently good as, Mandheling, from the north and the west-central regions.

Mandheling, with the deep, rich flavour and smoothness of a low-acidity coffee, merits the title "world's heaviest coffee", according to many experts. Ankola, also from the west-central region near the port of Padang, may not have quite the body of a Mandheling, but it is regarded by some connoisseurs as the world's finest unwashed arabica.

Above: Indonesian washed Java Jampit green beans.

Java The island of Java, which grows about 12 per cent of Indonesia's coffee, was where the Dutch began the first coffee-growing outside of Islam. About 300 years of intensive cultivation has left Java's soil a bit depleted. After the *hemileia vastatrix* (leaf rust), infestation of the late 19th century, only the highest-grown arabicas survived, and those scarce growths have recently been replaced with more productive arabica varieties, to the detriment of the flavour. "Estate Java" is now a wet-processed coffee, with more acidity, and less body, flavour and finish than the original Java arabicas, which had been known for rich smoothness, heavy body, and an earthy, mushroomy sort of flavour obtained only in unwashed coffees. There were five government-owned estates, including Jampit, Blawan and Pankur.

Above: Indonesian Sulawesi Kalossi Toraja roasted beans.

Sulawesi The third main island of arabica production is Sulawesi, which grows 9 per cent of all Indonesian coffee; under the Dutch, the island was called Celebes, the name under which much of the arabica coffee is today exported from the port of Ujung Pandang. The unwashed Kalossi coffees from the south-western region of Toraja are the true aristocrats of all Indonesian coffees. They have the heavy body and smooth texture associated with Indonesian coffees, as well as the deep earthy, mushroomy, sweetness; there is, as well, because of slightly increased acidity, a hint of fruit.

Overall, the best and most distinctive range of Indonesian coffees are those which have been aged. The coffees may be sold as "Old Government", "Old Brown" or "Old Java". Or they may simply be designated "aged" coffees, and may come from Java, Sulawesi or Sumatra. The ageing process carried out in the damp, warm climate – not the same as simply lengthy warehousing in another part of the world – lowers what acidity there may have been, enhances the sweetness and gives the already smooth, dense liquid an even heavier body. Other descriptors spring

Above: Indonesian "Old Brown" Javanese green beans.

to mind, like soft, velvety, golden and warm. In fact, an interesting suggestion is to replace the after-dinner liqueur with a small black cup of an "aged" Indonesian, particularly a Celebes Kalossi, as its concentrated, sweet, syrupy consistency is virtually liqueur without the alcohol. (And the cost is probably about the same!)

Other coffee growing areas Other arabica coffees known to be excellent are those grown on Bali, Flores and Timor, although Timor stopped growing coffee after annexation by Indonesia; one can hope production will resume again soon, as it seems Indonesia is in the process of reversing the annexation of the former Portuguese colony.

There is one more type of coffee obtainable from Indonesia, which is *kopi luak*. "Kopi" is the word for "coffee", and the luak is a small weasel-like animal particularly fond of coffee cherries. Villagers collect the animals' "droppings" and remove the hard coffee beans, which are then washed and further processed by less natural means. The flavour is exceptional, and the beans command a high price.

Laos

In recent years, the strongly communist Laos People's Democratic Republic has opened up to foreign investment, as well as receiving international aid and subsidies to encourage farmers to substitute cash crops for opium poppies. Laos' most important agricultural resources are currently listed as timber and coffee. Information on the type and quality of the coffee grown, and the regions of cultivation is not readily available, but in the past, the Laotian climate, soil and topography allowed the production of arabica, robusta and excelsa, which, during the 1970s, fell to amounts that could only sustain local consumption.

Malaysia

Although Malaysia grows arabica, robusta and excelsa, its main coffee crop is the higher-yielding and highly unpalatable liberica species, grown mostly in Western Malaya. Western Malaya is also the site of a small area of arabica trees, which is located in the higher altitudes of the Cameron Highlands. Because of the large population of the country, local consumption generally consumes all the coffee that can be grown. Malaysia is very concerned with economic success, and as coffee is not as lucrative a crop as some others, such as palm oil, rubber, timber and, of course, oil and gas, it is not usually seen to be a priority crop for cultivation.

New Caledonia

This small group of islands, called Kanaky by the natives, lying 1,497km/930 miles north-east of Australia, is still a French Overseas Territory, although independence seems possible. The windward (eastern)

Below: "Kopi Luak" comes from droppings of the luak animal, containing undigested coffee beans. The beans are collected, washed and processed – the resulting coffee is considered a rare delicacy by coffee lovers.

coast has the distinction of growing the world's best robusta, while the little arabica still grown comes from the western side of the island. The robusta is unusual for its type, as it is described as delicate, although the flavour of both coffees, known commercially as "Nouméa", is said to be aromatic and rich. The arabica is seldom exported, as the islands prefer to save the best for themselves, which they can afford to do, since New Caledonia has large deposits of nickel, accounting for 25 per cent of the world's supply.

Above: New Guinean "Y" grade roasted beans.

Papua New Guinea

It was probably extremely fortunate for all coffee lovers that coffee-growing came late to Papua New Guinea. Otherwise, the disastrous plague of *hemileia vastatrix* (leaf rust) that wiped out arabica plantations throughout South-east Asia and Oceania in the late 1800s, would have ensured that today Papua New Guinea would be growing mostly robusta, like so many other countries who replanted with resistant species at the cost of good flavour.

Much of New Guinea's arabica is grown, washed and further processed in varying degrees by natives of rural, and sometimes isolated, villages located in the high-altitude mountainous region which occupies so much of Papua New Guinea's landmass. These coffees are an extremely important source of revenue for Papua New Guinea, providing a living for hundreds of thousands of people, and the government provides encouragement and support by announcing, at the start of each year's crop, an ensured minimum price it will pay for the coffee, in the event that the market price should fall unexpectedly.

Gourmet quality coffee New Guinea coffee was cultivated from Blue Mountain variety stock, and the results make the New Guinea washed arabicas rather different from other coffees from this part of the world. Although New Guineas have good body and sweetness, as do many Indonesians, they also have a higher acidity closer in style to Central Americans. In short, a good New Guinea coffee can stand on its own, or be a terrific contribution to any high-quality blend, since it has literally everything to offer.

The sorting and grading, after some inconsistencies, is now regular and stringent. The top AA grade is very scarce, while about 60 per cent of beans make up the ordinary, decent "Y" grade. Quality names to look out for include Arona, Okapa and Sigri.

Philippines

The world's second-largest archipelago has everything it takes to grow good quality coffee in large amounts. In fact, it already grows all four of the main commercial species, robusta, liberica, excelsa and arabica, and is experimenting with hybrids.The small crop of good arabica, known for its full, slightly spicy flavour, is concentrated on the southern island of Mindanao.

At one time the Philippines were in fourth place for world coffee production, but that was before the terrible rust infestation that wiped out most of the arabica growths of South-east Asia, the Philippines included, in the late 1800s.

Above: Philippino arabica green coffee beans.

Above: Vietnamese robusta medium-roasted coffee beans.

As the arabica is not very acidic, and the flavour is fairly strong, this coffee works well where a darker roast is appreciated, as in after-dinner or espresso blends.

Sri Lanka

The world's greatest tea exporter, this island, which Tamils and Sinalese have cohabited in conflict for 14 centuries, grew a lot of good arabica coffee, until almost the entire crop was destroyed by *hemileia vastatrix* (leaf rust) in 1870. Although tea-growing basically replaced coffee cultivation, the British colonists introduced robusta, which still accounts for the majority of the generally poor-quality coffee, which is sold under the name Sinhala.

taipei

Taipei is known for its consumerism, and coffee is no exception. Trendy gourmet coffee houses vie for high-street prominence in Taipei. The small good-quality well-processed arabica crop, grown in the mountain region which dominates the island, is all consumed locally.

Thailand

Thailand's current coffee crop of about only a million bags is mostly robusta, grown primarily in the Malay Peninsula; some arabica is grown in the highlands of the north and north west. Recently Thailand seems to be eager to increase its coffee cultivation, which may be due to several reasons. Any increase will help to satisfy the consumption demands of its 58.8 million population, and at the same time utilize the potentially abundant workforce of hundreds of thousands of indigenous hill people and refugees from Laos and Cambodia in virtually all rural regions of the country. It will also help to redistribute the country's wealth and population from Bangkok, one of the world's most congested cities, by developing commercial interests in more remote provinces, and help to replace the growth of opium poppies in the Golden Triangle. There is one major problem for increased coffee production, as well as for other crops: there is a major national water shortage exacerbated by a lack of water storage facilities; deforestation has contributed to both flooding and droughts; and the massive amounts of water required to maintain numerous golf courses designed to improve the tourist industry adds to the problem.

Vanuatu

Previously the New Hebrides, this Pacific archipelago became independent from joint French and British rule in 1980. Copra and cocoa are the main exports, although coffee-growing had been introduced to the islands at the same time by the Europeans. Today, while Vanuatu, frightened by declining copra and cocoa prices, explores the possibilities of other export crops, cattle roam around the several hundred remaining robusta trees, which are basically untended except when the cherries are picked. The small crop is dry-processed completely by hand, loaded in 60 kg/ 132lb bags and sent to France. Although ungraded, it is described as fairly homogeneous and good.

Vietnam

As usual, the French first introduced coffee-growing to their colonies of Indo-China, but when most of the arabica succumbed to rust, it was replaced with robusta, the quality of which is fairly ordinary. What is not ordinary is the incredible growth in the Vietnamese coffee industry. After the devastation of the war, the remains of the French colonists' coffee estates were turned into state collectives. In 1980 Vietnam was 42nd in world coffee production. In 1982 it exported 67,000 bags.

In 1988, with the imminent break-up of the Soviet Union, the Vietnamese government encouraged private enterprise, and by 1993 it exported over three million bags of robusta, a figure which the 1997 crop saw more than doubled to 6.893 million bags, putting it third in world production behind Brazil and Colombia, with Indonesia close behind. And, while the coffee crop was burgeoning, so was the rice, as Vietnam became the third largest exporter after the US and Thailand. No wonder Vietnam is being billed as the next Asian "tiger".

Above: Though Colombia's coffee production outnumbers that of Vietnam by nearly two to one, Vietnam's rise from 42nd to 3rd place in world production rankings has been meteoric.

ROASTING

Of all the processes involved with coffee, the quickest and most critical is roasting. Roasting coffee is a terrible responsibility, because, in a few minutes, beans that cost hundreds of people time, effort and money can be completely ruined by ignorance or carelessness. Roasting coffee is an art, and like all true art, it takes years of practice before one becomes a master roaster; also, roasting is learned only by trial-and-error experience, and the errors may ruin many beans.

Above: These two samples of the same Ugandan Bugisu arabica bean show the differences that occur during roasting, not only in colour, but also size and shape.

The main reason that roasting is difficult is that virtually every batch of beans is different from every other. In factories, a small sample of every shipment is "batch" roasted to anticipate every potential problem that could arise in a commercial-size roast of perhaps 114kg/250lb of beans. A bright rather than a dull roast is desired, as dullness can indicate over-drying or poor processing; also, a good quality sample of beans will appear even, since a variety of colours, particularly "pales", among the coffee beans can indicate immature picking, poor sorting of cherries, and varying degrees of fermentation and drying on the plantation. Misshapen beans, broken beans, or simply an overly wide variety in bean sizes constitutes a "ragged" roast, as different-sized beans roast to different colours in the same roast.

The physical changes that occur to beans during roasting are many; the obvious changes are that the beans get bigger, gaining up to a third more of their former "green" size; this is because the decomposing carbohydrates create carbon dioxide, which literally causes the cells of the bean to expand. Meanwhile, most of the moisture remaining in the green beans after the plantation depulping, drying, storing and shipping, will be evaporated by the heat of roasting, and the beans will thus lose weight. Although moisture content can account for up to 23 per cent of green bean density, dehydration during roasting is usually kept to a maximum of about 15 per cent of the beans' weight, lest they become tasteless, brittle objects that reduce to powder at the first touch of a grinder's blade. The other very obvious physical change is that beans change colour during roasting.

Above: Sacks of different coffee samples, ready for roasting.

The Roasting Process

The most important effect of roasting beans is that the flavour is developed through the complex chemical changes caused by heat, which is the process of pyrolysis. It is estimated that a coffee bean contains more than 2,000 chemical substances, which may be broken down or changed during roasting into hundreds of "volatile aroma compounds". Various acids, oils, proteins, vitamins, sugars, starches, and caffeine are altered; some are enhanced and some are diminished. In certain cases, some substances are both developed and then burned away if the roasting time is extended.

A light roast is seldom used commercially, as it shows up all the flaws inherent in beans, many of which will disappear, or at least be hidden by other flavours, in a dark roast. For example, if a coffee has the distinctive, sometimes unusual, pleasant and expensively-acidic qualities of a high-grown arabica, it is better for it not to be dark-roasted. The darker the roast, the more uniform all coffees taste, as a truly dark roast will overwhelm the taste-buds, allowing them to perceive nothing of the coffee itself. A darker roast may sweeten some coffees, but only to a point; past a certain degree of roast all coffee becomes bitter. Also, the darker the roast, the greater the loss of acidity, that most sought-after quality.

Coffee roasters all vary in size and capacity, but the roasting process changes little from one size to another. All equipment should be pre-heated to a roasting temperature some minutes before the green beans are added, so all surfaces are uniformly hot. Many roasters are equipped with a revolving drum, often lined internally with curved metal strips which constantly toss the beans towards the centre of the drum. Above all, beans must be kept moving if they are to roast evenly, without burning. In fact, if a drum stops revolving while the heat is still on and the beans are hot, there is a danger of instant combustion within the drum. (The saying goes, "You're not a coffee roaster 'til you've had your first fire!")

Fine Tuning

The actual roast is a balancing act. Depending on the condition of the beans and the desired degree of roast, the beans are roasted at temperatures between about 200-240°C/392-464°F, give or take about 20°C/68°F on either side. Many roasters have devices for air ventilation, which, like fan-assisted ovens, cause the beans to cook faster. As the roast goes on (in total the process will take between about 8 and 14 minutes in a conventional-heat roaster), the beans retain more heat, and start to turn first yellow-green, then gold and into shades of brown. (All but the smallest drum roasters have devices allowing samples to be manually taken and returned to the drum.) The critical decision-making time is when the beans start to make popping sounds, as within seconds of this they turn dark very quickly. The drier the beans, the sooner the "popping" of pyrolysis begins; therefore, beans which are less green when unroasted, such as robusta, roast much quicker. Moisture-laden high-grown arabicas will take a bit longer to reach the same degree of roast.

The problem is deciding at what degree of roast each coffee tastes best, and the same coffee, roasted to

Above: Home roasting with a revolving drum over an outdoor fire.

different colours, will taste different. Even more complicated is the fact that the same coffee roasted to the same colour at a higher temperature for a shorter time, will taste different if roasted at a lower temperature for a longer time. With extremes of either time or temperature, the same colour roast can produce coffee that tastes under-cooked internally – cerealy or even green, or over-cooked – dried out, brittle when ground, or even burnt.

The last maddening fact of roasting is that the beans really need to be removed from the roaster immediately before the optimum colour is obtained, as they will darken in spite of cooling devices, such as revolving air-cooled trays outside the front of a drum roaster, or even the quick burst of water (quenching) of larger commercial machines, designed to stop the beans' continued cooking after they have left the drum. In later stages of roasting, beans release oils. Sometimes, even if a darker "oily" roast is not intended, the beans, if left in the roaster a fraction too long, will develop oil on their surfaces while in the cooling tray.

Types of Coffee Roasters

There are many sizes and types of coffee roasters available, ranging from factory machines, helped by sophisticated quenching-devices and automatic timers, with the capacity to roast hundreds of pounds of beans, down to tiny "professional" batch roasters which roast no more than a couple of hundred grams. Some companies use "high-yield" roasters, developed in the 1970s, which "roast" beans in relatively small amounts, but in a matter of precisely-timed seconds, perhaps up to two minutes, on fluidised "beds" of hot air rather than with the directly-transferred heat of metal drums. Called high-yield because the beans' surface areas expand so much as to produce more coffee when ground, these roasters are not favoured by many experts, who feel that the high-yield flavour is not as fully developed and round as that produced in conventional roasters.

There are small table-top roasters for the domestic market, but they can be hard to find, and expensive when located. Many people find it a joy to roast small amounts of coffee in frying pans over a cooker-burner (on the stove). (Oven-roasting is not recommended namely because it is not possible to keep the beans moving, and the roast is therefore usually very uneven and uncontrollable.) To roast coffee beans correctly, use a heavy, possibly cast-iron, frying pan, which has been warmed up. Add a single layer of beans over a low heat, increasing the heat to high as they roast, stirring constantly with a wooden spatula. In some Middle-Eastern countries whole spices such as cloves, cinnamon, cardamom, ginger, or fennel may be added, to be ground with them later. Other countries actually roast the beans in small amounts of butter or sugar, depending on the desired flavour.

When the beans are roasted to the desired colour, they must be cooled immediately, perhaps by putting them into a pre-chilled container, or onto a very cold surface. It is not advisable to grind beans for brewing immediately after roasting as the flavour will be sharp, green and sour. To achieve the desired mellowness of a good brew, do not grind until the coffee beans have had time to de-gas, preferably for a minimum of 12 hours.

Above: Roasted coffee beans spill out of the drum into the cooling tray below.

Above: Checking the beans after the roasting is completed.

Degrees of Roast

As in tasters' terminology, there is no standardized definition of different degrees of roast. "Light", "medium" and "dark" are the most-used terms, but coffees are seldom truly light-roasted, and there are many perceived degrees of medium and dark. (Also, it should be noted that Turkish coffee is not dark-roasted.) A combination of various opinions results in the following possibilities:

Light This roast is used only for extremely good-quality delicate or high-grown arabicas. Ideal for breakfast coffees when acidic coffees are mellowed by the addition of milk or cream. The American version of this roast, "Cinnamon", is so called because of the colour of cinnamon bark. It is high in acidity and low in body. Also sometimes called "half-city" or "New England" roast.

Medium "American roast"; or possibly "city" if slightly darker than medium. Also called "regular", "brown"; as dark as possible with no oily surfaces.

Viennese American term meaning slightly darker than medium roast. This roast is speckled with dark-brown spots, and a bit of oil on surface; also "light French", or "full city".

Dark "Spanish"; "Cuban"; there may be some oil on bean surface, "deep brown"; French roast.

Continental Can also be referred to as "Double roast"; "High"; in America, "French roast", "New Orleans roast" and "European". With a nearly bitter-chocolate colouring, this roast is variously described as very dark; dark French, heavy and Italian.

Italian In America, darker than in Italy; may be called "espresso" roasts (or may not!); almost black and very oily; the predominant taste is the roast rather than the coffee. Coffee beans should never be burned black.

Even if there were universal agreement on the meaning of the above roasting terms, there would not be general consensus as to how dark certain coffees should or should not be roasted. In America, all roasts are becoming darker, probably because of the emphasis on espresso and espresso-based drinks, which are seen to be the height of sophistication. In fact, in many other countries as well, there are those who think the goal of all roasting is to make the coffee taste pleasant and balanced even if this involves suppressing the more unique and unusual flavours. It must be remembered that dark roasts were originally designed to hide the flaws of inferior coffees, and to bring out the best in cheap blends loaded with inferior-tasting robusta. Surely true sophistication is to approach every coffee with an open mind, prepared to judge it on its own merits.

Light-roasted beans

Medium-roasted beans

Dark-roasted beans

Above: A very enjoyable facet of coffee is the fact that there are enormous differences, which can be appreciated only when each coffee is treated to its own best roast, even if its more unusual attributes are, if not shocking, at least outside the normal range of coffee tastes.

BLENDING

An ideal cup of coffee should have good aroma, good colour (if milk or cream is to be added), good body, and good tastes for whichever way the coffee will be roasted, brewed and served at any intended time of day. Out of the millions of bags of coffee processed every year, relatively few can provide the "ideal cup" criteria without a little help from their friends, the other coffees with whom they will be blended. Regarding the few that can stand alone, they will probably not provide an all-round, perfect, well-balanced cup; rather, they will have one or two particularly fine points which more than compensate for falling short on another aspect or two.

Above: Few coffees, on their own, can provide the perfect combination of good aroma, colour, body and taste. Blending seeks to achieve this in a consistent form.

Balancing Flavours

Each coffee used in a blend should make its own contribution. Dark roasting hides the not-so-desirable flavours of robustas, and of other coffees which may happen to have lower acidity, but usually have good body, which is only enhanced by the dark roast. Conversely, many high-grown arabicas, while producing a sharp flavour that can dominate the overall tastes of other less acidic coffees, are "thin-in-the-cup", and lack body. With these watery arabicas, the solution is not to roast darker, as roasting burns off the acids that contribute to the sharp, "expensive" taste. Other coffees may be pleasantly acceptable, having no particularly distinctive quality either to recommend or condemn them; these neutrals are ideal for bulking out a blend, as their flavours are not obtrusive, nor are they lacking in body.

There are no rules or taboos in blending coffees, but the idea is to combine coffees that complement each other, not those that are similar. A good starting point, therefore, for a middle-of-the-road, any-time-of-day well-rounded cup of coffee, would be a blend of perhaps 35 per cent high-grown arabica to provide the dominant flavour, 15 per cent darker-roasted robusta or heavier-bodied, lower-acidity coffee to provide the body, and 50 per cent of a more neutral and possibly more affordable coffee, like an average Brazilian Santos, or one of the slightly lower quality and less expensive Central American coffees. The character of this blend could be changed considerably just by altering the proportions. Also, lowering the proportions of each would allow for the addition of a small amount of a different, fourth, coffee, perhaps an unwashed arabica, as most "natural" arabicas are known for their sweetness.

All blends should be worked out in percentage weights with a taste or style in mind, whether the overall blend is to be, for example, a "fruity" blend; a "mild" breakfast coffee; a deep, rich, syrupy after-dinner indulgence; a naturally low-caffeine blend; a high-caffeine "pick-me-up" with lots of caffeine-rich robusta; or perhaps simply a strongish-flavoured coffee to provide the basis of an alcoholic coffee cocktail. If a blend is to be used often and remain consistent, the availability and affordability of each particular coffee must be considered.

Classic Combinations

A few combinations of particular coffees are so successful that they have become standards through the years. Mocha (either from Yemen or a reasonable second from Ethiopia) and Mysore from India are the most famous coffee marriage. Mocha-Java will be a bit earthier and heavy, but still winey, and wild (or gamey) from the Mocha. A very particular Mocha-Brazil combination is that favoured by Middle-Eastern roasters for the traditional "Turkish" coffee flavour: the Brazilian coffee is the famous, or infamous, rio-y flavour. A good Brazilian Santos will smooth out an average robusta to make a strong, smooth blend, while a blend requiring some lightness can be illuminated by the addition of some Kenyan coffee, or a high-grown Central American. A Haiti or a Peruvian adds some decent flavour without being too expensive. An aged coffee adds sweetness, and a Colombian can add aroma as well as body and flavour.

In America, a "New Orleans Blend", and in Britain a "French Blend", neither to be confused with any degree of roast, is a blend of coffee and the roots of the chicory plant, just as a "Viennese" blend in Britain contains roasted fig or fig-seasoning ground in with the coffee. Of these two "economy" blends, the Viennese is cheaper, being the least expensive coffee blend of the average British supermarket range.

STORAGE

No matter how carefully coffee is grown, processed, blended, roasted, ground and brewed, the ultimate quality depends on one overall factor: freshness. Considering the ready availability of ground coffee, there would never be any real reason to grind coffee beans at all – except, crucially, to obtain the freshest possible taste. When coffee is roasted, carbon dioxide develops within the beans; it escapes from the coffee for several hours, and does so with a force that ruptures seams in tin cans and causes softer packages to "balloon". Many roasters, therefore, allow the roasted beans or ground coffee to stand for hours before packing. Of course, while standing, the coffee goes stale, losing its volatile aromas and absorbing tasteless oxygen.

Given the practicalities of coffee packaging (which can be vacuum-sealed tins (cans), brick packs, one-way valve-lock bags, or gas-flushed packs, all trying to let the gas out and keep the freshness in), no coffee is ever 100 per cent fresh. It's no good trying to roast, grind and brew coffee within a few minutes because, until the coffee has degassed, it will not taste good.

However, the fact is that roasted beans do retain their freshness longer than ground coffee, as there is less cell surface exposed to the air. Assuming that the roasting company and the retailer have just roasted the beans and maintained their freshness, the obvious next question is how best to store them at home.

Experts differ widely in advice on storing coffee, particularly beans. Certainly coffee can absorb odours easily, and will taste of those odours when brewed. Therefore some people advise against keeping coffee in the fridge. Others advocate using an airtight container, which will keep out oxygen, but what about the oxygen sealed inside with the beans? The solution would be to keep the surface of the beans very high in the jar, but then one could never use the beans further down in the jar.

Even the freezing of beans has its opponents, who say that after freezing, the coffee will never taste the same. Certainly, freezing darker-roasted beans, which have an oily surface, is definitely not a good idea, as the oils congeal and never regain their original consistency and distribution throughout the coffee.

Above: Coffee pods for certain espresso machines are factory produced.

The ideal solution to the problem of keeping coffee fresh is to purchase smaller amounts more frequently. In Italy, for example, many people buy small amounts, perhaps 100-200g/3½-7oz of coffee several times a week from their local coffee bar; they choose a blend of roasted beans, and the *barista* (barman) grinds them. The ground coffee is then placed in a grease-lined paper bag. Similarly, a person who shops infrequently could still maximize the freshness of the coffee by buying several smaller packs of factory-sealed coffee instead of one or two large packs, as unopened factory-sealed containers will stay fresh for many months.

Helpful hints for keeping whole beans and ground coffee as fresh as possible

• Never pour dry coffee out of one container into another, as that is deliberate exposure.

• Keep the smallest air space between the top of the coffee and the lid, or top, of the container.

• If kept in the refrigerator, seal the original bag or packet as tightly around the coffee as possible, place a clip on it or a rubber band around it, and place it in a similar-sized airtight container.

• If the beans will not be used within a couple of weeks, pack them as for the refrigerator and store in the freezer. It is not a good idea to freeze ground coffee.

• Store small amounts of freshly-ground coffee in resealable bags, pressing down gently to trap as little oxygen as possible in the bag to maximize freshness.

The Art of Coffee Drinking

Many people derive as much pleasure from brewing coffee as from drinking it. For some, making coffee is a time-honoured traditional ritual, and the satisfaction is even greater with the knowledge that one is using the same equipment that yielded cups of the much-loved liquid to past generations. Other people delight in acquiring and using the latest trendy gadgets, and certainly coffee brewing and serving offer scope for constant design innovations, be they practical or aesthetic, or both. The following pages show you all you need to know to be able to select, grind and brew coffee with a range of different equipment – all part of the quest for the perfect cup.

HOME GRINDING

When purchasing a grinder, the choices may not be many, but the price range is wide, and it is best to bear in mind a particular brewing method when choosing a grinder, as the degree of grind required is dictated by this.

Hand Mills

For hundreds of years, coffee to be used at home was ground by hand with a box-type mill that held only a small amount of coffee. Anyone who uses one of these, and they are still available, realizes immediately that a greater storage capacity is not required; it takes so long to grind the beans that any ground coffee would be drunk before the little box could ever be full. Still, the hand mill can grind well, and with a surprising degree of uniformity in the particles. The grind is adjustable within a range that would qualify as "coarse", to a "medium" or even "fine", but it cannot grind fine enough for espresso. These are inexpensive, but it is an extremely time consuming method of grinding.

Below: Hand grinders have changed little for hundreds of years.

Using a hand mill

1 Rotating the lid reveals the aperture through which the beans are poured.

2 The coffee grounds, which fall into the drawer below, should be of a fairly consistent size, whether coarse, medium or fine.

Turkish Grinders

The prince of hand mills is the genuine Turkish grinder. The tall, heavy copper or brass mills are still used today throughout Turkey and other Middle Eastern countries for home grinding. The dome-like top pulls off to reveal the space where the whole beans go. The handle on the top is used to turn the mill; this detaches and fits over the grind adjustment screw which is revealed in the middle of the cylinder when the bottom half is removed. At the end of grinding – the range of which is all degrees of "extremely fine" – the bottom part of the cylinder holds the ground coffee. Middle Eastern coffee must be ground to the consistency of talcum powder, something no other type of domestic grinder can achieve. The difficulty in serving an authentic Middle Eastern coffee is not in getting the grind right; rather, it is in finding the right blend of coffee roasted to the right degree. (It is far easier just to buy a commercial brand, such as People's, imported from Nicosia, or Kurukahveçi, from Istanbul.)

Below: Turkish grinder.

Using a Turkish grinder

1 Remove the handle and dome top and insert the whole beans into the upper cylinder. Use the handle to adjust the grind screw to achieve the desired grind size.

2 After obtaining the desired grind consistency, replace the dome top and handle. Turn the handle to grind the beans. Remove the coffee from the bottom cylinder.

Electric Grinders

There is a wide range of electric coffee grinders available for the domestic market, most with some sort of receptacle or space for catching the ground coffee, which never needs to hold more than enough coffee for a day or two. There are two general designs for domestic grinders – those which simply cut the beans with a propeller-type blade, and those which truly grind the beans between metal discs.

Blade, or propeller, grinder The most common kind of home coffee grinder is the rotating blade, or propeller, grinder. This type, which sometimes comes as an accessory for a blender or some other food processor, is almost useless when it comes to coffee. The first problem is that it is nearly impossible to get uniformity of grind, which means that the coffee liquid will be very unevenly extracted. The larger chunks are wasted if they are too coarse for the water to penetrate; the fine powder particles will quickly saturate and yield bitterness, and can also clog a filter basket and create sediment in cups of plunger-pot coffee.

With a blade grinder it is best to grind small amounts of beans, shaking them up and down in the hope that the propellers will get to all the particles. Running the machine in short bursts will help you avoid scorching the beans from overheating. At least it is relatively easy to keep a blade-type grinder clean and avoid contamination with rancid coffee oils. With the machine unplugged, use a damp cloth or sponge to wipe the chamber and the blades. The plastic lid is washable, but must be carefully rinsed, so as not to leave a soapy taste for the beans to absorb.

Using an electric blade grinder

Always ensure the grinder is unplugged when adding or removing coffee, or when cleaning.

Below: Electric grinder.

Burr Mills By far the best all-round domestic grinder is a burr mill, which is the closest thing to a commercial grinder in that two metal discs perform the grinding. The uniformity of particles is amazingly precise considering the fairly compact size of the machines. The costs vary widely between brands, but even the cheapest will do a decent job. In fact, it is probably better to invest in a good burr mill than in an expensive coffee-maker, if the object is a good cup of freshly-ground coffee.

Burr mills are noisy and slow, but easy to operate, as the grind choice is made by selecting a number or degree on a knob. Manufacturers' instructions, which indicate certain settings for desired grinds, may not be entirely accurate, but once the desired grind is discovered, it is easy to get consistent results. Certain brands of burr mills are better at one range of grind, although all are adjustable. Some also have a timer, and will switch off automatically.

Never grind more coffee than will be used within a day or two. Before grinding, clear the discs of any old coffee remains, or of any coffee of a different origin or blend, by running the grinder with just a few beans of the new batch, before grinding in earnest.

For those that need an espresso grind, it is possible to buy a burr mill that specializes in very fine espresso grinds. They are precise and quick, but tend to cost more than those intended for a more general range of grinds; even so, in the espresso grinder category there are some models that can do an adequate job without requiring a bank loan. The price can be daunting, but it may be worth paying a higher price for a model with a measured espresso dose-dispenser, which makes the task of loading the filter-holder infinitely simpler and less messy, as the proper amount of coffee required is dispensed straight into the filter-holder. Espresso brewing, generally, benefits from buying proper equipment; a good grinder is just as important as the brewing machine, if not more so.

Below left and right: Two electric mills intended for espresso grind. The one on the right has a convenient dose-dispenser.

Degrees of Grind

Commercial coffee grinds vary from brand to brand. Coffee companies set and monitor coffee grinds by using mesh sieves stacked in a series with the coarsest mesh at the top. The level at which the particles of a grind stop falling, as well as the percentage of particles arrested in other sieves of the stacks, gauges not only the basic degree of grind, but also indicates the uniformity of particle size. If, for example, a coffee company wanted to check its medium-grind coffee, intended for a cafetière or percolator, it would expect that a high percentage of particles from a sample of ground coffee would stop at Gauge 9. If too many particles were to fall too far, or perhaps never even drop through to the Gauge 9 sieve, the company would know that the grind was faulty, and that the grinder might need re-calibrating.

Also, beans grind differently depending on the degree of roast. For example, darker-roasted beans become more brittle with moisture loss and are more prone to break into various sized pieces and powder. The grinder might need some adjustment in order to produce the same degree of grind as that obtained with a different roast.

An excellent way to determine the correct degree of grind to suit the brewing method, is to obtain a small sample of commercially ground coffee. Rubbed between thumb and forefinger, the degree of grind is relatively easy to judge. Commercial grinds are specifically designated as Turkish, espresso, filter fine, and medium grinds. Grinds coarser than medium are practically non-existent commercially. They are generally used only in *al fresco* or jug (carafe) brewing, and are not very economical, since the same amount of beans ground coarsely produces less volume, less extraction and therefore less flavour than if it were ground finer.

In recent years, certain coffee companies have attempted to gain a larger share of the market by producing in-between grinds, promising consumers of filter and cafetière coffee alike that the same "omnigrind" works for both. Another grind (which defies the laws of physics) is one that supposedly satisfies the requirements of both filter and espresso machines. Not only does the production of such grinds result in the wrong extraction in one or the other of the brewing methods, it also confuses people who want to understand why coffee is ground to different degrees.

One good result of the "omnigrind" for machines requiring a fine- or a medium-ground coffee, is that it provides the perfect alternative grind for the Neapolitan flip machine and the Cona vacuum machine. Both of these methods of brewing benefit from the greater extraction rate of a near-filter grind, and the fact that the very slightly larger particles of the "omnigrind" are not as prone to fall into the coffee liquid because of the machine design.

One tip for espresso perfectionists: in Italy, to maintain the production of a perfect espresso, the barman (barista) will alter his grinder to produce a very slightly coarser grind on a day of high humidity.

Turkish grind

Espresso grind

Fine (filter) grind

Omnigrind

Medium grind

BEFORE BEGINNING TO BREW

A coffee lover, setting out to make the best possible coffee, or at least a very enjoyable cup of coffee, should ponder several things before investing in any equipment. He or she must first consider which type of coffee is the preferred taste. It can be anything from the rich flavour of espresso or a mellow, high-grown arabica blend, whose acidity is softened by a touch of cream. Perhaps a full-bodied cup, providing pleasure in both taste and stimulation, is what is required. It is important to have the freedom to experiment with all sorts of blends and roasts.

Second, the time of day and how the choice of coffee is brewed needs to be taken into account. At breakfast, when time is short, volume and caffeine content are perhaps most welcome. After dinner, however, a small cup of pure flavour is more appropriate, ensuring that both the conversation continues and the palate is cleared of any lingering flavours of the meal still clinging to the taste-buds. At a quiet, reflective moment or when seeking to unwind, slowly savouring a deep, smoky, velvety black coffee transports the mind into another place and time.

The volume and strength of the coffee should also be considered. Is a small amount of coffee likely to be drunk all at once or are several cups required immediately? Perhaps one person may want to drink several cups over an extended period. Texture, too, is important. The liquid could slip down better if it were clean and clear of sediment, or one might prefer the roughness of a brew steeped in the particles from which it comes. Weak or strong, clear or thick, morning or evening, all of the requirements of coffee can be met by one or the other method of brewing.

Ensuring Lasting Flavour

Once the brewing method is decided, the question of "to grind or not to grind, and if so, what grind is necessary?" can be answered. The ultimate question is then "Can the magic of the moment last, can the coffee be maintained as fresh as it was brewed, until it is finished?" This question is perhaps the easiest to answer because it has been discovered that hot coffee stored in a preheated vacuum flask will taste good far longer than that kept hot by any other method. Nothing lasts forever, and the fresh flavour may very gradually deteriorate, but the coffee is not being heated up and cooled down and heated up again, which is what happens to the coffee molecules in a jug (carafe) on a hotplate.

Left: From elegant serving styles to tough durability, vacuum (or insulated) jugs and flasks can provide the solution to almost any situation where coffee quality needs to be maintained more than half an hour.

THE PRINCIPLES OF COFFEE BREWING

The beverage called coffee is the result of mixing dry coffee with water. The combination can be done by one of many methods – ranging from the very simple, with the minimum of equipment – to the use of complex machines which can cost thousands of pounds. Understanding a few facts about coffee brewing can help answer some of the questions which arise when wondering which brewing method to use.

Extracting the Flavour

A single coffee bean is an extremely complex entity, being composed of literally hundreds of substances, many of which are water-soluble. Nearly one-third of these water-soluble compounds can be removed in normal extraction processes. The goal of brewing coffee, however, is not to extract the greatest number of elements from ground coffee, because not all of them are desirable. Expert tasters generally agree that the overall coffee flavour, which consists of colour, aroma, taste and body, is best when about 18–22 per cent of the flavour components have left the solid coffee and infused into the water. When more than 22 per cent of the extractable materials permeate into the water, over-extraction occurs and harsh flavours are added to the brew, as the last substances to leave the grounds are unpleasant and bitter.

A second technical consideration is that, even if only the best flavoured components have been extracted from the coffee, the cup flavour can be too concentrated or too diluted, depending on how much water is used. Again, most expert tasters generally agree that a cup of coffee tastes best when the liquid consists of between 98.4–98.7 per cent water and 1.3–1.6 per cent "soluble solids", the latter being what would be left if a cup of liquid coffee was reduced back to dry ingredients by an evaporation process. This ideal coffee strength is easily achieved by controlling the proportion of ground coffee to water, which for European tastes ranges between 50–75g/2–3oz/ per 1 litre/33fl oz/4 cups of water. Many would consider normal strength coffee as one brewed at about 55g/ 10 tbsp per litre of water. Much of North America drinks a weaker cup.

The most beautiful and expensive coffee machines do not always produce the most satisfying cup of coffee, and when choosing coffee-brewing equipment, consideration must be given to whether the design allows for a correct balance of brewing factors, as well as taking into account various safety aspects.

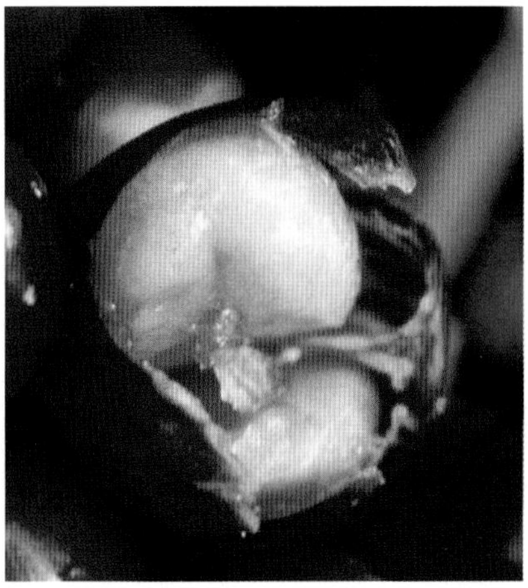

Above: From the coffee cherry spills two beans: the object of universal interest.

Key brewing factors

Correct coffee brewing depends on a balance of several factors, and each coffee will react differently and uniquely to exactly the same balance of factors. When brewing, consider the following factors:

- The degree of grind of the ground coffee.
- The ratio of coffee to water.
- The condition of the water.
- The water temperature.
- The contact time between the coffee and the water.

Above: These two glasses show the difference in strength when coffee is made with 50g/2oz of coffee per litre, left, and when made with only 75g/3oz, right.

Water Condition

People often buy coffee from a particular place where they have enjoyed an excellent cup. They take the coffee home, brew it correctly and wonder why it doesn't taste the same. As a cup of coffee is more than 98 per cent water, the condition and taste of the water are at least as important as the coffee used, and only water from the same source will recreate an exact taste. Coffee experts tend to agree that the best water for brewing coffee is slightly hard; a few minerals will

The importance of having the right grind

The finer the grind, the greater the surface area exposed to the water and the faster the extraction of soluble solids. Finely-ground particles of coffee are thus required for brewing methods where the contact time between the coffee and the water is shorter.

Conversely, a coarser grind will help to delay the extraction when grounds are left in the container from which the coffee will be served. A good grinder, whether manual or electric, will reduce the coffee beans to particles of a consistent size, so as to ensure an even extraction.

Comparing water types

You can easily do a few comparative tests for yourself on the effect different types of water have on the flavour of a cup of coffee. Try different waters, such as tap and distilled, and also add a pinch of salt to some distilled water to see if salt does in fact "bring out the flavour".

enhance the coffee flavour, hence the old custom of adding a pinch of salt to "bring out the flavour". If the brewing water is very hard, however, the calcium and magnesium ions can actually get between the water molecules and the coffee particles, interfering with the extraction process, and the resulting brew will have little flavour.

When considering the effect of soft water in brewing coffee, it is interesting to examine the softest water possible, which is distilled or de-ionized; as water it has virtually no taste, and no one would dream of making coffee with it. It could therefore be assumed that coffee made with distilled water would also be tasteless and would need a "pinch of salt to bring out the flavour". Wrong! Because it contains nothing to interfere with the extraction, coffee brewed with tasteless, distilled water has a very strong coffee flavour, which in the course of normal brewing, especially with a cheap blend, could easily be far too strong. Very soft water requires less coffee per brew, or a slightly coarser grind, or less contact time – any of which work to ensure that over-extraction does not occur. The old wives' habit of adding a pinch of salt may have worked not in "bringing out the flavour", but rather in toning it down, modifying the flavour for the better, if the original water was very soft.

Chlorinated or other chemically treated water, or water polluted by old pipes, rust or other tastes can affect the flavour of coffee. Filtering devices, which remove objectionable tastes, are available both in jug (carafe) form and in more permanent systems that attach to the kitchen main water pipe.

Generally, experts agree that fresh, cold water, which presumably has a higher oxygen content, makes the best coffee. Somewhat confusingly, however, it is oxygen that causes ground coffee to go stale, and it is from oxygen that vacuum flasks protect liquid coffee. Thus the need to have oxygen in the brewing water seems surprising, especially as convincing scientific explanations are rather scarce. (This calls for the challenge of a taste test: try brewing the same coffee with stale, warm water and with fresh, cold water and observe the difference.) Remember that most electric coffee-makers are equipped with thermostats which expect to start with cold water, and may not function very well if hot water is used.

Water Temperature

Water of any temperature will extract coffee, but hot water extracts faster than cold. Never pour boiling water on coffee, even on instant, as it brings out a harsh flavour. The optimum temperature range for coffee preparation is between 92–96°C/197–205°F. Conversely, if cooler water is used, the brew will be under-extracted. When coffee is intentionally boiled, as with Turkish brewing, sweetening offsets any bitterness.

Contact Time

When ground coffee and water are combined, a certain amount of time is needed for the water to saturate the coffee grounds and extract the various soluble solids, some of which take longer than others to pass into the water. For the first few minutes of the brewing cycle, the "blend" of the flavour compounds in the liquid is changing continuously. If the contact time is to be limited, the particles must be finer for the water to penetrate them and extract the flavour compounds. If the contact time is very long, the grounds should be coarser so as to slow the rate of extraction. In certain methods of brewing, such as those in which cold water drips very slowly through coffee grounds for several hours, the resulting brew will be extremely bitter, which is to be expected with such over-extraction, but will be offset later by dilution and sweetening.

Helpful Hints

• When using coffee equipment for the first time, follow the manufacturer's instructions. The following pages give recommended measures of coffee for each method of brewing. A good idea is to take one coffee scoop, and, having filled and weighed its capacity content, use it all the time for ease of measuring.

• If all the same equipment is to be used regularly and for the same amounts of coffee, note the number and size of the scoops of dry coffee required as well as the level of water in the measuring jug (cup). If it should happen that the first coffee brewed turns out to be weaker or stronger than preferred – all coffee is a matter of personal taste – make a note to adjust either the coffee, the water or perhaps the brewing time.

• Many coffee makers have indicators for the level of water required for a specific number of cups, but this rarely seems to correspond to the actual number of cups poured, no matter what size cup is being used. If in doubt about the ratio of coffee to water, it is far better to use more coffee than may be required; if the brew is too strong, it can be diluted after brewing. Coffee made too weak, that is, with too little dry coffee, cannot be "undone".

• Remember that coffee grounds absorb some water, so the yield of liquid coffee will always be less than the amount of water used in the brew; 600g of coffee will absorb 1.2 litres of water, which means that 1g of dry coffee will absorb 2ml of water.

• As much as possible, never reheat coffee and never use the same coffee grounds more than once.

• Any time a small amount of coffee (one or two cups) is being brewed, and the amount of coffee is not dictated by the size of the machine (as it is with the espresso pot, for example), use proportionally more dry coffee per cup. Approximately 50g coffee per litre of water is almost exactly 1oz per pint; this makes a slightly weakish "normal" brew and is a good starting point for determining preferred strength.

Above: The key to a good espresso machine is a mix of fine-tuning of the machine's pressure by the manufacturer, the skills of the roaster and blender, and the careful grinding and brewing of the barista (barman).

Some useful conversions

DRY MEASURES

28g = 1oz
440g = 1lb
5.7g coffee = 1 rounded tbsp
2.5g coffee = 1 heaped tsp
55g coffee = 10 tbsp/generous ⅔ cup

LIQUID MEASURES

50ml = 2fl oz/¼ cup
1 litre = 33fl oz/4 cups
600ml = 20fl oz/2½ cups

1 espresso cup (empty) = 2½fl oz

Liquid coffee for 1 espresso cup = 1½fl oz coffee (about 44ml)

Below: The basic equipment for brewing coffee couldn't be simpler – a scoop, measuring jug, saucepan and coffee – the trick is to familiarize yourself with your equipment and what amount and type of coffee and water best suit your equipment and tastes. Whatever the brewing method, measuring the coffee and water, noting the levels of each and the resulting flavour, makes successive brews easy.

COFFEE AND HEALTH

Caffeine ($C_8H_{10}N_4O_2$) is a white, slightly bitter alkaloid, sometimes also called "theine". It is a natural ingredient in coffee, where it comprises two to three per cent of the weight of each bean, or from about 60–90mg in an average cup of coffee. Robusta coffee has a much higher caffeine content than does arabica. As well as in coffee, caffeine is found in about 60 other plants, such as tea, cocoa, guarana and kola, and in products made from them, such as chocolate and cola-based soft drinks.

Because caffeine, as a stimulant of the central nervous system and cerebral circulation, imparts a feeling of energy and can often alleviate headaches, it is an ingredient in many pharmaceutical products, particularly those for headaches and colds. It is also a diuretic.

Tests have proved that caffeine increases mental alertness and the ability to concentrate, but the idea that strong coffee can offset the effects of too great a consumption of alcohol is a fallacy. Coffee does not "sober up" a truly inebriated person. Rather, it wakes one up, and as a sleepy drunk is preferable to a lively one, administering strong coffee to counter the alcohol is probably not a good idea. Also, the ensuing hangover seems to be worsened by the added complication of large doses of caffeine.

Excess Coffee

In general, too much caffeine consumption can cause palpitations, shaky hands, a feeling of anxiety and an inability to sleep. "Too much", however, varies enormously among caffeine consumers; for some people a single cup of coffee causes ill effects, while others thrive on ten cups a day. Coffee is one of the most widely-researched substances on earth, and yet scientific and medical opinions are still extremely divided. There is every reason to believe that the individual coffee drinker, exercising some degree of moderation according to his or her level of caffeine tolerance, can probably look forward to many years of "safe" coffee enjoyment.

Coffee is an acidic drink, especially if it is high-grown arabica, and many people, who find that coffee upsets their stomach, blame the caffeine content instead of the acidity. Decaffeination does not remove acidity, so drinking decaffeinated coffee is not the solution for stomach upset. Acid-neutralized coffees are difficult to find, but they are available in North America and the United Kingdom, in France (café allégé) and Germany (reizarmer Kaffee). They may not, however, be particularly tasty, as it is acidity that contributes so crucially to the flavours of high-grown arabicas and their blends.

Above: To many people, the difference in flavour between decaffeinated and regular coffee beans, will be slight. When market research indicated a growing niche for decaffeinated coffee, better quality beans were used by coffee companies.

Coffee and Medical Research

It has been proven that pregnancy greatly increases the time required for a woman's body to metabolize caffeine, and, as caffeine can be transferred to a foetus (fetus), it is recommended that a pregnant woman reduce her regular coffee intake by at least 50 per cent, with greater spaces of time between cups. If concerned, eliminate all caffeine from the diet during pregnancy.

For years, many thorough and exhaustive studies have been conducted to try to link coffee consumption with cancer or heart disease, but to no avail; nor does caffeine cause high blood pressure. One study indicating a definite link between coffee and high blood cholesterol (which in itself may cause cardiovascular problems), found that cholesterol was increased only in certain subjects who drank large amounts of coffee prepared by a particular Scandinavian method of excessive boiling and steeping of coffee. Filtering the boiled coffee before consumption, however, seemed to eliminate the cholesterol-raising oils. Other tests which link boiled coffee to an increase in cholesterol have proved that it is some other substance, and not caffeine which raises the cholesterol levels, as decaffeinated coffee – but only that which has been boiled and is consumed unfiltered – seems to contribute to higher cholesterol. Of course, if one suffers from low caffeine tolerance, is concerned about the safety of caffeine consumption, or simply wants to enjoy the taste of a late-night coffee drink without losing any sleep, a decaffeinated or even one brewed half-and-half, provides a perfectly acceptable alternative.

Decaffeinated Coffee

It is a fairly accurate statement that, although decaffeinated coffee has been produced since the early years of the 20th century, most of it was rather tasteless, at best, before about 1980. During the mid-80s, most likely due to numerous unfounded health scares about caffeine, there was an unprecedented interest in decaffeinated coffee. Almost immediately the flavour of decaffeinated coffee improved immensely, and all the major brands of supermarket coffee offered such a version. The decaffeination processes were changed very little, if at all. The Swiss Water Process, patented by

Coffex SA in 1979, needed several years to acquire a wide following, and many coffee companies are still producing decaffeinated beans that are not water-processed. So why did decaffeinated coffee start tasting good? The answer is that suddenly there was a market for it. For years only the very committed health enthusiast had drunk decaffeinated coffee, and coffee companies did not bother to use good beans for such a low-profile product. By about 1987, when decaffeinated sales represented around 25 per cent of the massive United States coffee market, coffee companies, in order to cash in on the phenomenal demand, started using higher quality beans for decaf products, and the flavour improved as quickly as the market grew.

Since caffeine is almost tasteless, except for a slight bitterness, its removal should not interfere with the coffee flavour at all, unless the decaffeination process inadvertently extracts flavour compounds as well as the caffeine. The goal of all decaf processors has been to remove only the caffeine, not the flavour. It is the quality of the beans that will ultimately determine the flavour of the coffee.

For around 200 years it has been known that, while caffeine survives roasting, retaining its properties through temperatures as high as 240°C/475°F, it is completely vulnerable to liquid, and will pass from green (unroasted) coffee beans into any liquid in which they are soaked. Some liquids extract the caffeine faster than others.

Left: Hide the package and most people would not know from taste alone if a coffee was decaffeinated.

The Decaffeination Process

The oldest method of decaffeinating coffee is that used by Kaffee Hag, among others, in which carbon dioxide, pressurized to a supercritical nearly-fluid state, is forced through steamed green beans, removing the caffeine. Many companies do not use this method simply because the equipment and facilities required are so expensive.

The most widespread means of decaffeination occurs when warmed or steamed green beans are soaked in a solution containing a chemical solvent, usually methylene chloride, which is selective in its target: all but about three per cent of the caffeine, and practically none of the flavour, passes into the solvent. The beans, rinsed and dried, go on to be roasted, and almost any trace of the solvent remaining with the beans is destroyed in the high roasting temperatures. In 1995 this method was banned in Europe because methylene chloride vapours, particularly in aerosol form, destroy the ozone layer. The United States Food and Drug Administration has limited methylene chloride residues in brewed coffee to ten parts per million, a figure which does not worry most coffee processors, who insist the actual residue is already less than one-millionth part anyway.

The slowest, and therefore most expensive, form of decaffeination is the patented Swiss Water Method, which uses only steamed beans, hot water and carbon filters to remove the caffeine. Unfortunately, some of the volatile flavour compounds also go with the caffeine, so the water is evaporated, and the remaining flavour concentrate is then sprayed on to the decaffeinated beans.

Although coffee lovers and experts alike are still convinced that decaffeination destroys the taste of coffee, many would find it extremely difficult to differentiate between a "regular" coffee and its "unleaded" version. In an exhaustive tasting project carried out over a period of several weeks at the International Coffee Organization, United Kingdom, a panel of trained tasters compared three cups of coffee, each made from beans from the same crop and same plantation; one cup was coffee decaffeinated with a solvent, one was water-processed decaffeinated, and the third was regular un-decaffeinated coffee. The tests were carried out time and again, not just with one set of coffee samples, but with coffees from Kenya, Colombia and Brazil. The results showed that often tasters could not tell which cups contained decaffeinated coffee, and, further, when tasters thought they could distinguish a difference, if asked for a preference, they often preferred the taste of the chemically decaffeinated coffee to the "regular" version of the same coffee.

Anyone who loves the taste of coffee, but is concerned about the effects of caffeine, should realize that today there are some fabulous decaffeinated coffees available, particularly from specialist shops. Cover the label, hide the box, and enjoy one of the luxuries of life: a cup of good coffee.

Left: Good beans make good flavour – decaf or not.

BREWING EQUIPMENT

Considering that there are a limited number of ways that coffee and water can be combined, it is amazing how many factors there are in brewing that make a difference to the resulting coffee flavour. But then it seems rather miraculous that anyone ever thought of combining the two substances anyway. Almost certainly, the first means of brewing coffee (probably only a few steps removed from the earliest practice of chewing on the fruit) was based on boiling the beans in water, although it was probably the entire coffee cherry that was first boiled.

The Turkish method of brewing coffee soon became the common way to prepare coffee, though Europeans did not take up the same means of brewing it. The first Europeans undoubtedly boiled the coffee, but not in a device like that retained throughout Islam for perhaps 600 years. We can only wonder why Europeans and their colonial descendants throughout the world have felt the need to constantly modify their coffee-makers. Museums around the world are filled with strange-looking pieces, such as beakers and tubes suspended above a flame, ceramic locomotives, complicated cylinders forcing water upwards, machines with pistons of near horse-power proportions which eke out tiny streams of coffee, cloth bags that could double as dirty socks and slow-drip devices like some form of water torture. The following brewing methods, perhaps less creative than the above, but generally more gratifying, are only some of those available to coffee lovers seeking the perfect cup.

Above: It is quite likely that very soon after coffee began to be used in Yemen, the brewing method we today call the Turkish became the common way to prepare coffee.

TURKISH IBRIK

The only real difficulty in making Turkish coffee is obtaining the right blend. The traditional Middle Eastern concoction has a very distinctive taste, due primarily to a penchant for rio-y flavoured Brazilian beans, which are usually blended with Ethiopian ones. Many people erroneously believe that Turkish coffee is dark-roasted, but the pulverized coffee is usually a reddish-brown shade, not dark at all.

The traditional brewing vessel, the *ibrik* (or Greek *briki*), is a small, long-handled copper- or brass-plated pan with a narrow neck. *Ibriks* come in different sizes, and usually each one has a tiny number underneath, which indicates how many cups it holds.

If an *ibrik* is not available, a small straight-sided pan for heating milk will do, although the coffee may not boil as easily. This is the only method which insists on breaking the "never boil coffee" rule, but as the coffee actually boils with sugar, the bitterness from boiling never affects the flavour. Adding spices to the brew, further adds to the flavour.

Left: Turkish coffee is usually served with a small glass of water and/or a piece of Turkish Delight. Turkish coffee is never served with milk or cream.

Using a Turkish *ibrik*

1 Remembering the proportions for Turkish coffee is simple: one of everything for each cup the *ibrik* holds. If it is a two-cup *ibrik*, place two very heaped teaspoons of Turkish coffee in the *ibrik*. (The coffee will heap high on the spoon very easily because of its fine consistency.)

2 Next, place two very heaped teaspoons of sugar in the *ibrik*. (The sugar will not heap quite as easily as the coffee, but it really needs to be somewhere between heaped and very heaped anyway, to achieve the "medium" sweet specification favoured by most Westerners.)

3 Lastly, using one of the tiny Turkish cups from which the coffee will be drunk, measure two cups of water into the *ibrik*. At this point possibilities for variations from the basic Turkish taste can be obtained by adding cardamom pods, a stick of cinnamon or aniseed to the brew.

4 Place the *ibrik* over a lowish heat and wait for it to boil. When the seething mixture threatens to run over the rim of the *ibrik*, quickly remove it from the heat, stir it, and return it to the heat. In a moment it will again start to boil over, so it must be instantly removed from the heat. Don't bother to stir again.

5 When the froth rises to the top the third time, carefully remove the *ibrik* from the heat and alternate pouring the contents of the *ibrik* between the two small Turkish cups, being careful to give some of the all-important froth to each.

COOK'S TIP

Returning the *ibrik* to boil the third time ensures the roundness of flavour and thorough blending of coffee and sugar.

Below: A number on the underside of an ibrik *indicates how many cups it holds.*

AL FRESCO

This is a simple method of making coffee when no proper serving jug (carafe) is available, or when the source of heat is a cooker or even an open fire. Any blend or roast of coffee is suitable, and brew for normal strength at 55g/10 tbsp per 1 litre/33fl oz/4 cups of water.

As *al fresco* brewing is useful in Spartan conditions, it is possible that the correct grind of coffee – medium if it is a commercial grind, slightly coarser if home-ground – may not always be available. If fine-grind coffee is used, shorten the brewing time to no more than three minutes and expect some sediment to remain in the bottom of each cup served.

Above: Al fresco *coffee requires only a saucepan, measuring jug and strainer.*

Making coffee *al fresco*

1 Measure the amount of cold water needed into a saucepan. If no measuring jug is available, use a coffee cup (multiplied by the number of cups to be served plus a little extra for absorption). Place the saucepan over the heat.

2 Measure out the amount of dry medium-to-coarse grind coffee needed. When the water is just beginning to boil, quickly add all the coffee to the water.

3 Immediately remove the saucepan from the heat, stirring well. Set aside for about four minutes. Strain the coffee into each cup.

JUG (CARAFE)

As with *al fresco* brewing, this infusion method is simple and requires little equipment. Any blend or roast of coffee is acceptable – though a medium grind is best, it can be a bit coarser, too.

Above: Earthenware jugs are ideal for this method of brewing coffee.

Making coffee with a jug or pot

1 Warm the jug by filling it with hot water, mentally noting the desired water level in the jug. Meanwhile, heat enough water for another jugful. Pour the first hot water out of the jug. (Measure the water capacity of the jug by pouring the water into a measuring jug.) Dry the jug and place medium-grind coffee in the bottom. Normal strength coffee for the jug would be about 55g/10 tbsp per 1 litre/$1\frac{3}{4}$ pints/4 cups of water.

2 When the water being heated is below boiling point – either just before or after it has boiled – pour the water over the coffee. Stir well, preferably with a wooden spoon, and wait about four minutes before straining the coffee into the cups.

COOK'S TIP

Do not try to keep jug coffee hot. If it is not to be drunk immediately, strain it into a preheated vacuum flask.

THE CAFETIÈRE (THE PRESS POT)

Making coffee in a cafetière (press pot) is almost exactly like making coffee in a simple jug (carafe). In fact, it is easier than using a jug in that it requires no separate strainer, and once one is accustomed to using it, it is easier to judge the correct water level. (It is not easier to clean, however.) The correct grind of coffee is medium, but if for some reason only finely ground is available, the brewing time should be reduced to no more than three minutes. Using a fine grind may make the plunging difficult – take care when pressing down, so that there is no danger of breaking the glass. Also, if using a fine grind, there will be more sediment in the bottom of the cup.

Cafetières, also called French presses, come in a variety of sizes, and there are various styles of "cosies" available to fit most; although cafetière coffee cannot be kept hot, its warmth can be slightly prolonged by wrapping a cosy around it. If the coffee is not to be drunk immediately, pour it into a preheated vacuum flask (thermos) directly after plunging.

There are many different sizes and brands of cafetières available, and the prices vary enormously. The more expensive ones, however, are generally better made, and the mesh sieve122 will last longer. In cheaper models the mesh may fray and curl around the edges, letting coffee grounds escape into the brew, and replacement meshes may not be available.

General Care and Maintenance

The cafetière is not as easy to clean as an ordinary jug because coffee grounds get trapped in the mesh and the metal disks on either side of it. These should be separated and cleaned after every use, as coffee grounds are oily and can go rancid, ruining the flavour of successive brews.When pressing the plunger pot down, be sure to press straight down and not at an angle, thus minimizing the risk of breaking the glass.

Above: Mesh sieves and also the strong glass jugs (carafes) can be replaced in the more expensive models, so it is worth enquiring about availability of spare parts when purchasing a cafetière (press pot).

Using a plunger pot

1 Preheat the glass cylinder by filling it with hot water; and while more water is heating for brewing, pour the water from the glass cylinder into a measuring jug and calculate the amount of coffee needed, working at 55g/10 tbsp per1 litre/33fl oz/4 cups of water.

2 Dry the glass and place the dry coffee in it. When the water for brewing is almost at boiling point (just before it boils or just after), pour it over the dry coffee.

3 Stir it very well with a large spoon. The more freshly ground the coffee, the more it has a tendency to float and seems more resistant to saturation by the water, so stir thoroughly to incorporate all the dry coffee.

4 Prop the sieve device, with the lid above it, just inside the top of the cylinder for about four minutes. When the brewing time is up, hold the lid down with one hand to stabilize the plunger shaft and, with the other hand, slowly push down the plunger. Serve the coffee as soon as possible.

THE NEAPOLITAN

Like the earliest large espresso machines, the Napoletana was claimed by Italians but was actually invented in France, where it is called the "café filtre", and indeed it is a form of filter machine, as the hot water, after the "flip", filters down through the ground coffee. Using a Neapolitan is a wonderful way of making a relatively small amount of coffee.

These unusual-looking pots are not particularly common, however, and well-made ones, in stainless steel, are even harder to come by, so no one quibbles about whether it's a two-cup or three-cup machine. Once a good Neapolitan is purchased, however, it should practically last forever, as long as the handle doesn't break. There are no glass parts to break, no disposable requirements to run short of, no seals or washers to wear out, and no electric coils to burn out.

Getting to Know Your Neapolitan

The trick when using this type of machine is getting the right grind, as all the aspects of brewing would indicate that the grind should be filter fine. The top and bottom of the coffee compartment, however, are both perforated, and the size of the holes can vary depending on the nationality of the manufacturer. The coffee must therefore be somewhere between medium and fine, so if a commercial grind is used, perhaps this method is one for "omnigrind".

Ascertaining that the water is the right temperature for flipping is not always easy. Some people therefore heat the water cylinder without attaching the coffee basket or the spouted cylinder until the water is hot, and ready for flipping. If the machine (or "macchinetta", as it is sometimes called in North America) is not assembled until the water is hot, care must be taken not to burn oneself; again, a non-metal handle is strongly recommended.

Occasionally, when the "flip" is done with a particular Neapolitan model, a small stream of water may arch out of the tiny steam vent, which at this stage is now towards the bottom of the top compartment. If this happens, it is only for a second or two, as it is just a few drops which get free before the coffee basket inside blocks the hole. Having the steam vent aligned with the spout below may ensure that the drops are caught by the spout. After the coffee is brewed and served, it is a good idea to let the apparatus cool down before attempting to separate the two halves for cleaning, and they usually fit together very tightly. When cooler, they contract and are less likely to burn anyone attempting the separation.

Choosing your Neapolitan

When purchasing a Neapolitan, look for sturdy, preferably stainless steel, construction, and an extremely welcome safety feature is a wooden or plastic-coated handle for holding when flipping over. The perforations in the top and bottom of the coffee basket can often vary in size from one manufacturer to the next, and generally speaking, the smaller the holes, the easier the operation of the machine, as fewer grounds will fall through and a finer grind is more desirable.

Above: Quirky and distinctive, the Neapolitan is a fun way to brew coffee.

Using a Neapolitan

1 When using the machine for the first time, measure the capacity of the unspouted cylinder. To make the coffee, fill this cylinder with water, then place the ground coffee in the coffee container, observing whether the grounds are falling through the bottom perforations; if they are, the grind is too fine and should not be used. Be generous with the coffee, especially if only one or two cups are being made; too few grounds will let the water zip through instead of holding it long enough for good extraction to take place.

2 If the grind is all right, place the coffee compartment on top of the pot with the water, and attach the spouted top in an upside-down position. The attachment varies depending on the manufacturer, but it should lock securely.

3 Place the Neapolitan over a low to medium heat and wait for the water to boil. It is not always easy to tell when the water in the lower chamber starts boiling. (Of course, by the time a bit of steam comes from the hole near the top of the lower chamber, it is definitely boiling.)

4 Remove the machine from the heat and wait a few seconds for the water to drop to just off the boil. Flip the machine over, being careful not to touch any hot parts, and set it on a heat-proof surface. The water will filter through the coffee for about three minutes, passing to the bottom cylinder, which now has a spout.

5 If the spout is set fairly low in its cylinder, the brew will not need stirring, as the first cup will get good-strength coffee and serving it will mix the remainder of the brew. If the spout is higher up the cylinder, remove the top half of the apparatus and the coffee compartment and stir the pot before serving the coffee.

COOK'S TIP

Although the Neapolitan is designed to sit on a burner, do not be tempted to try to keep the coffee hot over a low heat; it never works and the flavour will be ruined.

Above: Omnigrind coffee is best for Neapolitan brewing.

FILTER COFFEE MACHINES

Manual and One-Cup Filter Machines

For many years people have been letting water run through coffee grounds to extract the flavour instead of leaving the coffee to steep in the water. In a sense the electric percolator is a form of filtering, but the term "filter" (or filtre, as the French invented it) is understood by most people to mean some form of drip mechanism.

With filter coffee, the brew is clear and clean (although admittedly this can make the body seem thinner), and a stopwatch is no longer necessary, as the timing is all down to gravity, once the correct grind is obtained. Because the contact time between the ground coffee and the water is limited, a fine degree of grind is required for the proper amount of extraction to take place, but take care not to use too fine a grind or use too much coffee in the brew basket, lest the filter clog, causing over-extraction.

The invention of the electric drip machine about forty years ago meant that filter lovers were no longer required to stand over a filter device. However, the manual filter is cheaper to buy and maintain, easier to clean, requires less space and is far easier to control. Even its one disadvantage is actually another benefit: there is no hotplate on which to stew the coffee. The only equipment necessary is a kettle; a filter and filter paper, or a metal or synthetic filter which requires no paper; a jug for catching the liquid (a thermal jug (carafe) or vacuum flask (thermos) solves the problem of keeping the brew hot); and a spoon (wooden is best) with which to stir.

Plastic filter cones or baskets come in various sizes, and it is important to have a brew basket that corresponds to the number of cups to be brewed; the

Left and above: Manual filter cups come in a variety of sizes and shapes.

Making filter coffee using a manual filter machine

1 First, preheat the jug (carafe) or flask with hot water. It helps to know the desired level of the brewed coffee in the jug, in order to assess the amount of dry coffee to be used.

A good amount for normal strength filter coffee is about 55g/10 tbsp per 1 litre/33fl oz/4 cups, but if in doubt, use more coffee, as filter coffee can be diluted very successfully with a little hot water after the brewing is completed.

2 While the brewing water is heating, place the filter cone or brew basket on the jug. Measure the coffee into the cone.

3 Give the filter a gentle shake to level out the bed of coffee; this will help to ensure even extraction.

4 When the water has boiled, count to ten to let the temperature drop to about 95°C/203°F.

5 Pour a small amount of the water as widely as possible over the grounds just to moisten the surface, and pause a few seconds while the grounds form into a harder bed.

6 Continue slowly pouring the rest of the water over the grounds in a circular motion. If any grounds remain dry, or if the drip flow stops, stir the mixture in the filter basket.

7 When the water has all run through the grounds, remove the basket from the top of the jug, stir the coffee and serve, or seal the flask if the coffee is not to be drunk immediately.

Below: Individual-sized manual filter.

bed of coffee will be too shallow if less than 50 per cent of the basket capacity is used. A wedge-shaped filter is better for brewing smaller amounts of coffee (one to three cups) as it concentrates the grounds and provides a deeper bed of coffee to keep the water from rushing through too quickly. Flat-bottomed baskets work better for larger brews.

Commercial Products

For several years commercial coffee companies have produced individual one-cup or on-cup coffee filters. These are pre-measured, pre-packaged doses of filter coffee and a plastic holder with a lid, designed to sit on almost any-sized coffee cup or mug. Most companies offer these in both regular and decaffeinated versions. Some companies sell "sleeves" of usually ten of these filters, each designed to be disposed of entirely after using once; this seems a terrible waste of materials and packaging and space. Other companies sell boxes supplying two plastic filter-holders and lids, and ten individually vacuum-sealed pods of coffee, which fit neatly into a recess in the filter-holder. The same company will also sell boxes of just the ten pods of coffee without the filter-holders at a cheaper price, for regular return customers who have retained the plastic filter-holders from a previous purchase.

Commercial on-cup filters are extremely easy to use, requiring only a kettle or some other source of hot water, and a cup or mug for drinking. The coffee is good, well-packaged and correctly ground, and by simply filling the filter holder with hot water as it holds the coffee pod over the cup, there is little mess to clear up. In situations where two people require two vacuum flasks, if, for example one preferred decaffeinated coffee, or perhaps tea, to the other person's "regular" coffee, one good vacuum flask of extremely hot water could satisfy the demands of both people with the use of one or two on-cup filters.

There are only two drawbacks to on-cup disposable filters. One is that they are more expensive than an equivalent cup of just ground coffee, but, as they eliminate the need for any equipment other than a hot-water source, and as they are clean and convenient to use, the extra cost can be easily justified by many happy consumers.

The other negative aspect of on-cup commercial filters for the coffee "gourmet" is that one has very little choice or information about the origins of the coffee itself, although this aspect could be eliminated somewhat if a coffee company were to market a package containing perhaps two pods each of five different blends or coffees from five different countries of origin, with accompanying labelling.

Automatic Filter Machines

The many brands of electric filter machines vary as much in quality as they do in price, but there are a few points to consider when purchasing one. The first factor in choosing a machine is the capacity, which is critical in filter machines, as the filter cone or brew basket is of a particular size to accommodate a certain amount of coffee. Use too little coffee for the design (less than 50 per cent of the machine's capacity) and the water will rush through, not having time to extract the coffee flavour. Use too much coffee and the bed of coffee will be too deep, the water will be held too long in the basket and the coffee will be over-extracted. Even worse, brewing the full capacity of a badly-designed filter machine can easily result in the water/coffee mixture overflowing the sides of the brew basket, because there is not enough headroom at the top of the brew basket. Coffee grounds swell to nearly double their original volume during brewing, especially when freshly roasted and ground.

Another consideration is whether to buy a filter machine that comes with a permanent filter, which is probably made of metal mesh coated with gold (or of some sort of synthetic mesh), or a machine that requires paper liners for the filter basket. Generally, paper filters, easily disposed of, produce a cleaner, clearer cup of coffee, than do permanent filters, but what a nuisance to discover – at an inconvenient time of day or night – a lack of filter papers. Care must be taken to keep a permanent filter clean, however – a stiff brush is recommended – as its mesh can easily become clogged with old coffee grounds, causing a rancid taste and uneven extraction.

The importance of power Possibly the most important consideration in the choice of a filter machine will be the electrical power, as the greatest complaint against filter machines is a cold cup of coffee. The machine should take no longer than six minutes total to brew coffee, and should start the brewing cycle with a burst of water, which hits the grounds at a minimum temperature of 92°C/198°F. Whatever the wattage of the available machines, the higher the power, the better.

Many filter machines offer welcome options, such as a timer, so that the machine can be loaded with coffee and water at night to produce a morning brew at a specific time. However, any filter machine can be set to brew with the kind of timer that simply plugs into an electrical socket. The option of interrupting the brewing cycle by removing the jug (carafe) from the hotplate can be very convenient, but the coffee poured from the first half of an interrupted cycle will not be evenly extracted, and may be extremely strong and rather unpleasant. The best option possible on an electric filter machine is having a thermal vacuum jug to brew into instead of a conventional glass jug and hotplate.

Right: Permanent filters, besides eliminating the need to keep buying paper filters, allow more flavour (and a tiny bit of sediment) to come through.

General Care and Maintenance

An automatic filter machine needs to be descaled regularly to prevent calcium build-up in its internal tubes that can slow down the flow of water, extending the brewing time and causing over-extraction. Calcium scale can also shorten the life of the machine. Undiluted vinegar can be just as effective as a commercial descaler in cleaning a machine if the scale build-up is not excessive.

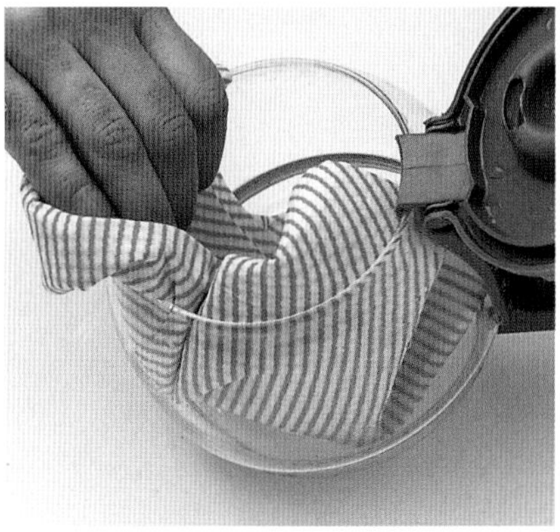

1 Keeping an electric machine clean is also important, as coffee is oily and can leave an invisible film which can turn rancid. Clean and rinse the jug (carafe) after every use.

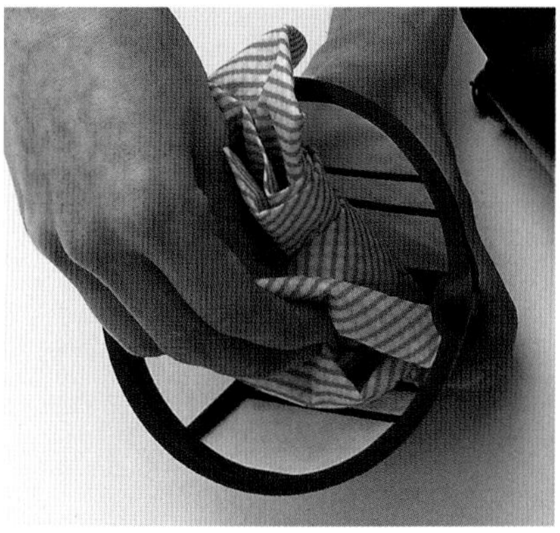

2 Do not allow the spray head to become clogged with old coffee grounds that will spoil the flavour of successive brews, as well as cause uneven extraction. Clean regularly with a soft cloth. Also, a hotplate will heat more efficiently and evenly if it is cleaned of liquid coffee residues.

Using domestic electric filter machines

It is always best to follow the manufacturer's instructions, which can vary from model to model. Most filter machines have markers on the side of the water reservoir indicating how many cups of coffee are made by certain water levels. These cups never seem to correspond to any exact cup size, so again, a trial-and-error system is best when getting used to a new machine. If in doubt about the number of cups and the amount of dry coffee required, use more coffee than may be correct, in the knowledge that the stronger coffee liquid can be diluted quite easily and successfully with hot water afterwards.

1 Begin with loading the electric filter machine with cold water and a level bed of dry, fine-grind coffee, at a ratio of about 55g/10 tbsp per 1 litre/33fl oz/4 cups of water.

It is not a good idea to try to hasten the brewing process by pouring preheated water into the machine, as it has a thermostat set to operate with cooler water. The time saved will be slight at any rate.

COOK'S TIP

Never re-use coffee grounds; after one brew cycle the flavour is completely extracted and the grounds produce only a weak and bitter liquid.

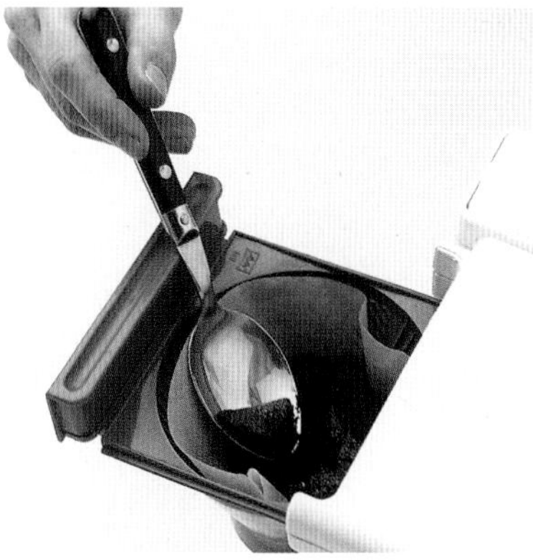

2 If it is a good machine, the brewing cycle will begin with a burst of water (which a thermometer will show to be between 92–96°C/198–205°F) wetting the grounds. Look at the coffee bed in mid-brew to check that all the grounds are wet and the surface of the mixture is fairly even; if it isn't, stir it.

3 When the brew is finished, stir the jug and serve. The hotplate should hold any remaining coffee at 80–85°C/176–185°F, but do not leave the jug on the hotplate longer than half an hour.

If the coffee is not to be drunk within this time, it should be stored in a preheated vacuum flask. Some machines supply jugs with funnel lids, which fill from the bottom, but by far the best optional feature of an electric filter machine is a thermal flask jug into which the coffee is brewed and which can be sealed.

MANUAL AND ELECTRIC PERCOLATORS

For many years, the "modern" means of making coffee was the percolator, which sat on a burner of the cooker (stove). It consisted of a metal jug (carafe), inside which was a central tube topped with a perforated metal brewing basket and its cover. The lid to the entire jug often had a glass knob through which coffee could be seen to be "perking".

Today's percolators are electric, but are still based on the same brewing principles: fresh, cold water in the bottom of the jug is brought to the boil, and passes up the hollow tube and out of the top, overflowing the perforated cover of the brew basket. It then filters through the dry coffee in the basket and drops back down into the bottom of the jug in the form of liquid coffee.

Contrary to the opinion of many connoisseurs, percolators can make excellent coffee, but the brewing cycle must occur only once. Better brands of electric percolators achieve this by switching to a lower heat after one cycle, which usually takes six to seven minutes. Remove the brew basket after one cycle. Even so, some, but hopefully not much, of the first coffee brewed is going to be boiled and re-passed through the grounds, which breaks all the rules. In spite of percolator brewing being basically a filter-drip method, a medium grind of coffee is required, to keep potentially disastrous over-extraction to a minimum. Again the ratio of coffee to water should be about 55g/10tbsp per 1 litre/33fl oz/4 cups.

Right: Today's electric percolators still rely on the same principles implemented by the original percolators first invented earlier this century.

Using electric percolators

1 Pour the fresh, cold water (allowing a bit extra for absorption by the grounds) into the pot. The water level should not be so high as to make contact with the bottom of the brew basket when the water boils.

2 Fill the brew basket with medium-grind coffee. Slide the brew basket on to the central tube and cover with the perforated lid.

As with the filter, even though the electric percolator can keep coffee warm, it is better to hold it in a preheated vacuum flask (thermos) if it is not for immediate drinking.

General Care and Maintenance

Cleaning the jug of an electric percolator is not easy, as most are not submersible, but it must be done. The invisible film left by coffee liquid can ruin the flavour of successive brews. Any surfaces touched by the grounds or the liquid should be washed with a mild detergent and well rinsed to avoid tainting future brews with a soapy taste.

CONA VACUUM POT

The vacuum pot, invented before 1840 by the Scottish engineer Robert Napier, is best known today by the name Cona, the principal manufacturer of these elegant and amazing machines. The method of brewing is actually steeping, or infusion, as the grounds are inundated by water for a few minutes before the natural law of cool air contraction takes over and separates the grounds from the brew. The Cona company supplies not only the machines (and replacement parts) and very good instructions for operating them, but also the choice of apparatus for one of two methods of heat: a spirit lamp and an electric coil. In addition to the source of heat, the vacuum mechanism consists of a glass jug (carafe), a glass bowl, a funnel, a plug and a holder frame. A large spoon will also be needed.

This is another machine that works best when the coffee is a grind somewhere between filter fine and medium, and the best choice of commercial grinds is "omnigrind". The ratio of coffee to water is the usual 55g/10 tbsp per 1 litre/33fl oz/4 cups, but as the machine works best at full capacity, it is not difficult to calculate, if the size of the model is known.

General Care and Maintenance

The Cona vacuum machine provides a science lesson by way of a fascinating visual experience, and it can be an interesting topic of conversation at the end of a dining table, but its greatest feat is producing an excellent pot of coffee. The disadvantages of this method of brewing are that it is definitely not fast and the delicacy and fragility of the glass parts, particularly the funnel, mean that it must be treated with great care during cleaning and handling to avoid breakage (although replacement parts are available from the Cona company).

Right: Perhaps one of the most striking designs for a domestic coffee machine, the Cona is perfect for making coffee at the table after dinner, as it is both beautiful and interesting to watch.

Using a Cona vacuum pot

1 As the glass jug (carafe) must be filled with hot water, it is quicker to heat the water in a kettle and add it to the jug. (The alternative is to let the water heat from cold in the jug, but it will take much longer, as neither the spirit lamp nor the electric coil can boil water quickly.)

2 Carefully insert the funnel plug into the funnel, place the glass bowl on top of the jug with the funnel in the water, and join the bowl and the jug by gently but firmly twisting together.

3 Light the spirit lamp or turn on the electric coil. Measure the dry coffee into the upper bowl and place the entire structure in the frame that will suspend it above the heat.

4 After the water boils, it will begin to move up the funnel into the upper bowl. When most of the water has risen, extinguish the spirit lamp or turn off the electric coil. The water will continue to rise. (Waiting a bit longer before reducing the heat will slightly prolong the brewing time, as the cooling of the air in the jug will be delayed.)

5 When enough water has risen to wet the ground coffee thoroughly, stir the mixture in the upper bowl, making sure that all the coffee is saturated. (Some water will remain below in the jug, as the funnel does not reach to the very bottom.)

6 When the temperature in the jug has dropped sufficiently, a partial vacuum will be created that will suck the liquid coffee back down into the jug, leaving the spent grounds above.

7 Very carefully detach the bowl and funnel, placing it in the hole provided over a small drip tray in the frame.

8 Serve the coffee immediately, or pour it into a preheated vacuum flask (thermos) if it is not to be drunk within a few minutes of brewing.

ALL ABOUT ESPRESSO

The simplest and most accurate definition of espresso is "hot water being forced under pressure through very finely ground, dark-roasted coffee". The idea of using steam to propel the brewing water for coffee was the brainchild of a Frenchman, Louis Bernard Rabaut, in the early 1820s. Another Frenchman, Edward Loysel de Santais, used the same principle to produce a machine that could make larger amounts of coffee; he exhibited it at the Paris Exposition of 1855. In Italy, around the turn of the century, changes were made that enabled several individual cups – instead of one large pot of coffee – to be brewed by steam pressure at a speed which gave rise to the name "espresso".

The improvements culminated in Luigi Bezzera's patented machine of 1902. Another milestone towards the perfection of the commercial espresso machine was Giovanni Achille Gaggia's 1948 use of a spring-powered piston to increase the amount of pressure on the brewing water, so that it no longer needed to be at such a high temperature, potentially scalding the coffee. Eventually the spring-powered pistons gave way to electric pumps, and today's *barista*, Italian barman, needs only to press a button to harness nine bars of pressure for a few sips of pure liquid energy.

Below: Manual espresso pots come in a wide variety of shapes and sizes, convenient for individual use or by two or more people.

Espresso *crema*

Making espresso to compare with that of a commercial machine is sometimes still beyond the limits of those espresso devices used domestically, many of which lack the capacity to produce that indication of espresso perfection, the *crema*. This is simply the light-brown foam on the espresso surface that results from the exact combination of fresh coffee and the correct degrees of grind, water temperature and pressure.

There are also definite differences between espresso made with a manual espresso pot and that produced by an electric domestic espresso machine. It is reassuring to remember, however, that probably 90 per cent of all Italian homes are still content to rely on the simple pot, which will never show signs of any *crema*, to provide the breakfast brew, consisting of half coffee and half milk, the latter heated in a saucepan. After a marathon midday Italian meal, the same simple pot will brew the small cups of black "caffè" (as many Italians call an espresso) which provide caffeine stimulation while the human body is trying to concentrate on digestion. (In Italy, evening coffee is often taken in a bar or restaurant.)

Making cappuccino at home

Electric home espresso machines can cost a fair amount of money and still do not guarantee a commercial-type cup of espresso, *crema* included. As for cappuccino, even if the little electric machine is capable of frothing cold milk – and not all are – the number of cups of cappuccino that can be produced in succession is directly dependent on the steam power and the price tag.

For owners of espresso pots and electric machines incapable of steaming milk, it is worth remembering that some electric machines offer accessory devices for frothing milk, and there are separate machines available which only steam and froth milk. Some of the latter are electric and others, are made to produce steam on the stove-top.

Above: There are a number of devices capable of frothing milk for home users.

MANUAL ESPRESSO POTS

There are numerous manufacturers of manual espresso pots, which vary in size and materials of construction as well as in price, although most operate in exactly the same way. As an espresso pot must be used to its full capacity, buying the right size is probably the most important priority. Bear in mind that the smallest pots may not balance over an average-size gas burner, so an adapter frame may be necessary to make the pot stable.

For more than 60 years, the most popular and affordable brand has been the Moka Express, but these, unfortunately, are made of aluminium, which can interact with coffee acids, producing off-flavours, and they conduct heat so well that they can burn the coffee. More expensive and reassuringly heavier are those models made of stainless steel, but even so, a high price does not guarantee the best results. Certain stainless steel designer models are disastrous when it comes to usage, as the handles are not heat resistant and are red-hot if touched during or after brewing. The lids, as well as being too hot to touch, have no hinge and are too tight to remove easily, which is a problem if one wants to check the level of the coffee in the upper half of the pot.

Safety and Hygiene

A few safety and hygiene tips for the espresso pot include:

- Never leave an espresso pot unattended on a hot stove top.
- Never let an espresso pot remain on the heat with no water in the bottom.
- Wash the espresso pot after every use.
- Check to make sure that the rubber seal underneath the upper half does not need replacing.
- Make sure the inside of the bottom chamber is thoroughly dry before storing it.

Above: Stove-top manual espresso.

Using a manual espresso pot

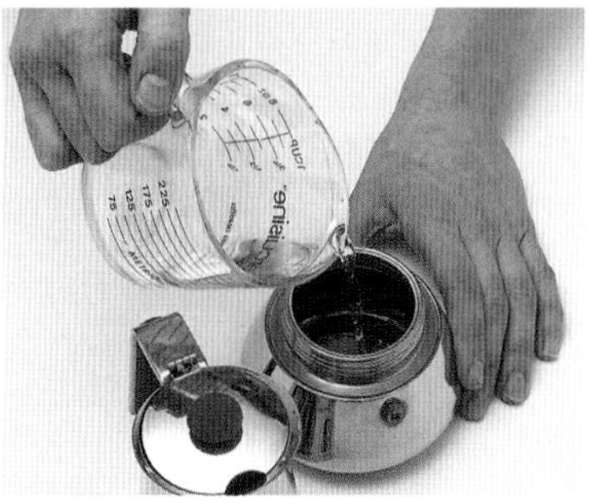

1 To make coffee in an espresso pot, fill the lower chamber with fresh water up to the bottom of the safety valve.

2 Fill the filter funnel basket with very finely ground dark-roasted coffee, using the back and edge of a spoon to eliminate any possible air pockets in the coffee and any gaps around the rim of the basket.

3 The ground coffee should always be level with the top of the basket. (The coffee should be very slightly compressed and any space in the top of the coffee basket filled; this holds the water longer in the coffee grounds and prevents the coffee being too watery.)

4 Using your finger, remove any loose coffee grounds from the outside of the basket rim, and place the coffee basket into the top of the lower chamber.

5 Very firmly screw the top half of the pot on to the bottom, keeping the bottom chamber containing the water upright, to avoid wetting the coffee grounds too soon.

6 Place the espresso pot on low to medium heat. After the water boils, its steam will start to push the remainder of the water up the funnel and into the coffee.

7 Immediately reduce the heat to very low. (If the heat remains too high, the coffee liquid will be acidic and thin, as the water will have passed through it too quickly.)

8 When most of the water has left the lower chamber the bubbling sound will become more intermittent, and it is very important to remove the pot from the heat at this time. Wait for the bubbling to ease before serving.

ELECTRIC DOMESTIC ESPRESSO MACHINES

Choosing an electric espresso machine for home use is not an easy matter, as there are many brands and the price range is wide. If money is no object, a few companies that make commercial machines offer models that are nearly more commercial than domestic. Sadly, only the most serious espresso lovers can justify paying several hundred pounds for this type of machine.

Looking at machines at a more average price level, the pump machines (not the piston) are the easiest to operate, although all may take some getting used to. Also, making espresso with an electric machine is always a bit messy, so it is a good idea to opt for the added accessory of a "knock-out" drawer as a means of clearing the filter holder of used grounds. When making a choice, consider weight and solidity an indication of strength; if the apparatus for holding the coffee filter (the "group") feels lightweight, it may reflect the flimsiness of the metal used overall. The newer thermal block machines have the advantage of being quieter, but a common complaint is that they lack pressure; as this is a prime consideration, a wiser choice might be to go for a noisy machine with normal boiler-generated pressure.

The machines which are made to brew only a particular pre-packaged "pod" or cartridge of espresso coffee can provide a temptingly easy solution to messy brewing, and worrying about the roast, the blend and the grind. The machine, however, is expensive and the cost of the coffee is also very high. Also, no real espresso lover wants to be tied to drinking the same coffee day after day, denied the opportunity to experiment with other tastes.

Another relatively recent addition is the filter holder with a valve that enables even cheaper machines to produce espresso with surface *crema* and good body. This is a very desirable feature, and obviously an important factor to consider when choosing a machine. Previously, the lack of *crema* highlighted the inferiority of a smaller machine to a commercial one.

Using electric espresso machines

1 To use an electric domestic espresso, follow the manufacturer's instructions, which, with most machines, will incorporate the following points. Assuming that the right roast and grind are being used, place a sufficient amount of water in the reservoir, and turn on the espresso machine.

2 Wait for a light to come on or go off indicating that steam is available, then decide on whether to brew one cup or two and, with the appropriate filter holder in place, use the "brew" mechanism to run some water through the filter to warm it.

3 Remove the filter holder, shaking out any water, and load it with espresso-grind coffee, allowing approximately 6g/1 tbsp per cup.

4 Press the coffee down evenly and firmly with the tamper supplied.

5 Clear any remaining coffee grounds from around the rim of the filter holder (or group). Position the filter holder under the water (brewing) aperture by holding the filter holder level, with the handle on the far left side (usually). Raise the filter holder to the brewing aperture until it feels securely in place.

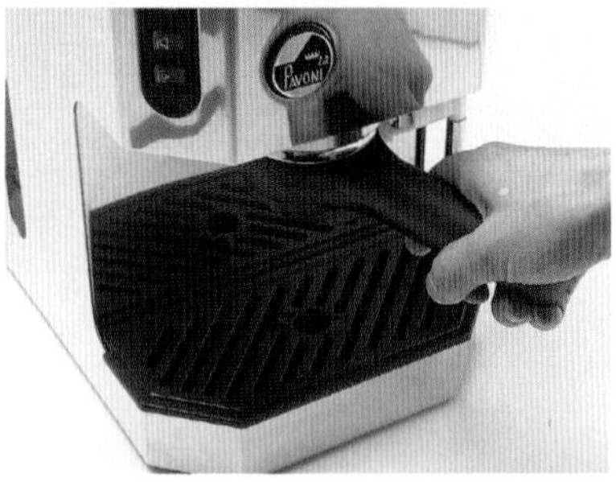

6 Lock the filter holder into place by pulling the handle to the far right.

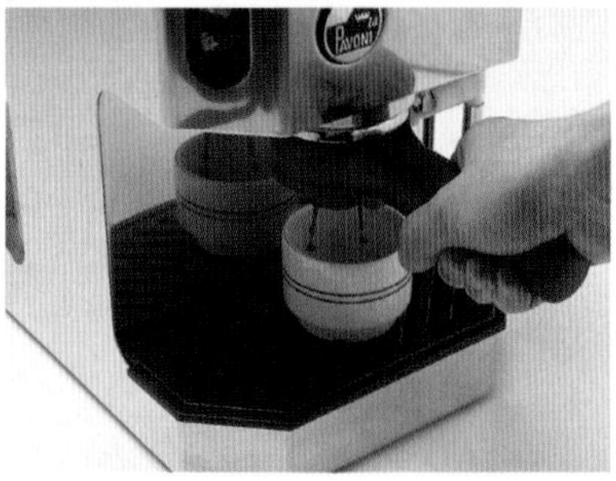

7 Place the cup(s) under the filter and press the brew button (with a valve-filter option), then open the valve by pulling the filter handle back to the left.

8 Stop the brew when the cups are slightly more than half-full (about 40ml/1½fl oz).

General Care and Maintenance

Cleaning an electric espresso machine can be tedious but it is an extremely important task that must be done regularly. A good idea is to clean the machine thoroughly each time it is turned off, if possible. A soft brush or soft cloth are suitable, but never use an abrasive cleaner or hard cloth that will scratch.

Below: Spend some time comparing the different electric espresso machines, as each machine's features can vary. It is important to keep in mind functional features, as well as appearance.

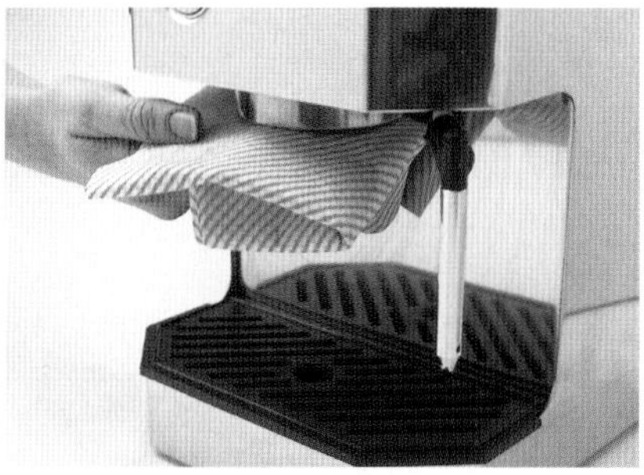

1 Keep the filter and filter holder clean and clear of any coffee grounds. Do not allow the spray head, above the filter holder lock, to become clogged with coffee grounds.

2 Empty and rinse the drip tray, where old sludge can turn into mould; the same applies to the knock-out box.

3 Get into the habit of wiping the steam nozzle after each use; a build-up of burnt milk around the nozzle is not only dirty, but it can easily cause a major clogging of the nozzle itself.

Ensuring the perfect espresso

Making slight adjustments to the grind, dosage and tamping pressure can result in the perfect cup that will take between 15–20 seconds to brew a maximum of 40ml/1½fl oz of coffee.

The appearance of the *crema* on the surface is an excellent diagnostic tool in determining why some cups of espresso are not perfect. If the *crema* is more white than brown, the coffee is under-extracted and needs either a finer grind and/or firmer tamping. If the *crema* looks burnt or is very dark in the middle, the coffee is over-extracted; perhaps the grind is too fine, the dose too large, the tamping too hard, or too much water was run through the coffee.

Espresso Types

Espresso is first a method of brewing coffee; second, it is the coffee produced by the brewing method; and third, it is a style of serving that coffee: for example, cappuccino is made with espresso coffee, but because of its milk and greater volume, it would never be called espresso.

Espresso (normale) Made from 6g/1 tbsp of very finely ground dark-roasted coffee extracted by highly pressurized water heated to 93–96°C/199–204°F water, the basic cup of espresso is approximately 40–50ml/1½–2fl oz (never more than 50ml/2fl oz) of strong black coffee served in a 60ml/2½fl oz cup.

Espresso romano This is a normal espresso served with a small piece of lemon peel. Brazil's *cafezinho*, its espresso equivalent, is also often served with a slice of lemon.

Espresso macchiato This is a normal espresso "marked" or "stained" with about 15ml/1 tbsp of foamed milk on top.

Espresso ristretto A basic espresso served in an espresso cup, but restricted in volume to about 25ml/1fl oz. Espresso ristretto is strong because it is made from the same amount of coffee as a normal espresso but is less diluted with water.

Espresso corretto A cup of normal espresso laced with an alcoholic spirit or liqueur; a northern Italian breakfast favourite is espresso "corrected" with grappa.

Espresso doppio Two doses of espresso coffee brewed in a two-group filter holder but dispensed into one 150ml/5fl oz cup; approximately the same volume as an espresso lungo, but twice the coffee, thus twice the caffeine, with less dilution. A real jolt of energy.

Espresso con panna or espresso tazza d'oro Espresso macchiato with a touch of luxury from the addition of whipped cream instead of foamed milk.

Espresso lungo or Caffè Americano A normal serving of espresso which is lengthened with hot water after it has been brewed to a volume of about 75–95ml/3–3½fl oz. The body of espresso lungo is like that of filter coffee, and it is usually served in a 150ml/5fl oz (small cappuccino) cup.

BEAN TO CUP MACHINES

For coffee lovers who want to get the freshest possible coffee straight from the coffee bean, bean to cup machines are a great but generally pricy option. They are very easy to use, do all the work and are less messy to use than other machines. They are usually automatic, which means the beans simply need to be added, then the machine grinds and dispenses the required amount of freshly ground coffee at the touch of a button. The grinding can be quite noisy and the machines are larger than capsule machines or traditional coffee makers, but the advantage is that a separate grinder is not needed, so there is no more tedious grinding, and less mess. Only the amount of beans needed are ground, which means really fresh coffee every time. Some versions also have an option to froth and steam milk. Bean to cup machines are the ideal choice for avid coffee drinkers who are especially particular about freshly ground coffee that can be made without any hassle.

Right: A bean to cup machine grinds and dispenses the required amount of coffee without making any mess.

CAPSULE MACHINES

Probably the easiest way to make a home-made espresso, coffee aficionados may consider this simple method of producing great coffee to be cheating, but the results are usually pretty good. Individual portions of ground coffee are kept fresh in little sealed pots, about the same size and shape as UHT milk portions, which are placed in the machine. Once the machine is turned on, the capsule is pierced, hot water is forced through the coffee and the espresso drips out.

This type of machine is a great time-saver, easy to use and clean, and very convenient. It is also ideal for those with limited dexterity, who cannot use a traditional espresso maker. Originally, the type of coffee that could be used in capsule machines was limited to the choice of varieties available for the specific machine or manufacturer, but an increasing number of compatible capsules are now on the market, offering a wider choice of coffee at more competitive prices. A final point worth bearing in mind before deciding which model to buy is whether the used pods can be recycled – some manufacturers offer a recycling service.

Left: Coffee capsules.

Below: A capsule machine is a quick and easy way to make home-made cups of espresso.

Coffee pods
These are often confused with the sealed pots used in capsule machines, but are actually quite different. Often referred to as ESE (easy serving espresso) pods, they are a single portion of ground coffee wrapped in filter paper and foil to keep them fresh, and are used in traditional espresso machines. They are easier and less messy to use than loose filter coffee.

Portable coffee maker: AeroPress®
A neat little lightweight gadget that is perfect for one-cup servings – great for using at home or work, or even for taking on holiday to guarantee an excellent cup of coffee while you're away. It's made up of two cylinders – the small one is plunged through the larger to force coffee through a paper or metal filter directly into a cup. Choose from a long Americano or espresso-style shot that is suitable for cappuccinos or lattes.

COLD BREW COFFEE MAKERS

Using a coffee maker to make cold brew coffee rather than filtering or plunging is more straightforward, and the coffee is less likely to contain any stray coffee grains. The coffee and water are combined in the upper container; when the coffee is ready to be filtered, a switch is flicked and the cold coffee concentrate starts to drip through. The resulting coffee concentrate can be stored for up to 2 weeks in the refrigerator. For iced coffee add cold water and ice to dilute, or for hot coffee add hot water or milk.

Right: Cold-brewing is becoming an increasingly popular trend among connoisseurs and baristas. Cold brew coffee makers create low-acid, sweeter-tasting cold coffee that brings out the full flavour of the bean.

Filter coffee mugs

Convenient, quick and easy to use, these are the ideal solution to coffee on the go. They produce a cup of filter coffee without the need for a large plunger. The coffee is made by placing freshly ground coffee and water in the cup, then once the coffee has time had time to brew, an integral plunger is pushed down. A wide range of individual lidded mugs are on the market, and most types are insulated to keep the coffee hot.

Cold brew method

This is an alternative to the traditional method of making coffee with hot water. Cold brew coffee is naturally slightly sweet and extracts less acid from the coffee beans, which is ideal for those who find hot-water brewed coffee too bitter. It is increasingly popular and as well as being easy to make at home, it can also be bought ready-made in bottles. Cold brew coffee bars are starting to emerge too, where cold brew is available on draught.

The basic method behind cold brew is that coarsely ground coffee is left to steep in cold water for up to 24 hours. The ratio for making cold brew depends on personal taste, but anything from 1 part coffee to 5–8 parts water – so 15ml/1 tbsp coffee to 75–120ml/2½–4fl oz cold water – is a good starting point. The coffee can either be made using a cafetière or a lined filter cone.

To use a cafetière, place the cold water and coffee in the jug and then transfer to the refrigerator for up to 24 hours. Then simply place the lid on and plunge the coffee as normal.

To use a filter, make the coffee in a jug and chill. When it is ready to be filtered, place a paper filter in a filter cone over a separate jug and pour the coffee through until it is all filtered.

Using either of these methods can result in stray coffee grains in the finished drink, so at this stage the once-filtered coffee can be re-filtered through a fine sieve or strainer lined with muslin or cheesecloth.

To serve, add cold water and ice for iced coffee, or hot water or milk for hot coffee. The coffee concentrate can be stored in the refrigerator for up to 2 weeks.

While cold brew can be used to make iced coffee, it is worth noting that cold brew is not the same as iced coffee – the latter is where chilled coffee is served over ice, often with milk and syrup.

Bulletproof coffee

This is a branded coffee drink that has been promised to aid cognition, boost IQ scores and trigger weight loss through ketosis (a metabolic process). The drink consists of "upgraded" black coffee blended with grass-fed, unsalted butter and "Brain Octane" oil, blended for 20–30 seconds until frothy. It was first created by David Asprey in 2009, after a trip to China during which he tried yak-butter tea drinks. Since its introduction, it has been consumed by sportspeople and Silicon Valley entrepreneurs, but dieticians are wary of its purported benefits.

You can make it yourself by preparing 1 cup hot coffee and pouring it into a blender. Add 15ml/1 tbsp grass-fed butter or ghee, and 15ml/1 tbsp coconut oil (preferably virgin), plus optional sweeteners and spices such as raw honey, pumpkin purée, cinnamon or cacao. Blend for 30 seconds until frothy and creamy (use caution when using a blender with hot liquids).

FLAVOURINGS AND GARNISHES

Of many tastes that seem to be natural partners with coffee, the most obvious are the flavours of milk or cream. Depending on the drink being concocted, the choice of milk or cream is wide. A simple cup of a high-grown arabica coffee, medium-roasted so as not to have lost its acidity, is wonderful with a splash of milk or cream. The acidity is slightly mellowed by the alkaline milk and the delicate, subtle arabica flavour is enhanced.

Milk and Cream

Many people making espresso-based drinks eventually ask the question, "Which milk is best for frothing?" as almost everyone has difficulty learning to froth or steam milk. There is disagreement on this topic. Any milk can be frothed, but some experts advocate skimmed (skim) milk because it froths very quickly; unfortunately, it also tastes like cardboard! Other choices include homogenized and heat-treated milks. Semi-skimmed (low fat) works adequately, but for real Italian-style flavour nothing beats pure whole milk, such as the British "gold top", and any rich, creamy milk is superb for complementing the flavour of espresso. Experience will show that the temperature factor is perhaps as important as the fat content; the milk to be steamed should be very cold.

Whipped cream should not be used as a substitute for milk intended for steaming, but it works well as a coffee garnish. Double (heavy) cream, especially with a tablespoon of milk to lessen the risk of over-whipping, adds richness and body.

Milk heated conventionally for hot coffee drinks curdles easily. To help avoid milk separation, heat it gently and do not let it boil. Also, the inclusion of sugar in hot drinks containing potentially milk-curdling ingredients helps to stabilize the milk compounds.

Below: Whether to add milk or cream to coffee is up to the individual, and it may be worth experimenting with skimmed and semi-skimmed milks when frothing milk. Use whipped or double cream for garnishing, though not for steaming.

Frothing milk with an electric espresso machine

1 First, pour the very cold milk into a cold half-litre metal jug (pitcher), with straight sides or sloping inwards towards the top.

2 To steam the milk, insert the steam nozzle to nearly the bottom of the jug, open the steam valve fully and rotate the nozzle around in the milk for 5–8 seconds. (The bottom of the milk jug should start to feel warm to the touch.)

3 Lower the jug until the nozzle is just below the milk surface; when the surface just begins to froth, place the nozzle slightly lower in the milk and turn the steam down. A deep purring sound signifies that the milk is steaming, and a few seconds is all that is needed for the milk to rise in volume.

4 When fine, smooth foam has just formed, close the steam valve and put the jug aside until ready to use. Cool if desired. Take care to stop frothing the milk before big airy bubbles form.

Below: Choose from a range of sugars; clockwise from back left: soft brown, demerara, dark muscovado, sugar cubes, cane sugar, caster (superfine) sugar.

Chocolate

In any form and any colour, chocolate provides a superb accompanying flavour for coffee, so much so that many coffee drinks include the word "mocha", which can imply a combination with chocolate. Also, as the Aztecs seem to have been the first chocolate drinkers, many coffee-chocolate recipes contain "Mexican" in their title. Powdered chocolate or cocoa powder (which is slightly bitter) can be sprinkled on top of any foamy, milky coffee surface. Chocolate syrup or melted chocolate of any type can be added to coffee to produce a happy combination. Chocolate mints or plain chocolate (milk, dark or white) wafers make a lovely garnish, as do chocolate-covered whole coffee beans.

Sugar

Sugar is an ingredient in many coffee drinks, not only to stabilize milk, but also to off-set the bitterness, which is almost always present to some degree in recipes using cold coffee. There are many types of sugar available, and a lot of people assume that one must be better for use in coffee than others.

Various sugars have different tastes depending on whether they are refined (all white sugars) or unrefined ("raw") cane sugar. Unrefined sugar has more flavour because of the molasses content, which varies from low in demerara to higher amounts in dark muscovado and darker soft brown sugar. Other brown sugars are made from white refined sugar to which molasses is added. The truth is that, like many aspects of coffee drinking, the choice of sugar is purely a matter of taste. Caster (superfine) sugar is excellent in recipes because it is quick-dissolving. Chunky rock sugar crystals, marketed specifically for coffee, are simply lumps of amber-coloured refined (white) sugar. Used in small cups of espresso, which is not normally brewed at a particularly high temperature, rock sugar has little chance of dissolving before the coffee is consumed, and it contributes little flavour. It could therefore be considered a waste of time, although admittedly, it looks good in a sugar bowl.

Right: Chocolate powder and chocolate garnishes.

Essences and Flavourings

Vanilla, in the form of syrup, powder or even vanilla sugar, goes well with coffee. A drop of vanilla essence (extract) can convert an ordinary drink into an addictive elixir.

Many people consider cinnamon, either in the natural stick form, as an essence, or more commonly as a sprinkling powder, a suitable coffee accompaniment. Sometimes coffee concoctions containing cinnamon have the word "Viennese" somewhere in their title – these are not to be confused with coffee marketed in Britain as "Viennese style", which is normal coffee bulked out with no more than 4 per cent fig or fig seasoning. The addition of fig makes the blend less expensive, as well as altering the coffee taste slightly.

The early 1980s saw a widening of flavours considered suitable coffee companions with the development of "flavoured" coffees. Just after roasting, flavour concentrates in the form of oil or powder are mixed with the hot coffee beans to produce combinations of fruit, nut and liqueur tastes in the brewed coffee. These are still very popular, particularly in North America, and perhaps also with people who prefer another taste than that of coffee. They can, however, provide a welcome change or round off a special meal. Any coffee equipment which touches a flavoured coffee must be thoroughly washed and rinsed afterwards, as the flavourings can cling persistently and influence the taste of future brews adversely.

Just as all coffee is a matter of taste, there are no hard and fast rules concerning combinations of other flavours with that of coffee. Somehow the "gourmet" coffee craze which began in the United States has led to all sorts of taste combinations, many of which are obtained by the use of simple syrups, essences, or liqueurs, as well as the natural product itself. If a cold coffee recipe calls for milk or cream, as most do, a scoop of flavoured ice cream can be substituted (with amendments to the proportions, of course).

Left: Adding a drop of essence (extract) or a flavouring can greatly change the taste of an ordinary coffee drink.

Above: Fruit and nuts make versatile flavourings and garnishes.

Left: Cinnamon sticks, nutmeg, star anise, and ground ginger all combine well with coffee.

Fruit, Nuts and Spices

Fruit flavour possibilities include banana, blackcurrant, blueberry, cherry, coconut, lemon, orange, peach, pineapple, raspberry and strawberry. These can be combined with coffee in various ways, depending on the desired texture and length of the concoction. The use of a blender can provide a smooth mélange of coffee and fresh fruit. Alternatively, fruit pieces or slices can be used in the drink or as a garnish. Fruit syrups, concentrates and essences are easy ways of obtaining a coffee and fruit flavour mix.

Nuts seem to provide a more indisputably happy marriage with coffee, and the tastes of hazelnut, almond, pecan and even peanut, obtained from powders, essences (extracts), or the nuts themselves used as garnish, work very well in coffee drinks.

Caramel and maple are flavours that enhance coffee well, as does mint, and a mint leaf or a dollop of whipped cream makes a lovely garnish.

Ginger, cardamom, cinnamon, nutmeg and cumin are spices which might be overlooked as coffee companions, but those flavours, if used in small proportions, provide a subtle difference to a coffee drink. The best way to add a ginger or nutmeg flavour is to grind small amounts of the fresh spice. A single cracked cardamom seed or a stick of cinnamon work particularly well in hot coffee drinks. A few cumin seeds or a sprinkle of ground cumin can provide a delicate undertone to a cold, milky coffee drink.

Alcohol

Coffee and alcohol can be a delightful combination. In general, orange-based liqueurs, such as Cointreau, curaçao and orange-flavoured brandy, are wonderful coffee partners. "Normal" brandy, Armagnac, cognac, Calvados and poire each individually blend well with the flavour of coffee, as do grappa, marc and raki.

More individual tastes are achieved with Benedictine, Galliano, kirsch, Strega, Southern Comfort, crème de menthe, Drambuie, vodka, or, of course, the classic Caribbean standard, rum. Numerous variations on the established Irish coffee are possible with Scotch whiskey or American bourbon. In fact, used in the right proportions with usually quite strong coffee, there are few alcoholic beverages that would not make a suitable addition to a coffee-based concoction.

Right: Alcohol and coffee have made many classic combinations.

HOT NON-ALCOHOLIC DRINKS

Be it a classic cappuccino with snowy-white frothed milk on top or a Spanish combination of coffee and molasses, there can be nothing more enjoyable than a steaming hot cup of coffee on a cold winter's day.

Cappuccino

The classic espresso and milk drink.

SERVES TWO

INGREDIENTS

- 160–250ml/generous 5–8fl oz/ ½–1 cup very cold whole milk
- about 15g/½oz/2 tbsp dark-roast espresso finely-ground coffee
- chocolate or cocoa powder (optional)

1 Pour very cold milk into a metal jug or frothing device, steam until a fine, smooth foam has formed, and set aside.

2 Next, brew two cups of espresso into cappuccino or regular 150ml/6fl oz/ ⅔ cup coffee cups.

3 Pour the steamed milk over the coffee, holding back the froth with a spoon until last, when it can be spooned on to the surface.

4 The ideal cappuccino should be about one-third each espresso coffee, steamed milk and frothed milk. (After brewing the coffee you may need to re-steam the milk for just a moment if it has begun to "fall" or lose the froth.) If the milk has boiled or has been too aerated, throw the milk away and start again.

5 Top with a sprinkle of chocolate or cocoa powder, if desired.

Caffè Latte (Café au Lait)

The is a very basic breakfast drink, as served in homes and bars throughout Italy and France. It can be made with only a manual espresso pot and a saucepan to heat the milk.

SERVES TWO

INGREDIENTS

- 2 parts espresso or very strong coffee
- 6 parts boiled milk
- sugar (optional)
- steamed, frothed milk for topping (optional)

1 Pour the brewed coffee into glasses or large French coffee bowl. Add the hot milk and sugar, if using, and stir well.

2 Top each glass with a spoonful of steamed, frothed milk if desired.

VANILLA VARIATION

1 Pour 700ml/24fl oz/scant 3 cups milk into a saucepan. Add a vanilla pod and place over a low heat until hot. Set aside to infuse for about 10 minutes, then remove the vanilla pod.

2 Mix strong coffee with 500ml/16fl oz/2 cups milk in a large heatproof jug. Add sugar to taste.

3 Return the saucepan of milk to the heat and add 45ml/3 tbsp vanilla sugar. Bring to the boil,then reduce the heat. Add 115g/4 oz dark chocolate. Heat until melted. Pour the chocolate milk into the jug and whisk. Serve in tall mugs with whipped cream and a cinnamon stick.

Normandy Coffee

Normandy, like Washington State in the United States of America, is known for its apple orchards, and gives it name to many dishes made with apple juice or apple sauce. This recipe blends the flavour of apples with spices for a delicious, tangy coffee drink.

SERVES FOUR

INGREDIENTS
- 475ml/16fl oz/2 cups strong black coffee (espresso strength, or filter/plunger brewed at 75g/13 tbsp/scant 1 cup coffee per 1 litre/33fl oz/4 cups of water)
- 475ml/16fl oz/2 cups apple juice
- 30ml/2 tbsp brown sugar, to taste
- 3 oranges, thinly sliced
- 2 small cinnamon sticks
- pinch of ground allspice
- pinch of ground cloves
- cinnamon stick, to serve

1 Bring all the ingredients to the boil over a moderate heat, then reduce the heat and simmer for 10 minutes.

COOK'S TIP
This recipe could be made into an alcoholic drink if one-fourth of the apple juice were replaced with Calvados, added when the heat is reduced to simmer in step 1. Do not allow the Calvados to boil.

2 Strain the liquid into a preheated flask or serving jug. Pour into cappuccino-style cups, adding a cinnamon stick to each, if you wish.

Georgia 'n Ginger

This is named after the US state of Georgia, famous for its peaches.

SERVES SIX

INGREDIENTS
- 1 can (450–500g/1–1¼lb) sliced peaches in syrup
- 750ml/26fl oz/3 cups strong coffee
- 120ml/4fl oz/½ cup whipping cream
- 25ml/1½ tbsp brown sugar
- 1.5ml/¼ tsp ground cinnamon
- ⅛ tsp (generous pinch) ground ginger
- zest of orange rind, to decorate

1 Drain the peaches, retaining the syrup. In a blender, process half of the coffee and the peaches for 1 minute.

2 In a clean bowl, whip the cream, taking care not to over whip.

3 Place 250ml/8fl oz/1 cup cold water, the sugar, cinnamon, ginger and peach syrup in a saucepan and bring to the boil over a moderate heat; reduce the heat and simmer for 1 minute.

4 Add the blended peaches and the remaining coffee to the pan and stir well. Serve topped with whipped cream and decorated with orange zest.

Mexican Coffee

The Aztec Indians were the first known chocolate addicts, and chocolate is an ingredient in many Mexican recipes. Combined with coffee, it makes a rich, smooth drink.

SERVES FOUR

INGREDIENTS
- 30ml/2 tbsp chocolate syrup
- 120ml/4fl oz/½ cup whipping cream
- 1.5ml/¼ tsp ground cinnamon
- 30ml/2 tbsp brown sugar
- pinch of ground nutmeg
- 475ml/16fl oz/2 cups strong black coffee
- whipped cream and cinnamon shavings, to decorate

1 Whip together the chocolate syrup, cream, cinnamon, sugar and nutmeg.

2 Pour the hot coffee into the mixture and stir well, before dividing between four mugs. Top with a generous dollop of whipped cream and decorate with a few shavings of cinnamon.

COOK'S TIP
This recipe can be made with filter or plunger brewed coffee using 40g/7 tbsp/½ cup coffee per 475ml/16fl oz/2 cups of water, to taste.

Café de Olla

This recipe is traditionally brewed in large quantities over a wood fire in a heavy earthenware Mexican cooking pot, called an "olla".

SERVES FOUR

INGREDIENTS
- 1 litre/33fl oz/4 cups water
- 150g/5oz/⅔ cup dark brown sugar
- 5ml/1 tsp molasses
- 1 small cinnamon stick
- aniseeds (optional)
- 50g/9 tbsp/⅔ cup darker-roasted coffee, medium grind

1 Place the water, sugar, molasses, cinnamon and aniseeds, if using, in a saucepan and slowly bring to the boil.

2 Stir thoroughly to dissolve the sugar and molasses.

3 When the mixture reaches boiling point, stir in the dry coffee, remove from the heat, cover, and steep for 5 minutes. Strain into earthenware mugs and serve immediately. Add a few of the aniseeds, if you wish.

COOK'S TIP
Use a French or Viennese roast coffee, dark but not as dark as that for espresso, so that the spice and molasses flavours aren't overwhelmed.

HOT ALCOHOLIC DRINKS

There are any number of combinations of alcohol with hot brewed coffee, some more successful than others. The following recipes include six of the classic mixes, and provide the perfect starting place for discovering your own personal favourite blends and flavours.

Jamaican Black Coffee

This delicious version of black coffee is only slightly alcoholic.

SERVES ABOUT EIGHT

INGREDIENTS
- 1 lemon and 2 oranges, finely sliced
- 1.5 litres/50fl oz/$6\frac{1}{4}$ cups black coffee (filter/plunger brewed using 55g/10 tbsp/generous $\frac{2}{3}$ cup coffee per 1 litre/33fl oz/4 cup of water)
- 45ml/3 tbsp rum
- 85g/14 tbsp/$\frac{1}{3}$ cup caster (superfine) sugar
- 8 lemon slices, for serving

1 Place the lemon and orange slices in a saucepan. Add the coffee and heat.

2 When the mixture is about to boil, pour in the rum and sugar, stirring well until the sugar is dissolved, and immediately remove from the heat.

3 While the coffee is still very hot, pour or ladle into glasses, and decorate with a lemon slice.

COOK'S TIP
This recipe uses hot normal-strength coffee. Any degree of roast is suitable, but a medium-to-darker roast will allow more perception of the citrus and rum flavours than would a dark roast.

French Toddy

This is a variation of a very old French recipe – said to have been a favourite of Flaubert – to which coffee and sugar have been added.

SERVES TWO

INGREDIENTS
- 120ml/4fl oz/$\frac{1}{2}$ cup Calvados
- 50ml/2fl oz/$\frac{1}{4}$ cup apricot brandy
- 20–30ml/4–6 tsp sugar, to taste
- 300ml/10fl oz/$1\frac{1}{4}$ cups very strong coffee (filter brewed at about 45g/8 tbsp/generous $\frac{1}{2}$ cup coffee per 500ml/17fl oz/2 cups of water)
- 25ml/$1\frac{1}{2}$ tbsp double (heavy) cream

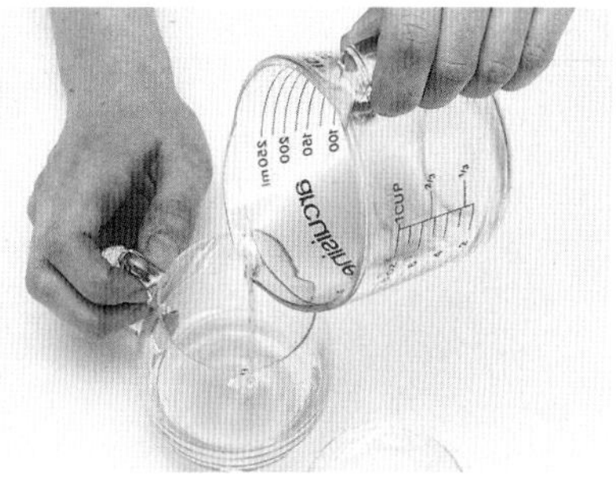

1 Very gently warm the Calvados and brandy together over a low heat, and transfer to large balloon glasses.

2 Dissolve the sugar in the coffee and add to the liqueurs. Stir.

3 While the contents are still rotating from the stirring, pour the cream over the surface in a circular motion. Do not stir, just sip and savour.

COOK'S TIP
This French Toddy can be drunk without cream and/or with poire (pear *eau de vie*) substituted for the Calvados, if you would prefer.

Café à l'Orange

This is one of numerous drink possibilities in which the flavours of orange and coffee are combined.

SERVES FOUR

INGREDIENTS
- 120ml/4fl oz/½ cup whipping cream
- 30ml/2 tbsp icing (confectioner's) sugar
- 5ml/1 tsp orange zest
- 600ml/20fl oz/2½ cups hot coffee
- 150ml/5fl oz/⅔ cup any orange-flavoured liqueur, such as Grand Marnier, Filfar, Cointreau, triple sec
- 4 orange wedges, to decorate

1 In a clean bowl, whip the cream until stiff. Fold in the icing sugar and zest.

2 Chill for 30 minutes, or until the cream mixture is firm enough to hold a wedge of orange on top.

3 Divide the black coffee equally between tall glass mugs and stir about 30ml/2 tbsp of the liqueur into each. Top with chilled whipped cream and place an orange wedge on the cream. Serve immediately.

COOK'S TIP
The flavour of this drink will vary depending on which orange liqueur is used, as some are quite subtle.

Hot Mint Julep

Instead of a long cool sip on a shady Southern veranda, here the bourbon and mint are combined with coffee to produce something comforting for colder weather as well.

SERVES TWO

INGREDIENTS
- 100–150ml/4–5fl oz Bourbon
- 30ml/2 tbsp sugar
- 450ml/15fl oz/scant 2 cups hot strong black coffee
- 30ml/2 tbsp double (heavy) cream
- 2 sprigs mint leaf, to decorate

1 Put the bourbon and sugar into two warmed large wine glasses. Add the hot coffee and stir to dissolve the sugar.

2 Top with cream by pouring it over the back of a spoon. Do not stir. Decorate with the chopped mint leaf.

VARIATION
This simple recipe can be adapted for use with any one of the many different forms of alcohol available. For example, Southern Comfort or Wild Turkey will certainly add a different flavour from that of ordinary bourbon.

Grasshopper Coffee

This drink is named for the crème de menthe flavour suggestive of a green grasshopper colour.

SERVES TWO

INGREDIENTS

- dark and white chocolate "after-dinner" style chocolate mints
- 50ml/2fl oz/¼ cup green crème de menthe
- 50ml/2fl oz/¼ cup coffee liqueur, such as Tia Maria, Sangster's
- 350ml/12fl oz /1½ cups hot strong coffee
- 50ml/2fl oz/¼ cup whipping cream

1 Cut the dark and white chocolate mints diagonally in half.

2 Divide the two liqueurs equally between two tall, strong latte glasses. Combine well.

3 Fill each glass with the hot coffee and top them with whipped cream. Decorate with the chocolate mint triangles, dividing the white and dark chocolate evenly between the drinks.

COOK'S TIP

Use coffee strong enough so as not to taste watery or be too diluted by the liqueurs, though weaker than espresso.

Easy Café Brûlot

This is a traditional coffee drink from New Orleans, where all the ingredients except the coffee are heated by being "flamed" in a heat-proof bowl at the table; the flame is extinguished by pouring the coffee into the bowl. Except for the dramatic visual effects, this recipe achieves the same flavour with less fuss.

SERVES THREE TO FOUR

INGREDIENTS

- 80ml/3fl oz/6 tbsp brandy or rum
- 50ml/2fl oz/¼ cup Cointreau or other orange-flavoured liqueur
- 30ml/2 tbsp sugar
- 6–8 cloves
- 2 sticks cinnamon
- 1 strip of lemon peel and/or 1 strip of orange peel
- 700ml/24fl oz/3 cups strong hot coffee
- cinnamon sticks and orange rind, to decorate (optional)

1 Gently heat the brandy or rum, Cointreau, sugar, cloves, cinnamon sticks and lemon or orange peel in a large saucepan. Stir continuously to dissolve the sugar.

2 Pour the black coffee, brewed at about 65g/11½ tbsp/¾ cup per 1 litre/33fl oz/4 cups of water by the filter or cafetière method, into the mixture. (A slightly darker-roast is best, as espresso would be too overwhelming.) Stir and serve, ladling the mixture into coffee cups. Garnish with a cinnamon stick and orange rind, if you wish.

COOK'S TIP

For greater visual impact, ignite the brandy mixture just before the coffee is added. Slowly add the coffee in a continuous stream, extinguishing the brandy mixture.

COLD NON-ALCOHOLIC DRINKS

Perhaps one reason for coffee's enduring popularity is its sheer versatility. Drunk cold, and mixed with a variety of flavourings, nothing could be more refreshing.

Coffee Milk-shake

This is a cold coffee drink that does not require an electric blender, as any closed container used as a shaker will work equally well.

SERVES TWO

INGREDIENTS
- 200ml/7fl oz/scant 1 cup chilled strong coffee (about 4 generous cups of espresso, or filter/plunger brewed using 70g/12 tbsp/generous ¾ cup coffee per 1 litre/33fl oz/ 4 cups of water)
- 2 eggs, well-beaten
- 450ml/¾ pint/scant 2 cups cold milk
- 100ml/3½fl oz/½ cup single (light) or double (heavy) cream
- 15ml/1 tbsp sugar
- pinch of salt
- 4 drops of vanilla or almond essence (extract)
- ginger bisuits, crumbled, to decorate

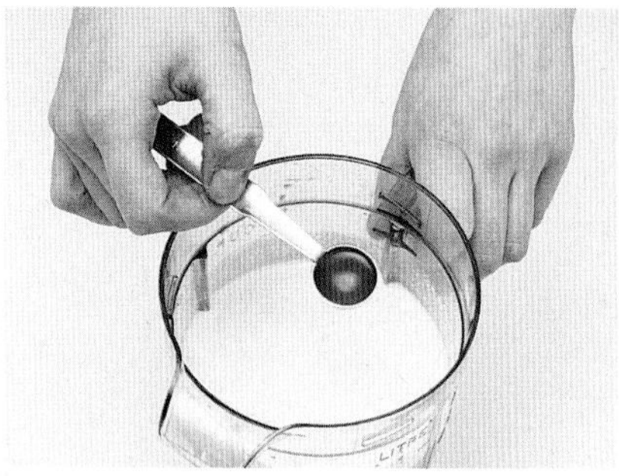

1 Combine all the ingredients in a shaker or blender until well-mixed.

2 Serve at once, sprinkled with biscuit.

Coffee Frappé

Similar to a milk-shake, this frappé recipe is another long, cold coffee drink that is both refreshing and uplifting.

SERVES TWO

INGREDIENTS
- 450ml/15fl oz/scant 2 cups cold strong coffee (brewed using about 80g/14 tbsp/1 cup coffee per 1 litre/33 fl oz/4 cups of water)
- 8 drops vanilla essence (extract)
- 300ml/10fl oz/1¼ cups crushed ice
- 60ml/4 tbsp condensed milk
- whipped cream and sliced banana, to decorate (optional)

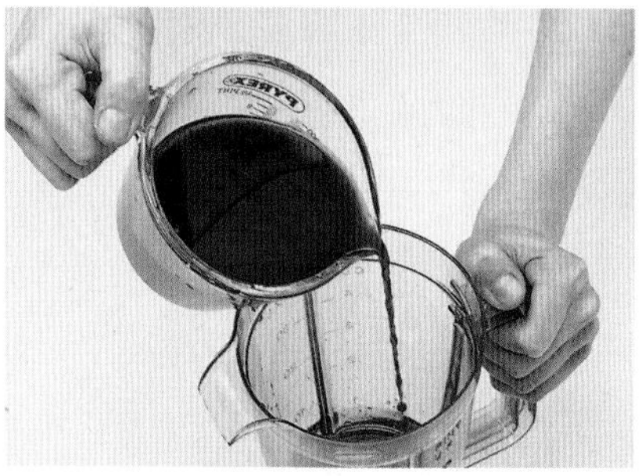

1 Add the cold brewed coffee to a large blender.

2 Next, add the vanilla essence (extract), crushed ice and condensed milk. Blend well until a smooth texture is obtained.

3 Pour into tall, clear glasses and stir in sugar to taste. Decorate with some whipped cream and banana slices, if you wish.

VARIATION

There are countless variations on the classic frappé. Any of the following essences would be suitable: try almond, banana, maple and peppermint.

Coffee Yogurt

This is really a variation on a "lassi", the refreshing yogurt drink of Indian restaurants. It can be made as either a sweet drink (traditionally with sugar and ground cinnamon) or salty (using salt and a little cumin).

SERVES TWO

INGREDIENTS

- 350ml/12fl oz/$1\frac{1}{2}$ cups cold black coffee (filter/plunger brewed using about 65g/$11\frac{1}{2}$ tbsp/$\frac{3}{4}$ cups coffee per 475ml/16fl oz/2 cups of water)
- 350ml/12fl oz/$1\frac{1}{2}$ cups natural (plain) yogurt
- 20ml/4 tsp sugar
- a pinch of ground cinnamon, to taste

VARIATION

For a salty version, use 5ml/1 tsp salt and a pinch of ground cumin, instead of the cinnamon, possibly with some sugar to taste, if desired.

1 Combine all the ingredients in a blender. Mix until creamy.

2 Serve sprinkled with cinnamon.

Chilled Coffee Caribbean

Use coffee that is not too strong; filter coffee gives a clean, clear texture.

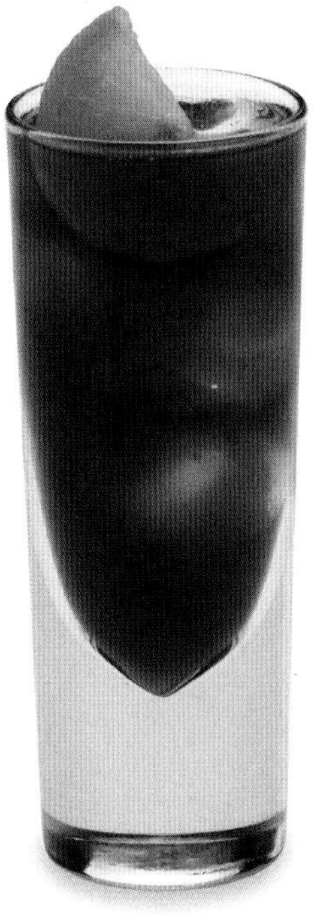

SERVES TWO

INGREDIENTS

- 600ml/20 fl oz/$2\frac{1}{2}$ cups strong filter coffee, cooled for about 20 minutes
- $\frac{1}{2}$ orange and $\frac{1}{2}$ lemon, thinly sliced
- 1 pineapple slice
- sugar, to taste
- 1–2 drops Angostura bitters, optional
- 3 ice cubes per serving
- slice of orange or lemon, to decorate

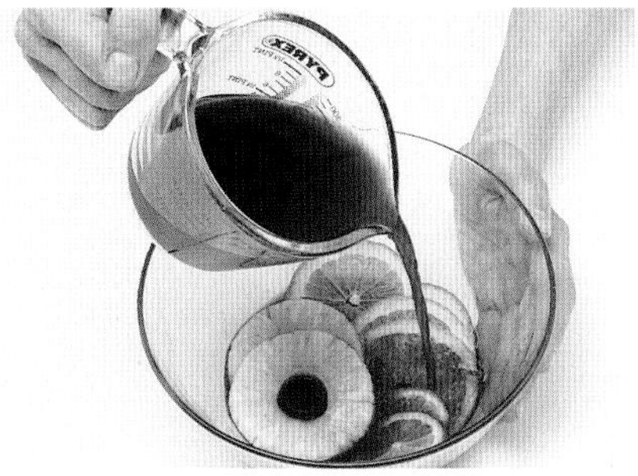

1 Add the cooled coffee to the fruit slices in a large bowl.

2 Stir and chill in the freezer for about 1 hour or until very cold.

3 Remove from the freezer and stir again. Remove the fruit slices from the liquid. Add sugar to taste, and stir in the bitters, if using.

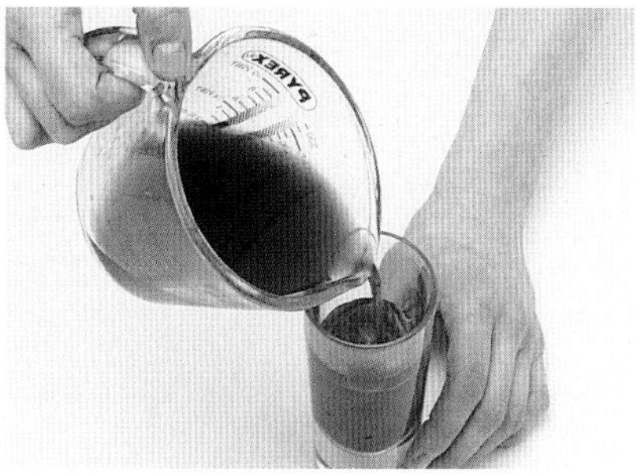

4 Add three ice cubes per drink to tall glasses, or whisky tumblers, then pour over the chilled coffee drink. Decorate with a half-slice of orange or lemon on the rim or add to the drink, if preferred.

Granita di Caffè

This is basically coffee ice, or slush. Makes just over 1 litre/33fl oz/4 cups.

SERVES FOUR

INGREDIENTS

- 200ml/7fl oz/scant 1 cup strong coffee (about 5 generous cups of espresso or filter/plunger brewed using 80g/14 tbsp/1 cup coffee per 1 litre/33fl oz/4 cups of water)
- 400ml/14fl oz/$1\frac{2}{3}$ cups water
- 140g/5oz/$\frac{3}{4}$ cup sugar
- 2.5ml/$\frac{1}{2}$ tsp vanilla essence (extract) (optional)
- 1 egg white (optional)
- 120ml/4fl oz/$\frac{1}{2}$ cup whipped cream, to decorate

1 Pour the brewed coffee into a large bowl or blender and set aside.

2 Boil half the water with the sugar, stirring to dissolve the sugar. Place in the refrigerator.

3 When the sugar syrup is cold, add it, the remaining water, and the vanilla to the coffee. Stir until well-blended.

4 If using, whisk the egg white and fold it into the mixture; it will make the granita much smoother.

5 Pour the mixture into a shallow freezer-proof tin (pan), such as an ice cube tray or baking tin (sheet), and place in the freezer.

6 About every 30 minutes, break the freezing mixture up with a fork to create the traditional grainy shaved-ice consistency. When it is well-frozen serve it in individual cups, and top them with a little whipped cream.

Coffee-chocolate Soda

This is a fun, refreshing drink that looks as good as it tastes.

SERVES TWO

INGREDIENTS

- 250ml/8fl oz/1 cup strong cold coffee (4 espresso cups of coffee)
- 60ml/4 tbsp double (heavy) cream or 30ml/2 tbsp evaporated milk (optional)
- 250ml/8fl oz/1 cup cold soda water
- 2 scoops chocolate ice cream
- chocolate-covered coffee beans, roughly chopped, to decorate

1 Pour the coffee into tall glasses. Add the cream or evaporated milk if desired.

2 Add the soda water and stir. Gently place a scoop of ice cream into the mixture. Decorate with some of the roughly chopped chocolate-covered coffee beans. Serve with a long spoon or a straw.

VARIATION

Try also chocolate mint, vanilla, hazelnut or banana ice cream and sprinkle with chocolate shavings, fruit slices or even a few roughly chopped up pieces of hazelnut.

COLD ALCOHOLIC DRINKS

Chilled and served in pretty glasses, coffee and alcohol make delicious and simple desserts.

Coffee Egg Nog

This is a rather special coffee drink, particularly suitable for daytime summer holiday festivities.

SERVES SIX TO EIGHT

INGREDIENTS

- 8 eggs, separated
- 225g/8oz/generous 1 cup sugar
- 250ml/8fl oz/1 cup cold strong coffee (espresso strength or filter/plunger brewed at 75g/13 tbsp/scant 1 cup coffee per 1 litre/33fl oz/4 cups of water)
- 220ml/7½fl oz/scant 1 cup whisky, Bourbon, rum or brandy, or combination of these
- 220ml/7½fl oz/scant 1 cup cold double (heavy) cream
- 120ml/4fl oz/½ cup whipped cream
- ground nutmeg, to decorate

1 In a clean bowl, thoroughly beat the egg yolks, then slowly add the sugar, mixing well.

2 Place in a large saucepan, and heat gently over a low heat, stirring all the time with a wooden spoon.

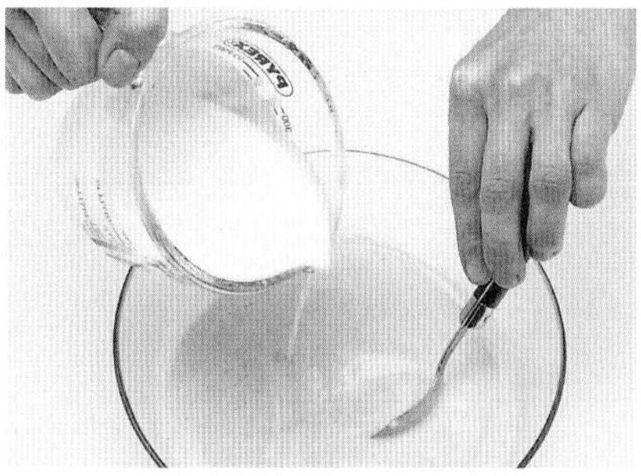

3 Remove the saucepan from the heat, allow to cool a few minutes, stir in the coffee and whisky, and then slowly add the cream, stirring well.

4 Beat the egg whites until stiff and stir into the egg nog, mixing well. Pour into punch (small round) cups, top each with a small dollop of whipped cream and sprinkle nutmeg on top.

COOK'S TIP

Use a little more sugar, if necessary, to avoid the cream and alcohol separating and curdling.

African Coffee

In parts of Africa, coffee is often drunk with condensed milk. This recipe is an adaptation of an African brew with a luxurious liqueur finish.

SERVES ONE

INGREDIENTS

- 250ml/8fl oz/1 cup strong coffee (4 generous *espressi* or cafetière coffee brewed using 70g/12 tbsp/generous ¾ cup coffee per 1 litre/33fl oz/4 cups of water)
- 40ml/8 tsp condensed milk
- 20ml/4 tsp crème de cacao
- ice cubes, to serve, optional

COOK'S TIP

Other chocolate- and coconut-based liqueurs, such as Malibu, work equally well in this recipe.

1 Add the coffee, condensed milk and liqueur to a shaker and mix well.

2 Serve over ice-cubes in tall glasses.

Caffè Vermouth

Vermouth is not an obvious choice to partner coffee, but the resulting flavour is good; different and sophisticated. Use a little less if unsure of the flavour.

SERVES TWO

INGREDIENTS

- 120ml/4fl oz/$\frac{1}{2}$ cup red vermouth
- 60ml/4 tbsp very strong cold coffee (espresso strength or filter/plunger brewed at 75g/13 tbsp/scant 1 cup coffee per 1 litre/33fl oz/4 cups of water)
- 250ml/8fl oz/1 cup milk
- 30ml/2 tbsp crushed ice
- 10ml/2 tsp sugar
- coffee beans, to decorate

COOK'S TIP

This is another combination in which the milk product may have a tendency to separate in some cases. The use of a slightly higher sugar content can prevent this.

1 In a cocktail shaker, combine all the ingredients and shake well.

2 Serve immediately in cocktail glasses or glass tumblers. Decorate with a few roasted coffee beans.

VARIATION

Different flavours and textures can be obtained by varying the type of milk used, or by using a little cream instead of milk for a richer version.

Lisbon Flip Coffee

Here the coffee is not so much a main ingredient; rather it provides a flavourful undertone in an interesting and satisfying cocktail.

SERVES TWO

INGREDIENTS

- 120ml/4fl oz/$\frac{1}{2}$ cup port
- 45ml/3 tbsp curaçao
- 20ml/4 tsp very strong coffee
- 10ml/2 tsp icing (confectioner's) sugar
- 2 eggs
- 20ml/4 tsp condensed milk
- 60ml/4 tbsp crushed ice
- grated chocolate and orange rind shavings, to decorate

1 Place all the ingredients in a cocktail shaker, including the crushed ice.

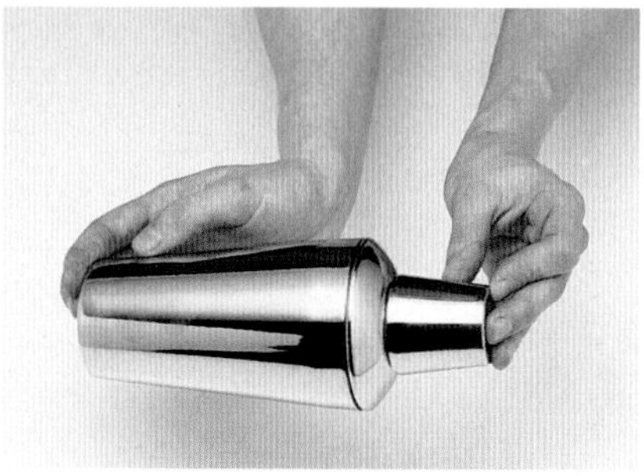

2 Shake vigorously and serve immediately in cocktail glasses. Top with the finely grated chocolate and orange rind.

COOK'S TIPS

- To make this drink, espresso ristretto is the strength required.
- Most orange-based liqueurs, such as Grand Marnier, Cointreau, Orange Nassau and triple sec, could be used in place of the curaçao, if not available.

Coffee Colada

This coffee cocktail is a riot of bold Caribbean flavours. A jug can be made up a couple of hours in advance, then allowed to partially freeze, like a frozen margarita, before topping with plenty of whipped cream.

SERVES FOUR

INGREDIENTS

- 450ml/15fl oz/scant 2 cups cold, very strong coffee (filter or cafetière brewed using 80g/14 tbsp/1 cup coffee per 1 litre/33fl oz/4 cups of water)
- 50ml/2fl oz/¼ cup tequila (or white rum)
- 50ml/2fl oz/¼ cup Malibu
- 100ml/3½fl oz/½ cup cream of coconut
- 2.5ml/½ tsp vanilla essence (extract)
- 350ml/12fl oz/1½ cups crushed ice
- 60ml/4 tbsp whipped cream and toasted coconut shavings, to decorate

1 In a blender, combine all the ingredients and blend on high.

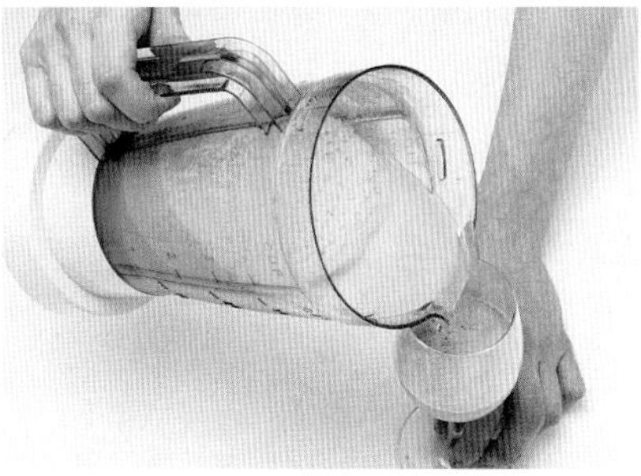

2 Serve in tall wine glasses.

3 Decorate with whipped cream, and top with toasted coconut shavings.

Coffee Cognac Cooler

This drink is unabashedly decadent – not for those counting calories!

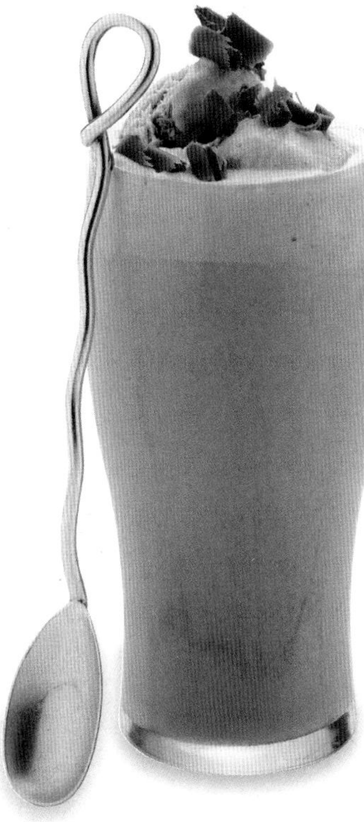

SERVES TWO

INGREDIENTS

- 250ml/8fl oz/1 cup cold strong darker-roast coffee
- 80ml/3fl oz/6 tbsp cognac or brandy
- 50ml/2fl oz/¼ cup coffee liqueur
- 50ml/2fl oz/¼ cup double cream
- 10ml/2 tsp sugar
- 250ml/8fl oz/1 cup crushed ice
- 2 scoops coffee ice cream
- chocolate shavings, to decorate

1 Shake or blend all the ingredients except the ice cream together.

2 Pour into tall glasses and gently add a scoop of ice cream to each. Decorate with chocolate shavings and serve with a long-handled spoon.

COOK'S TIP

The coffee liqueur can be either a cream-based one, such as Kahlua, or a non-cream based liqueur, such as Tia Maria.

Cooking with Coffee: The Recipes

This section contains over 70 recipes presented in a beautifully illustrated step-by-step format. All the classic coffee recipes are included, such as Tiramisu, Coffee Coeurs `a la Crème, Mocha Sponge Cake and Cappuccino Torte. There are also recipes for all occasions, from fruit and frozen desserts, sumptuous tortes, rich pies and pastries and irresistible biscuits and breads. All of the recipes demonstrate just how versatile an ingredient coffee is; it combines effortlessly with so many other flavours, such as alcohol, fruit, chocolate and cream. Always use good-quality coffee, and experimenting with coffees from around the world will make each dish a delicious culinary adventure.

Cream Desserts and Hot Puddings

Smooth creamy custards form the base of many cold desserts, such as Coffee Crème Caramel and Petits Pots de Cappuccino, as well as hot ones such as Apricot Panettone Pudding. Served in tall elegant glasses, light airy mousses feature frequently among the most memorable desserts. Many are also blissfully simple; such as Coffee Cardamom Zabaglione and Chocolate and Espresso Mousse.

CLASSIC COFFEE CRÈME CARAMEL

THESE LIGHTLY SET COFFEE CUSTARDS ARE SERVED IN A POOL OF CARAMEL SAUCE. FOR A RICHER FLAVOUR, MAKE THEM WITH HALF SINGLE CREAM, HALF MILK.

SERVES SIX

INGREDIENTS
- 600ml/1 pint/2½ cups milk
- 45ml/3 tbsp ground coffee
- 50g/2oz/¼ cup caster sugar
- 4 eggs
- 4 egg yolks
- spun sugar, to decorate (optional)

For the caramel sauce
- 150g/5oz/¾ cup caster sugar
- 60ml/4 tbsp water

1 Preheat the oven to 160°C/325°F/ Gas 3. To make the caramel sauce, gently heat the sugar in a small heavy-based pan with the water, until the sugar has dissolved. Bring to the boil and boil rapidly until the syrup turns a rich golden brown.

2 Quickly and carefully, pour the hot syrup into six warmed 150ml/¼ pint/ ⅔ cup ramekins.

3 To make the coffee custard, heat the milk until almost boiling. Pour over the ground coffee and leave to infuse for about 5 minutes. Strain through a fine sieve into a jug.

4 In a bowl, whisk the caster sugar, eggs and yolks until light and creamy. Whisk the coffee-flavoured milk into the egg mixture. Pour into the ramekins.

5 Put the ramekins in a roasting tin and pour in enough hot water to come two-thirds of the way up the sides of the dishes. Bake for 30–35 minutes or until just set. Test by gently shaking one of the custards; it should wobble like a jelly. Remove the custards from the hot water and leave to cool.

6 Chill the coffee custards for at least 3 hours. To turn out, carefully loosen the sides with a palette knife then invert on to serving plates. Decorate with spun sugar, if using.

COOK'S TIP

To make spun sugar, gently heat 75g/ 3oz/scant ½ cup caster sugar, 5ml/1 tsp liquid glucose and 30ml/2 tbsp water in a heavy-based pan until the sugar dissolves. Boil the syrup to 160°C/325°F, then briefly dip the base of the pan into cold water. Put a sheet of greaseproof paper on the work surface to protect it. Holding two forks together, dip them into the syrup and flick them rapidly backwards and forwards over an oiled rolling pin. Store in an airtight container until ready to use.

TIRAMISU

THE NAME OF THIS CLASSIC DESSERT TRANSLATES AS "PICK ME UP", WHICH IS SAID TO DERIVE FROM THE FACT THAT IT IS SO GOOD THAT IT LITERALLY MAKES YOU SWOON WHEN YOU EAT IT.

SERVES FOUR

INGREDIENTS

- 225g/8oz/1 cup mascarpone
- 25g/1oz/¼ cup icing sugar, sifted
- 150ml/¼ pint/⅔ cup strong brewed coffee, chilled
- 300ml/½ pint/1¼ cups double cream
- 45ml/3 tbsp coffee liqueur such as Tia Maria, Kahlúa or Toussaint
- 115g/4oz Savoiardi (sponge finger) biscuits
- 50g/2oz bittersweet or plain chocolate, coarsely grated
- cocoa powder, for dusting

1 Lightly grease and line a 900g/2lb loaf tin with clear film. Put the mascarpone and icing sugar in a large bowl and beat for 1 minute. Stir in 30ml/2 tbsp of the chilled coffee. Mix thoroughly.

2 Whip the cream with 15ml/1 tbsp of the liqueur until it forms soft peaks. Stir a spoonful into the mascarpone mixture, then fold in the rest. Spoon half the mascarpone mixture into the loaf tin and smooth the top.

3 Put the remaining strong brewed coffee and liqueur in a shallow dish just wider than the Savoiardi biscuits. Using half the biscuits, dip one side of each biscuit into the coffee mixture, then arrange on top of the mascarpone mixture in a single layer.

4 Spoon the rest of the mascarpone mixture over the biscuit layer and smooth the top.

5 Dip the remaining biscuits in the coffee mixture, and arrange on top. Drizzle any remaining coffee mixture over the top. Cover the dish with clear film and chill for at least 4 hours. Carefully turn the tiramisu out of the loaf tin and sprinkle with grated chocolate and cocoa powder; serve cut into slices.

COOK'S TIP

Mascarpone is a silky-textured, soft, thick cream cheese, originally from Lombardy, and made with cows' milk.

COFFEE CARDAMOM ZABAGLIONE

THIS WARM ITALIAN DESSERT IS USUALLY MADE WITH ITALIAN MARSALA WINE. IN THIS RECIPE COFFEE LIQUEUR IS USED ALONG WITH FRESHLY CRUSHED CARDAMOM.

SERVES FOUR

INGREDIENTS
- 4 cardamom pods
- 8 egg yolks
- 50g/2oz/4 tbsp golden caster sugar
- 30ml/2 tbsp strong brewed coffee
- 50ml/2fl oz/¼ cup coffee liqueur such as Tia Maria, Kahlúa or Toussaint
- a few crushed roasted coffee beans, to decorate

1 Peel away the pale green outer husks from the cardamom pods and remove the black seeds. Crush these to a fine powder using a pestle and mortar.

2 Put the egg yolks, caster sugar and crushed cardamom seeds in a large bowl and whisk with an electric hand whisk for 1–2 minutes, or until the mixture is pale and creamy.

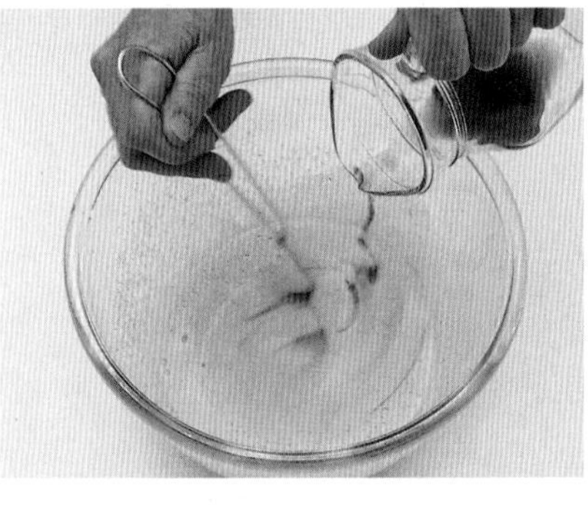

3 Gradually whisk the coffee and the liqueur into the egg yolk mixture.

4 Place the bowl over a saucepan of near-boiling water and continue whisking for about 10 minutes.

5 Continue whisking until the mixture is very thick and fluffy and has doubled in volume, making sure the water doesn't boil – if it does the mixture will curdle. Remove the bowl from the heat and carefully pour the zabaglione into four warmed glasses or dishes. Sprinkle with a few crushed roasted coffee beans and serve immediately.

COOK'S TIP

Cardamom is a fragrant spice from northern India. It may be bought ready-ground, but freshly crushed cardamom is much sweeter.

PETITS POTS DE CAPPUCCINO

THESE VERY RICH COFFEE CUSTARDS, WITH A CREAM TOPPING AND A LIGHT DUSTING OF DRINKING CHOCOLATE, LOOK WONDERFUL PRESENTED IN FINE CHINA COFFEE CUPS.

SERVES SIX TO EIGHT

INGREDIENTS
- 75g/3oz/1 cup roasted coffee beans
- 300ml/½ pint/1¼ cups milk
- 300ml/½ pint/1¼ cups single cream
- 1 whole egg
- 4 egg yolks
- 50g/2oz/4 tbsp caster sugar
- 2.5ml/½ tsp vanilla extract

For the topping
- 120ml/4fl oz/½ cup whipping cream
- 45ml/3 tbsp iced water
- 10ml/2 tsp drinking chocolate

1 Preheat the oven to 160°C/325°F/Gas 3. Put the roasted coffee beans in a saucepan over a low heat for about 3 minutes, shaking the pan frequently.

2 Pour the milk and cream over the beans. Heat until almost boiling; cover and leave to infuse for 30 minutes.

3 Whisk the egg, the egg yolks, sugar and vanilla together. Return the milk to boiling and pour through a sieve on to the egg mixture. Discard the beans.

4 Pour the mixture into eight 75ml/5 tbsp coffee cups or six 120ml/4fl oz/½ cup ramekins. Cover each with a small piece of foil.

5 Put in a roasting tin with hot water reaching about two-thirds of the way up the sides of the dishes. Bake them for 30–35 minutes, or until lightly set. Let cool. Chill in the fridge for at least 2 hours.

6 Whisk the whipping cream and iced water until thick and frothy and spoon on top of the custards. Dust with drinking chocolate before serving.

COOK'S TIPS
These petits pots may also be served warm, topped with a spoonful of clotted cream. Serve straight away, with the clotted cream just starting to melt.

COFFEE AND BRANDY SYLLABUB

THIS HEAVENLY DESSERT COULDN'T BE EASIER – A FROTH OF WHIPPED COFFEE AND BRANDY CREAM TOPS JUICY GRAPES. CRISP BISCUITS ARE A DELICIOUS CONTRAST.

SERVES SIX

INGREDIENTS
- 75g/3oz/6 tbsp soft light brown sugar
- finely grated rind of ½ orange
- 120ml/4fl oz/½ cup brandy
- 120ml/4fl oz/½ cup cold strong brewed coffee
- 400ml/14fl oz/1⅔ cups double cream
- 225g/8oz white seedless grapes
- sugared grapes, to decorate
- crisp biscuits, to serve

COOK'S TIP
For sugared grapes, wash and dry the fruit, then snip into small clusters. Use a fine brush to paint lightly beaten egg white evenly on to the grapes, then dust with caster sugar. Shake off excess sugar and leave to dry before using.

1 Put the brown sugar, orange rind and brandy into a small bowl. Stir well, then cover with clear film and leave to stand for 1 hour.

2 Strain the mixture through a fine sieve into a clean bowl. Stir in the coffee. Slowly pour in the cream, whisking all the time.

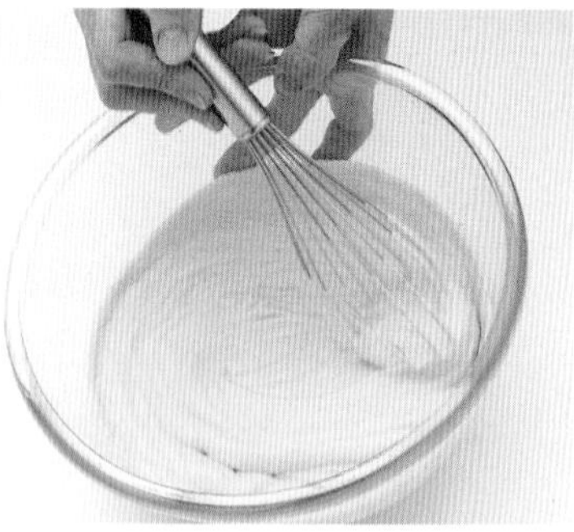

3 Continue whisking for 3–4 minutes, until the mixture thickens enough to stand in soft peaks.

4 Divide the grapes between the glasses. Pour or spoon the syllabub over the grapes. Chill in the fridge for 1 hour. Decorate the glasses with clusters of sugared grapes and serve with crisp biscuits.

COFFEE JELLIES

SERVE THESE SPARKLING COFFEE JELLIES AS A LIGHT AND REFRESHING END TO A RICH MEAL.

SERVES FOUR

INGREDIENTS
- 20ml/4 tsp powdered gelatine
- 75ml/5 tbsp cold water
- 600ml/1 pint/2½ cups very hot strong brewed coffee
- 40g/1½oz/3 tbsp caster sugar

For the bay cream
- 300ml/½ pint/1¼ cups whipping cream
- 15ml/1 tbsp bay-scented caster sugar
- fresh bay leaves, to decorate

VARIATION
For a creamy version of these jellies, make the coffee with hot milk and serve with fresh fruit instead of bay cream.

COOK'S TIP
To make bay-scented caster sugar, add 2–3 dried bay leaves to caster sugar. Leave for at least a week before using.

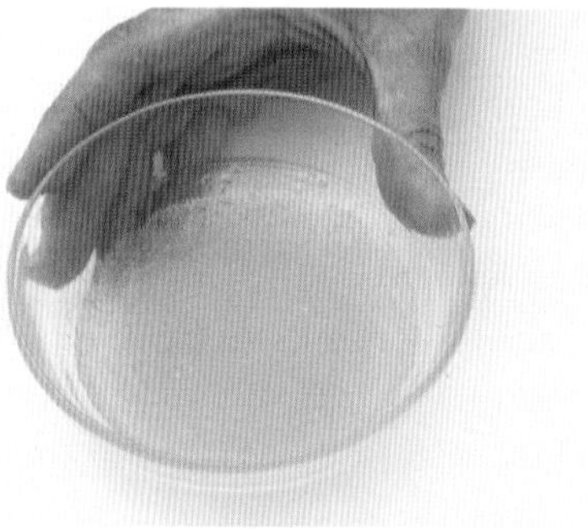

1 To make the jellies, sprinkle the gelatine over the cold water. Leave to soak for 2–3 minutes. Add to the hot strong brewed coffee with the sugar and stir to dissolve.

2 Allow the coffee to cool, then pour into four 150ml/¼ pint/⅔ cup metal moulds. Chill in the fridge for 3 hours or until set.

3 To make the bay cream, lightly whisk the cream and bay scented caster sugar until very soft peaks form. Spoon into a serving bowl.

4 To serve, dip the moulds in a bowl of hot water for a few seconds, then invert on to individual serving plates. Serve with the bay cream and decorate with fresh bay leaves.

COFFEE COEUR À LA CRÈME

THESE PRETTY HEART-SHAPED CREAMS, SPECKLED WITH ESPRESSO-ROASTED COFFEE BEANS, ARE SERVED WITH A FRESH FRUIT SAUCE. USE WILD STRAWBERRIES, IF AVAILABLE, FOR THEIR WONDERFUL PERFUME.

SERVES SIX

INGREDIENTS

- 25g/1oz/generous ¼ cup espresso-roasted coffee beans
- 225g/8oz/1 cup ricotta or curd cheese
- 300ml/½ pint/1¼ cups crème fraîche
- 25g/1oz/2 tbsp caster sugar
- finely grated rind of ½ orange
- 2 egg whites

For the red fruit coulis

- 175g/6oz/1 cup raspberries
- 30ml/2 tbsp icing sugar, sifted
- 115g/4oz/⅔ cup small strawberries, (or wild ones, if available), halved

1 Preheat the oven to 180°C/350°F/Gas 4. Evenly spread the espresso-roasted coffee beans on to a baking sheet and toast for about 10 minutes. Allow to cool, then put in a large plastic bag and crush into tiny pieces with a rolling pin.

2 Thoroughly rinse 12 pieces of muslin in cold water and squeeze dry. Use to line six coeur à la crème moulds with a double layer, allowing the muslin to overhang the edges.

3 Press the ricotta or curd cheese through a fine sieve into a bowl. Stir the crème fraîche, sugar, orange rind and crushed roasted coffee beans together. Add to the cheese and mix well.

4 Whisk the egg whites until stiff and fold into the mixture. Spoon into the prepared moulds, then bring the muslin up and over the filling. Leave in the fridge overnight to drain and chill.

5 To make the red fruit coulis, put the raspberries and icing sugar in a food processor and blend until smooth. Push through a fine sieve to remove the pips. Stir in the strawberries. Chill until ready to serve.

6 Unmould the hearts on to individual serving plates and carefully remove the muslin. Spoon the red fruit coulis over before serving.

COOK'S TIP

Muslin has a fine weave which allows the liquid from the cheese to drain through. If you haven't got any muslin, use a new all-purpose disposable cloth instead.

CHILLED CHOCOLATE AND ESPRESSO MOUSSE

HEADY, AROMATIC ESPRESSO COFFEE ADDS A DISTINCTIVE FLAVOUR TO THIS SMOOTH, RICH MOUSSE. SERVE IT IN STYLISH CHOCOLATE CUPS FOR A SPECIAL OCCASION.

SERVES FOUR

INGREDIENTS

- 225g/8oz plain chocolate
- 45ml/3 tbsp brewed espresso
- 25g/1oz/2 tbsp unsalted butter
- 4 eggs, separated
- sprigs of fresh mint, to decorate (optional)
- mascarpone or clotted cream, to serve (optional)

For the chocolate cups

- 225g/8oz plain chocolate

1 For each chocolate cup, cut a double thickness 15cm/6in square of foil. Mould it around a small orange, leaving the edges and corners loose to make a cup shape. Remove the orange and press the bottom of the foil case gently on a surface to make a flat base. Repeat to make four foil cups.

2 Break the plain chocolate into small pieces and place in a bowl set over a pan of very hot water. Stir occasionally until the chocolate has melted.

3 Spoon the chocolate into the foil cups, spreading it up the sides with the back of a spoon to give a ragged edge. Refrigerate for 30 minutes or until set hard. Gently peel away the foil, starting at the top edge.

4 To make the chocolate mousse, put the plain chocolate and brewed espresso into a bowl set over a pan of hot water and melt as before. When it is smooth and liquid, add the unsalted butter, a little at a time. Remove the pan from the heat then stir in the egg yolks.

5 Whisk the egg whites in a bowl until stiff, but not dry, then fold them into the chocolate mixture. Pour into a bowl and refrigerate for at least 3 hours.

6 To serve, scoop the chilled mousse into the chocolate cups. Add a scoop of mascarpone or clotted cream and decorate with a sprig of fresh mint, if you wish.

Apricot Panettone Pudding

Slices of light-textured panettone are layered with dried apricots and cooked in a creamy coffee custard for a satisfyingly warming dessert.

SERVES FOUR

INGREDIENTS

- 50g/2oz/4 tbsp unsalted butter, softened
- 6 x 1cm/½in thick slices (about 400g/14oz) panettone containing candied fruit
- 175g/6oz/¾ cup ready-to-eat dried apricots, chopped
- 400ml/14fl oz/1⅔ cups milk
- 250ml/8fl oz/1 cup double cream
- 60ml/4 tbsp mild-flavoured ground coffee
- 90g/3½oz/½ cup caster sugar
- 3 eggs
- 30ml/2 tbsp demerara sugar
- pouring cream or crème fraîche, to serve

1 Preheat the oven to 160°C/325°F/Gas 3. Brush a 2 litre/3½ pint/8 cup oval baking dish with 15g/½oz/1 tbsp of the butter. Spread the panettone with the remaining butter and arrange in the baking dish. Cut to fit and scatter the apricots among and over the layers.

2 Pour the milk and cream into a pan and heat until almost boiling. Pour the milk mixture over the coffee and leave to infuse for 10 minutes. Strain through a fine sieve, discarding the coffee grounds.

3 Lightly beat the caster sugar and eggs together, then whisk in the warm coffee-flavoured milk. Slowly pour the mixture over the panettone. Leave to soak for 15 minutes.

4 Sprinkle the top of the pudding with demerara sugar and place the dish in a large roasting tin. Pour in enough boiling water to come halfway up the sides of the baking dish.

5 Bake for 40–45 minutes until the top is golden and crusty, but the middle still slightly wobbly. Remove from the oven, but leave the dish in the hot water for 10 minutes. Serve warm with pouring cream or crème fraîche.

COOK'S TIP

This recipe works equally well with plain or chocolate-flavoured panettone.

Sticky Coffee and Ginger Pudding

This coffee-capped feather-light sponge is made with breadcrumbs and ground almonds. Serve with creamy custard or scoops of vanilla ice cream.

SERVES FOUR

INGREDIENTS
- 30ml/2 tbsp soft light brown sugar
- 25g/1oz/2 tbsp stem ginger, chopped
- 30ml/2 tbsp mild-flavoured ground coffee
- 75ml/5 tbsp stem ginger syrup (from a jar of stem ginger)
- 115g/4oz/generous ½ cup caster sugar
- 3 eggs, separated
- 25g/1oz/¼ cup plain flour
- 5ml/1 tsp ground ginger
- 65g/2½oz/generous 1 cup fresh white breadcrumbs
- 25g/1oz/¼ cup ground almonds

1 Preheat the oven to 180°C/350°F/Gas 4. Grease and line the base of a 750ml/1¼ pint/3 cup pudding basin, then sprinkle in the soft light brown sugar and chopped stem ginger.

2 Put the ground coffee in a small bowl. Heat the ginger syrup until almost boiling; pour into the coffee. Stir well and leave for 4 minutes. Pour through a fine sieve into the pudding basin.

3 Beat half the caster sugar and egg yolks until light and fluffy. Sift the flour and ground ginger together and fold into the egg mixture with the breadcrumbs and ground almonds.

4 Whisk the egg whites until stiff, then gradually whisk in the remaining caster sugar. Fold into the mixture, half at a time. Spoon into the pudding basin and smooth the top.

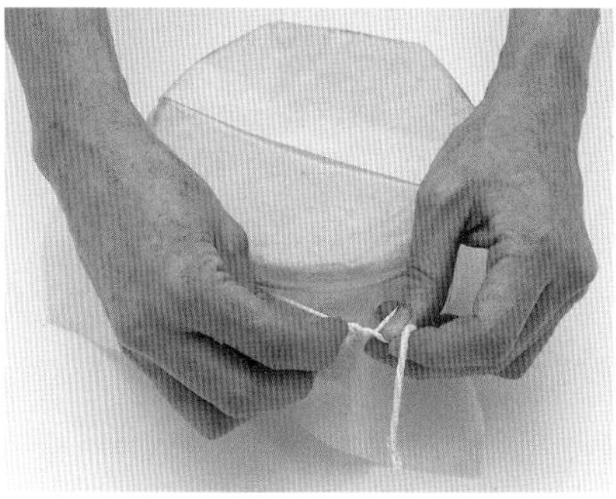

5 Cover the basin with a piece of pleated greased greaseproof paper and secure with string. Bake for 40 minutes, or until the sponge is firm to the touch. Turn out and serve immediately.

COOK'S TIP

This pudding can also be baked in a 900ml/1½ pint/3¾ cup loaf tin and served thickly sliced.

Soufflés and Meringues

Fluffy soufflés that rise to the occasion and melt-in-the-mouth meringues – these are coffee desserts to tempt your eye and your palate. The basic ingredients for meringues couldn't be simpler – just egg whites and sugar, to which coffee lends a sophisticated touch. For the perfect finish to a meal, try spicy Floating Islands, or the tropical taste of Mango and Coffee Meringue Roll.

CHILLED COFFEE AND PRALINE SOUFFLÉ

A smooth coffee soufflé with a crushed praline topping that is spectacular and easy.

SERVES SIX

INGREDIENTS

- 150g/5oz/¾ cup caster sugar
- 75ml/5 tbsp water
- 150g/5oz/generous 1 cup blanched almonds, plus extra, for decoration
- 120ml/4fl oz/½ cup strong brewed coffee, e.g. hazelnut-flavoured
- 15ml/1 tbsp powdered gelatine
- 3 eggs, separated
- 75g/3oz/scant ½ cup soft light brown sugar
- 15ml/1 tbsp coffee liqueur, such as Tia Maria, Kahlúa or Toussaint
- 150ml/¼ pint/⅔ cup double cream
- about 150ml/¼ pint/⅔ cup double cream, for decoration (optional)

1 Cut a paper collar from a double layer of greaseproof paper, 5cm/2in deeper than a 900ml/1½ pint/3¾ cup soufflé dish. Wrap around the dish and tie in place with string. Refrigerate.

2 Oil a baking sheet. Put the caster sugar in a small heavy-based pan with the water and heat gently until the sugar dissolves. Boil rapidly until the syrup becomes pale golden. Add the almonds and boil until dark golden.

3 Pour the mixture on to the baking sheet and leave to set. When hard, transfer to a plastic bag and break into pieces with a rolling pin. Reserve 50g/2oz/½ cup and crush the remainder.

4 Pour half the coffee into a small bowl; sprinkle over the gelatine. Leave to soak for 5 minutes, then place the bowl over a pan of hot water; stir until dissolved.

5 Put the egg yolks, soft light brown sugar, remaining coffee and liqueur in a bowl over a pan of simmering water. Whisk until thick and foamy, then whisk in the dissolved gelatine.

6 Whip the cream until soft peaks form, then whisk the egg whites until stiff. Fold the crushed praline into the cream, then fold into the coffee mixture. Finally, fold in the egg whites, half at a time.

7 Spoon into the soufflé dish and smooth the top; chill for at least 2 hours or until set. Put in the freezer for 15–20 minutes before serving. Remove the paper collar by running a warmed palette knife between the set soufflé and the paper. Whisk the cream for decoration, if using, and place large spoonfuls on top. Decorate with the reserved praline pieces and whole blanched almonds.

TWICE-BAKED MOCHA SOUFFLÉ

THE PERFECT WAY TO END A MEAL, THESE MINI MOCHA SOUFFLÉS CAN BE MADE UP TO 3 HOURS AHEAD, THEN REHEATED JUST BEFORE YOU SERVE THEM.

SERVES SIX

INGREDIENTS
- 75g/3oz/6 tbsp unsalted butter, softened
- 90g/3½ oz bittersweet or plain chocolate, grated
- 30ml/2 tbsp ground coffee
- 400ml/14fl oz/1⅔ cup milk
- 40g/1½oz/⅓ cup plain flour, sifted
- 15g/½ oz/2 tbsp cocoa, sifted
- 3 eggs, separated
- 50g/2oz/¼ cup caster sugar
- 175ml/6fl oz/¾ cup creamy chocolate or coffee liqueur, such as Crème de Caçao, Sheridans

1 Preheat the oven to 200°C/400°F/Gas 6. Thickly brush six 150ml/¼ pint/⅔ cup dariole moulds or mini pudding basins with 25g/1oz/2 tbsp of the butter. Coat with 50g/2oz of the grated chocolate.

2 Put the ground coffee in a small bowl. Heat the milk until almost boiling and pour over the coffee. Infuse for 4 minutes and strain, discarding the grounds.

3 Melt the remaining butter in a small pan. Stir in the flour and cocoa to make a roux. Cook for about 1 minute, then gradually add the coffee milk, stirring all the time to make a very thick sauce. Simmer for 2 minutes. Remove from the heat and stir in the egg yolks.

VARIATION

Good quality white or milk cooking chocolate can be use instead of plain, if preferred.

4 Cool for 5 minutes, then stir in the remaining chocolate. Whisk the egg whites until stiff, then gradually whisk in the sugar. Stir half into the sauce to loosen, then fold in the remainder.

5 Spoon the mixture into the dariole moulds and place in a roasting tin. Pour in enough hot water to come two-thirds of the way up the sides of the tins.

6 Bake the soufflés for 15 minutes. Turn them out on to a baking tray and leave to cool completely.

7 Before serving, spoon 15ml/1 tbsp chocolate or coffee liqueur over each pudding and reheat in the oven for 6–7 minutes. Serve on individual plates with the remaining liqueur poured over.

CLASSIC CHOCOLATE AND COFFEE ROULADE

THIS RICH, SQUIDGY CHOCOLATE ROLL SHOULD BE MADE AT LEAST 12 HOURS BEFORE SERVING, TO ALLOW IT TO SOFTEN. EXPECT THE ROULADE TO CRACK A LITTLE WHEN YOU ROLL IT UP.

SERVES EIGHT

INGREDIENTS
- 200g/7oz plain chocolate
- 200g/7oz/1 cup caster sugar
- 7 eggs, separated

For the filling
- 300ml/½ pint/1¼ cups double cream
- 30ml/2 tbsp cold strong brewed coffee, e.g. mocha-flavoured
- 15ml/1 tbsp coffee liqueur, such as Tia Maria, Kahlúa or Toussaint
- 60ml/4 tbsp icing sugar, for dusting
- little grated chocolate, for sprinkling

1 Preheat the oven to 180°C/350°F/Gas 4. Grease and line a 33 x 23cm/13 x 9in Swiss roll tin with non-stick baking parchment.

2 Break the chocolate into squares and melt in a bowl over a pan of barely simmering water. Remove from the heat and leave to cool for 5 minutes.

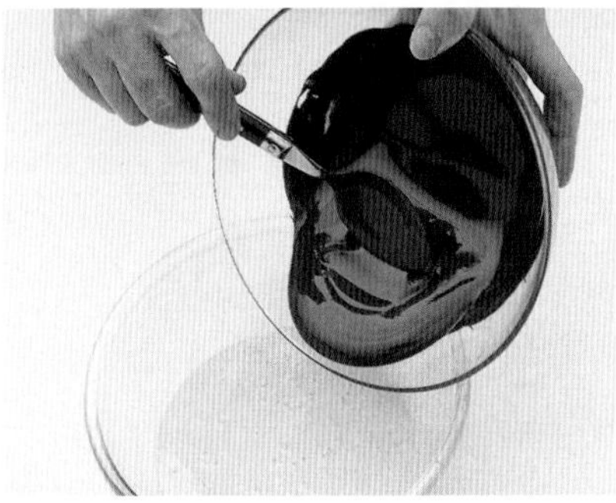

3 In a large bowl, whisk the sugar and egg yolks until light and fluffy. Stir in the melted chocolate.

4 Whisk the egg whites until stiff, but not dry, and then gently fold into the chocolate mixture.

5 Pour the chocolate mixture into the prepared tin, spreading it level with a spatula. Bake for about 25 minutes until firm. Leave the cake in the tin and cover with a cooling rack, making sure it doesn't touch the cake.

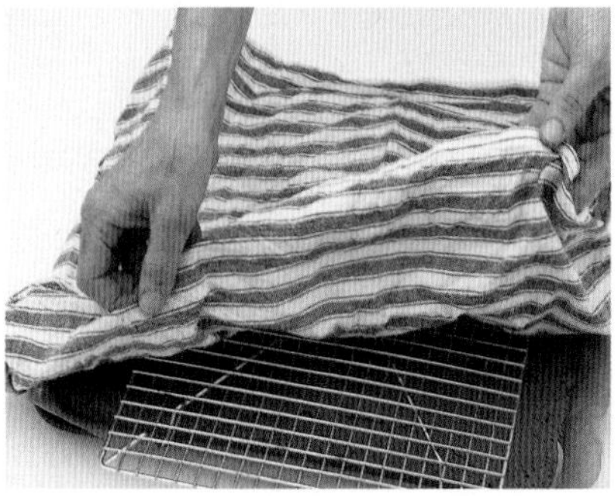

6 Cover the rack with a damp tea towel, then wrap in clear film. Leave in a cool place for at least 8 hours or overnight, if possible.

7 Dust a large sheet of greaseproof paper with icing sugar and turn out the roulade on to it. Peel off the lining.

8 To make the filling, whip the double cream with the coffee and liqueur until soft peaks form. Spread the cream over the roulade. Starting from one of the short ends, carefully roll it up, using the paper to help.

9 Place the roulade, seam-side down, on to a serving plate; dust generously with icing sugar and sprinkle with a little grated chocolate before serving.

COOK'S TIP

If liked, decorate the roulade with swirls of whipped cream and chocolate coffee beans or with clusters of raspberries and mint leaves.

MANGO AND COFFEE MERINGUE ROLL

A LIGHT AND FLUFFY ROLL OF MERINGUE IS THE IDEAL CONTRAST TO THE UNSWEETENED FILLING OF COFFEE, MASCARPONE AND JUICY RIPE MANGO.

SERVES SIX TO EIGHT

INGREDIENTS
- 4 egg whites
- 225g/8oz/generous 1 cup caster sugar

For the filling
- 45ml/3 tbsp strong-flavoured ground coffee
- 75ml/5 tbsp milk
- 350g/12oz/1½ cups mascarpone
- 1 ripe mango, cut into 1cm/½in cubes

COOK'S TIP
If you like, the meringue can be sprinkled with 50g/2oz/½ cup of skinned chopped hazelnuts before baking.

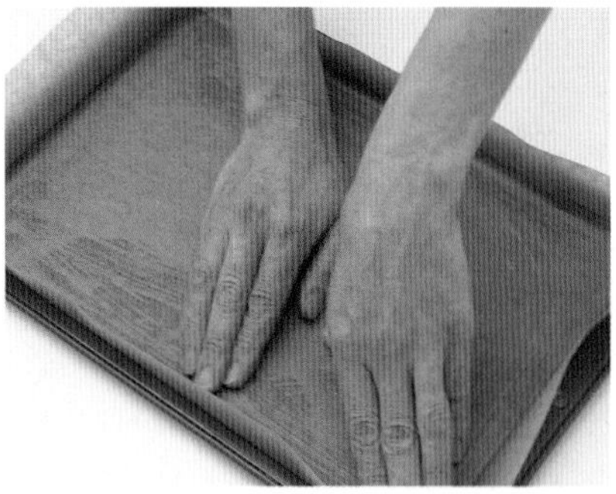

1 Preheat the oven to 190°C/375°F/Gas 5. Line a 33 x 23cm/13 x 9in Swiss roll tin with lightly greased non-stick baking parchment. Whisk the egg whites until stiff. Gradually add the sugar, whisking after each addition until thick and glossy.

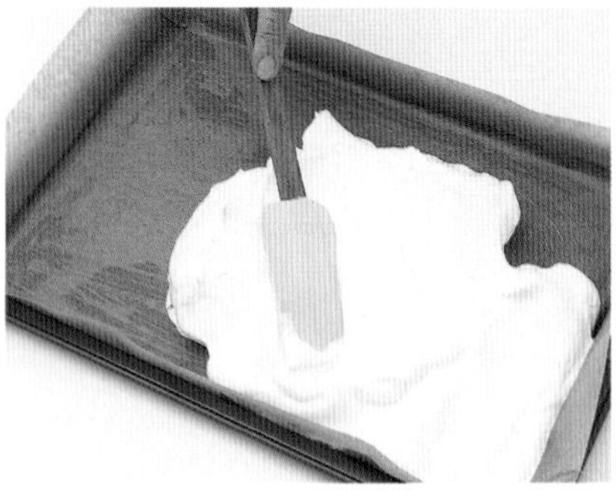

2 When the meringue is thick and glossy, spoon it into the prepared tin and smooth the surface. Bake for 15 minutes or until firm and golden.

3 Turn the meringue out on to a sheet of non-stick baking parchment. Remove the lining paper and leave until cold.

4 To make the filling, put the coffee in a small bowl. Heat the milk until it is nearly boiling and pour over the coffee. Leave to infuse for 4 minutes, then strain through a fine sieve, discarding the coffee grounds.

5 Beat the mascarpone until soft, then gradually beat in the coffee. Spread over the meringue, then scatter with the chopped mango.

6 Gently roll up the meringue from one of the short ends, with the help of the baking parchment. Transfer to a serving plate seam-side down. Chill for at least 30 minutes before serving.

GINGERED COFFEE MERINGUES

WHAT COULD BE MORE ENTICING THAN TO BREAK THROUGH THE COATING OF CRISP MERINGUE TO REVEAL JUST-MELTING COFFEE ICE CREAM ON A MOIST GINGER SPONGE?

SERVES SIX

INGREDIENTS
- 275g/10oz bought ginger cake
- 600ml/1 pint/2½ cups coffee ice cream
- 4 egg whites
- 1.5ml/¼ tsp cream of tartar
- 150g/5oz/¾ cup caster sugar
- 25g/1oz/2 tbsp preserved ginger, finely chopped

1 Preheat the oven to 230°C/450°F/Gas 8. Cut the ginger cake lengthways into three slices. Stamp out two rounds from each slice, using a 5cm/2in cutter, and put on a baking tray.

2 Top each cake round with a large scoop of coffee ice cream, then place the baking tray in the freezer for at least 30 minutes.

3 Whisk the egg whites and cream of tartar until soft peaks form. Gradually add the sugar and continue whisking until the mixture forms stiff peaks. Fold in the preserved ginger.

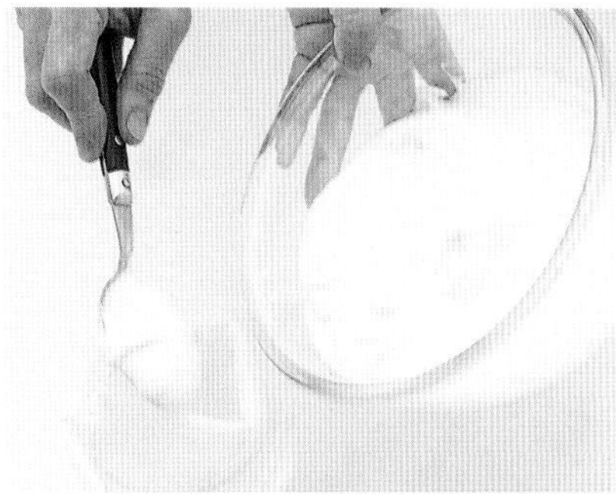

4 Carefully spoon the meringue and ginger mixture into a piping bag fitted with a large plain nozzle.

COOK'S TIP
The ice cream is insulated in the oven by the tiny bubbles of air in the meringue, so ensure it is completely covered. Once coated, the ice cream cakes could be frozen until ready to cook.

5 Quickly pipe the meringue over the ice cream, starting from the base and working up to the top.

6 Bake in the oven for 3–4 minutes, until the outside of the meringue is crisp and lightly tinged with brown. Serve immediately.

FLOATING ISLANDS

THIS WELL-KNOWN DESSERT GETS ITS NAME FROM THE POACHED MERINGUES SURROUNDED BY A "SEA" OF CRÈME ANGLAISE. THIS VERSION IS GIVEN A TOUCH OF THE EXOTIC THROUGH THE ADDITION OF STAR ANISE AND IS SERVED WITH A RICH COFFEE SAUCE.

SERVES SIX

INGREDIENTS

For the coffee crème Anglaise
- 150ml/¼ pint/⅔ cup milk
- 150ml/¼ pint/⅔ cup single cream
- 120ml/4fl oz/½ cup strong brewed coffee
- 4 egg yolks
- 25g/1oz/2 tbsp soft light brown sugar
- 5ml/1 tsp cornflour

For the caramel sauce
- 90g/3½oz/½ cup caster sugar

For the poached meringues
- 2 egg whites
- 50g/2oz/¼ cup caster sugar
- 1.5ml/¼ tsp ground star anise
- pinch of salt

1 To make the coffee crème Anglaise, pour the milk, cream and coffee into a pan and heat to boiling point.

2 In a large bowl, whisk the egg yolks, brown sugar and cornflour together until creamy. Whisk in the hot coffee mixture, then pour the entire mixture back into the pan.

3 Heat for 1–2 minutes, stirring until the sauce thickens. Take off the heat and allow to cool, stirring occasionally.

COOK'S TIP
Once poached, the meringues will keep their shape for up to 2 hours.

4 Cover the bowl containing the sauce with clear film and place in the fridge.

5 For the caramel, put the sugar in a small heavy-based pan with 45ml/3 tbsp water and heat very gently until dissolved. Boil rapidly until the syrup turns a rich golden colour. Off the heat, carefully add 45ml/3 tbsp hot water – it will splutter. Leave to cool.

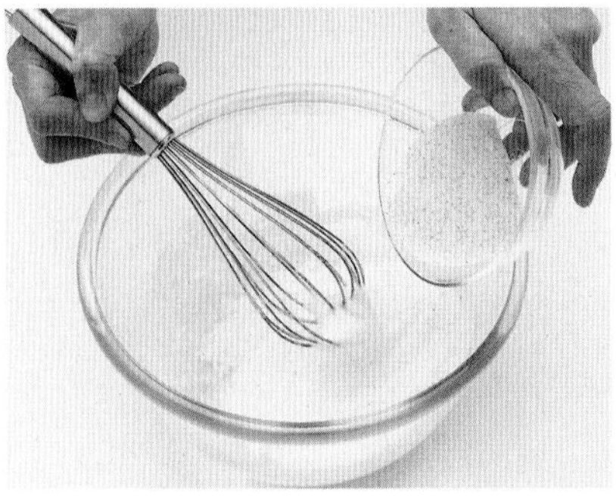

6 To make the meringues, whisk the egg whites until stiff. Combine the sugar and star anise; add to the egg whites.

7 Pour 2.5cm/1in of boiling water into a large frying pan. Add the salt and bring to a gentle simmer. Shape the meringue into small ovals, using two spoons, and add to the water. Poach four or five of the meringues at a time for about 3 minutes, until firm.

8 Remove with a slotted spoon and drain on kitchen paper. Repeat with the remaining mixture.

9 To serve, spoon a little coffee crème Anglaise on to each serving plate. Float two or three "islands" on top, then drizzle with caramel sauce.

COFFEE MERINGUES WITH ROSE CREAM

THESE SUGARY MERINGUES, WITH CRUSHED ESPRESSO-ROASTED COFFEE BEANS, ARE FILLED WITH A DELICATE ROSE-SCENTED CREAM. LIGHTLY SPRINKLE ROSE PETALS FOR A ROMANTIC FINISH.

MAKES TWENTY PAIRS OF MERINGUES

INGREDIENTS

- 25g/1oz/generous ¼ cup espresso-roasted coffee beans
- 3 egg whites
- 175g/6oz/scant 1 cup caster sugar
- 25g/1oz/¼ cup pistachio nuts, roughly chopped
- few rose petals, for decoration

For the rose cream

- 300ml/½ pint/1¼ cups double cream
- 15ml/1 tbsp icing sugar, sifted
- 10ml/2 tsp rose water

1 Preheat the oven to 180°C/350°F/Gas 4. Spread the coffee beans on a baking sheet and toast for 8 minutes. Allow to cool, then put in a plastic bag and crush with a rolling pin. Turn the oven to 140°C/275°F/Gas 1.

2 Whisk the egg whites and sugar in a bowl over a pan of hot water until thick.

3 Remove from the heat and continue whisking until the meringue holds stiff peaks. Whisk in the crushed beans.

4 Fill a piping bag fitted with a large star nozzle with the mixture and pipe about 40 small swirls on to two baking sheets lined with non-stick baking parchment. Leave some space between each swirl.

5 Sprinkle with the pistachio nuts. Bake the meringues for 2–2½ hours, or until dry and crisp, swapping the position of the baking trays halfway through the cooking time. Leave to cool, then remove from the paper.

6 To make the rose cream, whip the cream, icing sugar and rose water until soft peaks form. Use to sandwich the meringues together in pairs. Arrange on a serving plate and serve scattered with rose petals for decoration.

VARIATION

Orange-flower water may be used instead of rose water in the cream and a drop of pink food colouring added, if you like.

Coffee Pavlova with Exotic Fruits

Both Australia and New Zealand claim to have invented this fluffy meringue named after the ballerina Anna Pavlova. The secret of success is to leave the meringue in the oven until completely cooled, as a sudden change in temperature will make it crack.

SERVES SIX TO EIGHT

INGREDIENTS
- 30ml/2 tbsp ground coffee, e.g. mocha orange-flavoured
- 30ml/2 tbsp near-boiling water
- 3 egg whites
- 2.5ml/½ tsp cream of tartar
- 175g/6oz/scant 1 cup caster sugar
- 5ml/1 tsp cornflour, sifted

For the filling
- 150ml/¼ pint/⅔ cup double cream
- 5ml/1 tsp vanilla orange-flower water
- 150ml/¼ pint/⅔ cup crème fraîche
- 500g/1¼lb sliced exotic fruits, such as mango, papaya and kiwi
- 15ml/1 tbsp icing sugar

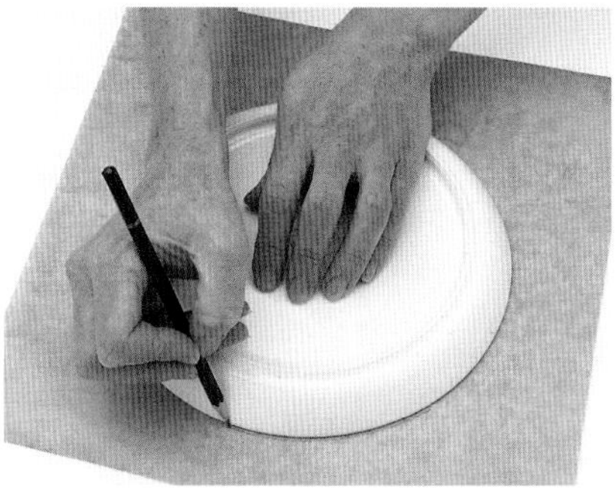

1 Preheat the oven to 140°C/275°F/Gas 1. Draw a 20cm/8in circle on non-stick baking parchment. Place pencil-side down on a baking sheet.

2 Put the coffee in a small bowl and pour the hot water over. Leave to infuse for 4 minutes, then strain through a very fine sieve.

3 Whisk the egg whites with the cream of tartar until stiff, but not dry. Gradually whisk in the sugar until the meringue is stiff and shiny, then quickly whisk in the cornflour and coffee.

VARIATION
450g/1lb soft fruit, such as wild or cultivated strawberries, raspberries and blueberries, may be used instead of the exotic fruits, if you wish.

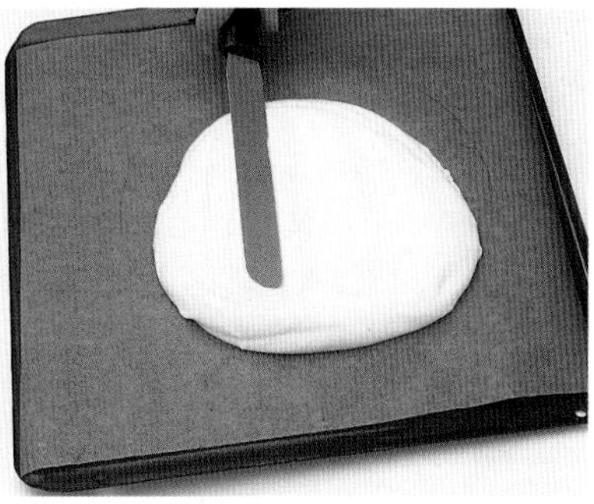

4 Using a long knife or spatula, spoon the meringue mixture on to the baking sheet, spreading to an even 20cm/8in circle. Make a slight hollow in the middle. Bake in the oven for 1 hour, then turn off the heat and leave in the oven until cool.

5 Transfer the meringue to a plate, peeling off the lining. To make the filling, whip the cream with the orange-flower water until soft peaks form. Fold in the crème fraîche. Spoon into the meringue. Arrange the fruits over the cream and dust with icing sugar.

Fruit Desserts

If you're looking for colour, flavour and freshness and something a little out of the ordinary, opt for one of these fruit and coffee combinations. Fruit always makes the perfect pudding, no matter how simple or grand the meal, but it doesn't have to be chilled. Try steeping oranges in a hot coffee syrup or serve a slice of Sticky Pear Pudding for pure indulgence.

ORANGES IN HOT COFFEE SYRUP

THIS RECIPE WORKS WELL WITH MOST CITRUS FRUITS; TRY PINK GRAPEFRUIT OR SWEET, PERFUMED CLEMENTINES, PEELED BUT LEFT WHOLE, FOR A CHANGE.

SERVES SIX

INGREDIENTS

- 6 medium oranges
- 200g/7oz/1 cup sugar
- 50ml/2fl oz/¼ cup cold water
- 100ml/3½fl oz/scant ½ cup boiling water
- 100ml/3½fl oz/scant ½ cup fresh strong brewed coffee
- 50g/2oz/½ cup pistachio nuts, chopped (optional)

COOK'S TIP

Choose a pan in which the oranges will just fit in a single layer.

1 Finely pare the rind from one orange, shred and reserve the rind. Peel the remaining oranges. Cut each one crosswise into slices, then re-form with a cocktail stick through the centre.

2 Put the sugar and cold water in a heavy-based pan. Heat gently until the sugar dissolves, then bring to the boil and cook until the syrup turns pale gold.

3 Remove from the heat and carefully pour the boiling water into the pan. Return to the heat until the syrup has dissolved in the water. Stir in the coffee.

4 Add the oranges and the shredded rind to the coffee syrup. Simmer for 15–20 minutes, turning the oranges once during cooking. Sprinkle with pistachio nuts, if using, and serve hot.

FRESH FIG COMPOTE

LIGHTLY POACHING FIGS IN A VANILLA AND COFFEE SYRUP BRINGS OUT THEIR WONDERFUL FLAVOUR.

SERVES FOUR TO SIX

INGREDIENTS

- 400ml/14fl oz/1⅔ cups brewed coffee
- 115g/4oz/½ cup clear honey
- 1 vanilla pod
- 12 slightly under-ripe fresh figs
- Greek yogurt, to serve (optional)

COOK'S TIPS

- Rinse and dry the vanilla pod; it can be used several times.
- Figs come in three main varieties – red, white and black – and all three are suitable for cooking. Naturally high in sugar, they are sweet and succulent and complement well the stronger flavours of coffee and vanilla.

1 Choose a frying pan with a lid, large enough to hold the figs in a single layer. Pour in the coffee and add the honey.

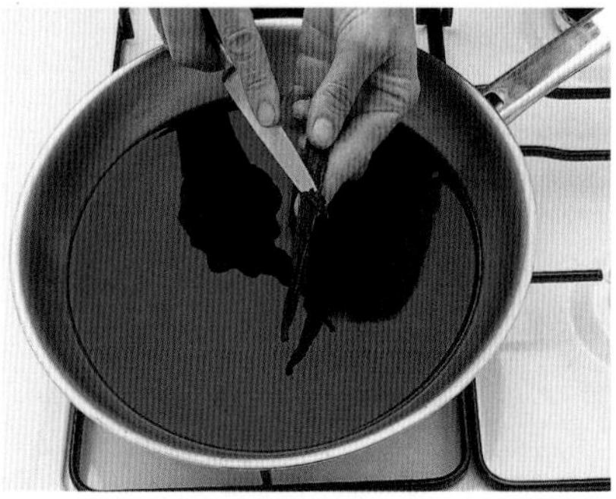

2 Split the vanilla pod lengthways and scrape the seeds into the pan. Add the vanilla pod, then bring to the boil. Bring the syrup to a rapid boil and cook until reduced to about 175ml/6fl oz/¾ cup. Leave to cool.

3 Wash the figs and pierce the skins several times with a sharp skewer. Cut in half and add to the syrup. Lower the heat, cover and simmer for 5 minutes. Remove the figs from the syrup with a slotted spoon and set aside to cool.

4 Strain the syrup over the figs. Allow to stand at room temperature for 1 hour before serving with yogurt, if liked.

STICKY PEAR PUDDING

CLOVES ADD A DISTINCTIVE FRAGRANT FLAVOUR TO THIS HAZELNUT, PEAR AND COFFEE PUDDING.

SERVES SIX

INGREDIENTS
- 30ml/2 tbsp ground coffee, e.g. hazelnut-flavoured
- 15ml/1 tbsp near-boiling water
- 50g/2oz/½ cup toasted skinned hazelnuts
- 4 ripe pears
- juice of ½ orange
- 115g/4oz/8 tbsp butter, softened
- 115g/4oz/generous ½ cup golden caster sugar, plus an extra 15ml/1 tbsp, for baking
- 2 eggs, beaten
- 50g/2oz/½ cup self-raising flour, sifted
- pinch of ground cloves
- 8 whole cloves, optional
- 45ml/3 tbsp maple syrup
- fine strips of orange rind, to decorate

For the orange cream
- 300ml/½ pint/1¼ cups whipping cream
- 15ml/1 tbsp icing sugar, sifted
- finely grated rind of ½ orange

1 Preheat the oven to 180°C/350°F/Gas 4. Lightly grease a 20cm/8in loose-based sandwich tin. Put the ground coffee in a small bowl and pour the water over. Leave to infuse for 4 minutes, then strain through a fine sieve.

COOK'S TIP
If you can't find ready-toasted skinned hazelnuts, prepare your own. Toast under a hot grill for 3–4 minutes, turning frequently until well browned. Rub off the skins and cool before grinding.

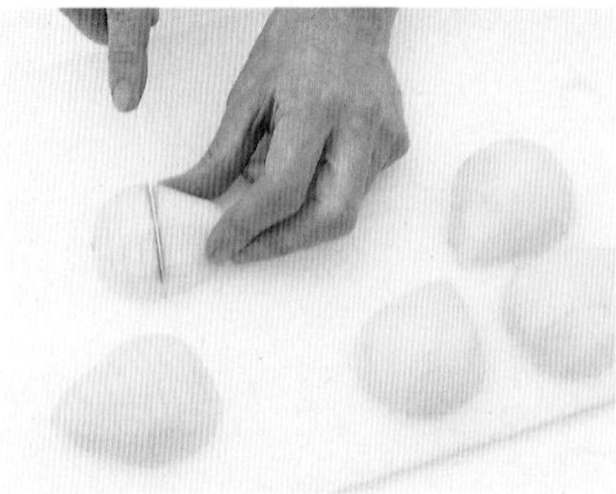

2 Grind the hazelnuts in a coffee grinder until fine. Peel, halve and core the pears. Thinly slice across the pear halves part of the way through. Brush with orange juice.

3 Beat the butter and the 115g/4oz/generous ½ cup caster sugar together in a large bowl until very light and fluffy. Gradually beat in the eggs, then fold in the flour, ground cloves, hazelnuts and coffee. Spoon the mixture into the tin and level the surface.

4 Pat the pears dry on kitchen paper, then arrange in the sponge mixture, flat side down.

5 Lightly press 2 whole cloves into each pear half, if using. Brush the pears with 15ml/1 tbsp maple syrup.

6 Sprinkle the pears with the 15ml/1 tbsp caster sugar. Bake for 45–50 minutes or until firm and well-risen.

7 While the sponge is cooking, make the orange cream. Whip the cream, icing sugar and orange rind until soft peaks form. Spoon into a serving dish and chill until needed.

8 Allow the sponge to cool for about 10 minutes in the tin, then remove and place on a serving plate. Lightly brush with the remaining maple syrup before decorating with orange rind and serving warm with the orange cream.

COFFEE CRÊPES WITH PEACHES AND CREAM

JUICY GOLDEN PEACHES AND CREAM CONJURE UP THE SWEET TASTE OF SUMMER. HERE THEY ARE DELICIOUS AS THE FILLING FOR THESE LIGHT COFFEE CRÊPES.

SERVES SIX

INGREDIENTS
- 75g/3oz/⅔ cup plain flour
- 25g/1oz/¼ cup buckwheat flour
- 1.5ml/¼ tsp salt
- 1 egg, beaten
- 200ml/7fl oz/scant 1 cup milk
- 15g/½oz/1 tbsp butter, melted
- 100ml/3½ oz/scant ½ cup strong brewed coffee
- sunflower oil, for frying

For the filling
- 6 ripe peaches
- 300ml/½ pint/1¼ cups double cream
- 15ml/1 tbsp Amaretto liqueur
- 225g/8oz/1 cup mascarpone
- 65g/2½oz/generous ¼ cup caster sugar
- 30ml/2 tbsp icing sugar, for dusting

1 Sift the flours and salt into a mixing bowl. Make a well in the middle and add the egg, half the milk and the melted butter. Gradually mix in the flour, beating until smooth, then beat in the remaining milk and coffee.

2 Heat a drizzle of oil in a 15–20cm/6–8in crêpe pan. Pour in just enough batter to thinly cover the base of the pan. Cook for 2–3 minutes, until the underneath is golden brown, then flip over and cook the other side.

COOK'S TIP
To keep the pancakes warm while you make the rest, cover them with foil and place the plate over a pan of barely simmering water.

3 Slide the crêpe out of the pan on to a plate. Continue making crêpes until all the mixture is used, stacking and interleaving with greaseproof paper.

4 To make the filling, halve the peaches and remove the stones. Cut into thick slices. Whip the cream and Amaretto liqueur until soft peaks form. Beat the mascarpone with the sugar until smooth. Beat 30ml/2 tbsp of the cream into the mascarpone, then fold in the remainder.

5 Spoon a little of the Amaretto cream on to one half of each pancake and top with peach slices. Gently fold the pancake over and dust with icing sugar. Serve immediately.

PLUM AND RUM BABAS

A Polish king thought up these spongy yeast cakes after hearing the story of Ali Baba. Soaked in a coffee and rum syrup, their middles are filled with juicy plums.

SERVES SIX

INGREDIENTS
- 65g/2½oz/5 tbsp unsalted butter, softened
- 115g/4oz/1 cup strong plain flour
- pinch of salt
- 7.5ml/1½ tsp easy-blend dried yeast
- 25g/1oz/2 tbsp soft light brown sugar
- 2 eggs, beaten
- 45ml/3 tbsp warm milk
- crème fraîche, to serve

For the syrup
- 115g/4oz/generous ½ cup granulated sugar
- 120ml/4fl oz/½ cup water
- 450g/1lb plums, halved, stoned and thickly sliced
- 120ml/4fl oz/½ cup brewed coffee
- 45ml/3 tbsp dark rum

1 Preheat the oven to 190°C/375°F/Gas 5. Thickly brush six 9cm/3½in ring tins with 15g/½oz/1 tbsp of the butter.

2 Sift the flour and salt into a mixing bowl and stir in the yeast and soft light brown sugar.

3 Make a well in the middle and add the eggs and warm milk. Beat for about 5 minutes with a wooden spoon to make a very sticky dough that is fairly smooth and elastic.

COOK'S TIP
The babas may also be split in half horizontally, filled with whipped cream and sandwiched back together.

4 Cover with clear film and leave to rise for 40 minutes.Cut the remaining butter into cubes and mix into the dough. Put the tins on a baking tray and drop the dough into the moulds. Cover with oiled clear film and leave until the dough has almost risen to the top. Remove the film and bake for 15–20 minutes.

5 Meanwhile make the syrup. Put 25g/1oz/2 tbsp of the sugar in a pan with the water. Add the plums and cook over a low heat until barely tender; remove with a slotted spoon. Add the remaining sugar and coffee to the pan. Heat gently until dissolved, but do not boil. Remove from the heat and stir in the rum.

6 Turn out the babas on to a wire rack and leave to cool for 5 minutes. Dunk them in the warm syrup until well soaked. Return them to the wire rack with a plate underneath to catch any drips. Leave to cool completely.

7 Put the babas on a serving plate and fill the middles with the sliced plums. Spoon a little extra syrup over each and serve with crème fraîche.

Coconut and Coffee Trifle

Dark coffee sponge, laced with liqueur, coconut custard and a coffee cream topping makes this a lavish dessert. Serve in a large glass bowl for maximum impact.

SERVES SIX TO EIGHT

INGREDIENTS

For the coffee sponge
- 45ml/3 tbsp strong-flavoured ground coffee
- 45ml/3 tbsp near-boiling water
- 2 eggs
- 50g/2oz/¼ cup soft dark brown sugar
- 40g/1½oz/⅓ cup self-raising flour, sifted
- 25ml/1½ tbsp hazelnut or sunflower oil

For the coconut custard
- 400ml/14fl oz/1⅔ cup canned coconut milk
- 3 eggs
- 40g/1½oz/3 tbsp caster sugar
- 10ml/2 tsp cornflour

For the filling and topping
- 2 medium bananas
- 60ml/4 tbsp coffee liqueur, such as Tia Maria, Kahlúa or Toussaint
- 300ml/½ pint/1¼ cups double cream
- 30ml/2 tbsp icing sugar, sifted
- ribbons of fresh coconut, to decorate

1 Preheat the oven to 160°C/325°F/ Gas 3. Grease and line an 18cm/7in square tin with greaseproof paper.

2 Put the coffee in a small bowl. Pour the hot water over and leave to infuse for 4 minutes. Strain through a fine sieve, discarding the grounds.

3 Whisk the eggs and soft dark brown sugar in a large bowl until the whisk leaves a trail when lifted.

4 Gently fold in the flour, followed by 15ml/1 tbsp of the coffee and the oil. Spoon the mixture into the tin and bake for 20 minutes, until firm. Turn out on to a wire rack, remove the lining paper and leave to cool.

5 To make the coconut custard, heat the coconut milk in a saucepan until it is almost boiling.

6 Whisk the eggs, sugar and cornflour together until frothy. Pour on the hot coconut milk, whisking all the time. Add to the pan and heat gently, stirring for 1–2 minutes, until the custard thickens, but do not boil. Set aside to cool for about 10 minutes, stirring occasionally.

7 Cut the coffee sponge into 5cm/2in squares and arrange in the base of a large glass bowl. Slice the bananas and arrange on top of the sponge. Drizzle the coffee liqueur on top. Pour the custard over and leave until cold.

8 Whip the cream with the remaining coffee and icing sugar until soft peaks form. Spoon the cream over the custard. Cover and chill for several hours. Sprinkle with ribbons of fresh coconut before serving.

COOK'S TIP

To make coconut ribbons, use a vegetable peeler to cut thin ribbons from the flesh of a fresh coconut, or buy shredded coconut and toast until it is pale golden.

Flambéed Bananas with Caribbean Coffee Sauce

This dessert has all the flavour of the Caribbean; bananas, dark sugar, coffee and rum.

SERVES FOUR TO SIX

INGREDIENTS
- 6 bananas
- 40g/1½oz/3 tbsp butter
- 50g/2oz/¼ cup soft dark brown sugar
- 50ml/2fl oz/¼ cup strong brewed coffee
- 60ml/4 tbsp dark rum
- vanilla ice cream, to serve

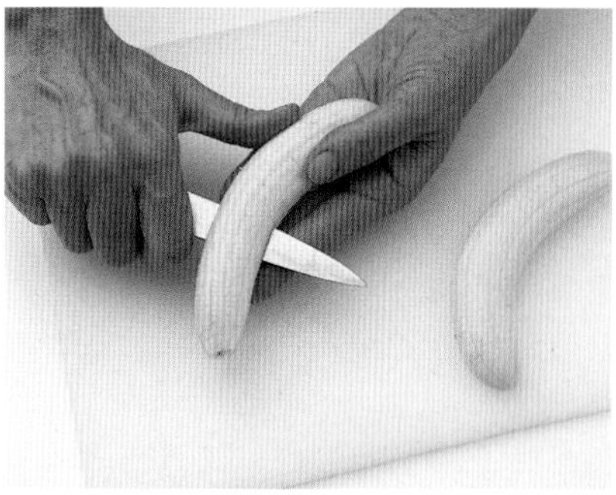

1 Peel the bananas and cut in half lengthways. Melt the butter in a large frying pan over a medium heat. Add the bananas and cook for 3 minutes, turning halfway through cooking time, taking care not to break them.

COOK'S TIP
These hot bananas taste equally good served with coconut or coffee ice cream.

2 Sprinkle the sugar over the bananas, then add the coffee. Continue cooking, stirring occasionally, for 2–3 minutes, or until the bananas are tender.

3 Pour the rum into the pan and bring to the boil. With a long match or taper and tilting the pan, ignite the rum. As soon as the flames subside, serve the bananas with vanilla ice cream.

Grilled Nectarines with Coffee Mascarpone Filling

This simple dessert is perfect for nectarines that are still slightly hard, as they're grilled with a delicious honey and butter glaze and filled with chilled coffee cream.

SERVES FOUR

INGREDIENTS
- 115g/4oz/½ cup mascarpone
- 45ml/3 tbsp cold very strong brewed coffee
- 4 nectarines
- 15g/½oz/1 tbsp butter, melted and cooled
- 45ml/3 tbsp clear honey
- pinch of ground mixed spice
- 25g/1oz/¼ cup slivered brazil nuts

1 Beat the mascarpone until softened, then gradually mix in the cold brewed coffee. Cover with clear film and chill for 20 minutes.

2 Cut the nectarines in half and remove the stones. In a small bowl, mix the butter, 30ml/2 tbsp of the honey and ground mixed spice. Brush the spicy butter all over the cut surfaces.

3 Arrange the nectarines, cut-side up on a foil-lined grill pan. Cook under a hot grill for 2–3 minutes. Add the brazil nuts to the grill pan for the last minute of cooking and toast until golden.

4 Put a spoonful of the chilled cheese mixture in the centre of each hot nectarine. Drizzle with the remaining honey and sprinkle with the toasted brazil nuts before serving.

COOK'S TIP
If possible, choose a scented honey for this dessert: orange blossom and rosemary are both delicious.

Vanilla Poached Pears with Frothy Cappuccino Sauce

Vanilla-scented pears are served with a bubbly espresso sauce and finished with a faint dusting of spicy chocolate for a light, elegant dessert.

SERVES SIX

INGREDIENTS
- 1 vanilla pod
- 150g/5oz/¾ cup granulated sugar
- 400ml/14fl oz/1⅔ cups water
- 6 slightly under-ripe pears
- juice of ½ lemon

For the frothy cappuccino sauce
- 3 egg yolks
- 25g/1oz/2 tbsp caster sugar
- 50ml/2fl oz/¼ cup brewed espresso coffee
- 50ml/2fl oz/¼ cup single cream
- 10ml/2 tsp drinking chocolate
- 2.5ml/½ tsp ground cinnamon

1 Split the vanilla pod lengthways and scrape out the black seeds into a large saucepan. Add the split pod, sugar and water. Heat gently until the sugar has completely dissolved.

2 Meanwhile, peel and halve the pears, then rub with lemon juice. Scoop out the cores with a melon baller or teaspoon. Add the cored pears to the syrup and pour in extra water to cover.

3 Cut out a circle of greaseproof paper and cover the top of the pears. Bring to a light boil, cover the pan with a lid and simmer for 15 minutes, or until tender.

4 Using a slotted spoon, transfer the pears to a serving bowl. Bring the syrup to a rapid boil and cook for 15 minutes, or until reduced by half.

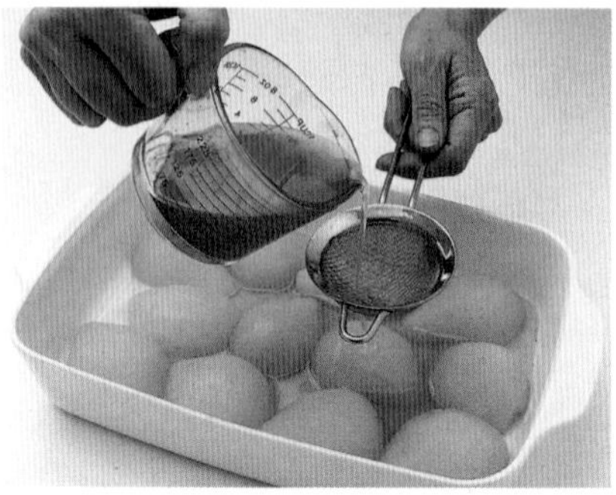

5 Strain over the pears and leave to cool. Cover with clear film and chill for several hours. Allow to come back to room temperature before serving.

6 To make the sauce, put the egg yolks, sugar, coffee and cream into a heatproof bowl over a pan of barely simmering water. With a balloon whisk, beat until the mixture is very thick and frothy. Remove from the heat and continue beating for 2–3 minutes.

7 Arrange the pears on individual plates and pour a little sauce over each. Mix together the drinking chocolate and cinnamon and sprinkle over the sauce. Serve immediately.

FRAGRANT FRUIT SALAD

THE SYRUP OF THIS EXOTIC FRUIT SALAD IS FLAVOURED AND SWEETENED WITH LIME AND COFFEE LIQUEUR. IT CAN BE PREPARED UP TO A DAY BEFORE SERVING.

SERVES SIX

INGREDIENTS

- 130g/4½oz/½ cup sugar
- thinly pared rind and juice of 1 lime
- 60ml/4 tbsp coffee liqueur, such as Tia Maria, Kahlúa or Toussaint
- 1 small pineapple
- 1 medium mango
- 1 papaya
- 2 pomegranates
- 2 passion fruits
- fine strips of lime peel, to decorate

1 Put the sugar and lime rind in a small saucepan with 150ml/¼ pint ⅔ cup water. Heat gently until the sugar dissolves, then bring to the boil and simmer for 5 minutes. Leave to cool, then strain into a large serving bowl, discarding the lime rind. Stir in the lime juice and liqueur.

2 Using a sharp knife, cut the plume and stalk end from the pineapple. Peel thickly and cut the flesh into bite-sized pieces, discarding the woody central core. Add to the bowl.

3 Cut the papaya in half and scoop out the seeds. Cut away the skin, then cut into slices. Cut the pomegranates in half and scoop out the seeds. Break into clusters and add to the bowl.

COOK'S TIP

To maximise the flavour of the fruit, allow the salad to stand at room temperature for an hour before serving.

4 Cut the mango lengthways, along each side of the stone. Peel the skin off the flesh. Add with the rest of the fruit to the bowl. Stir well.

5 Halve the passion fruits and scoop out the flesh using a teaspoon. Spoon over the salad and serve, decorated with fine strips of lime peel.

CARAMELIZED APPLES

A TRADITIONAL DESSERT WITH A DIFFERENCE – BAKED APPLES BATHED IN A RICH COFFEE SYRUP.

SERVES SIX

INGREDIENTS

- 6 eating apples, peeled, but left whole
- 50g/2oz/4 tbsp unsalted butter, melted and cooled
- 90g/3½oz/½ cup caster sugar
- 1.5ml/¼ tsp ground cinnamon
- 90ml/6 tbsp strong brewed coffee
- whipped or clotted cream, to serve

COOK'S TIP

This recipe is equally good made with pears, but reduce the cooking time by 10–15 minutes and use mixed spice in place of the cinnamon.

1 Preheat the oven to 180°C/350°F/Gas 4. Cut a thin slice from the bottom of each apple to give them a flat base. Using a pastry brush, thickly coat each apple with melted butter.

2 Mix the caster sugar and cinnamon in a shallow dish. Holding each apple by its stalk, roll in the mixture to coat.

3 Arrange the apples in a shallow baking dish into which they just fit. Stand them upright.

4 Pour the coffee into the dish then sprinkle over any remaining sugar mixture. Bake the apples for 40 minutes, basting with the coffee two or three times throughout. Baste a last time, then pour the juices into a small pan, returning the apples to the oven.

5 Boil the juices rapidly until syrupy and reduced to about 60ml/4 tbsp. Pour over the apples and cook for 10 more minutes, or until the apples are tender. Serve hot with a spoonful of cream.

SUMMER BERRIES WITH COFFEE SABAYON

FOR A LIGHT AND DELICIOUSLY REFRESHING FINALE, SERVE A PLATTER OF FRESH SUMMER FRUIT WITH A FLUFFY COFFEE SAUCE, WHICH HAS THE ADDED ADVANTAGE OF BEING DELIGHTFULLY EASY TO MAKE.

SERVES SIX

INGREDIENTS

- 900g/2lb/6–8 cups mixed summer berries such as raspberries, blueberries and strawberries (hulled and halved, if large)
- 5 egg yolks
- 75g/3oz/scant ½ cup caster sugar
- 50ml/2fl oz/¼ cup brewed coffee
- 30ml/2 tbsp coffee liqueur, such as Tia Maria, Kahlúa or Toussaint
- strawberry or mint leaves, to decorate (optional)
- 30ml/2 tbsp icing sugar, to dust

COOK'S TIP

Ensure that the water doesn't get too hot when making the sauce, or it may curdle.

1 Arrange the fruit on a serving platter and decorate with strawberry or mint leaves, if you like. Dust with icing sugar.

2 Whisk the egg yolks and caster sugar in a bowl over a pan of simmering water until the mixture begins to thicken.

3 Gradually add the coffee and liqueur, pouring in a thin, continuous stream and whisking all the time. Continue whisking until the sauce is thick and fluffy. Serve warm, or allow to cool, whisking occasionally, and serve cold with the fruit.

Frozen Desserts

Frozen desserts are an ideal choice for all occasions as they can be made in advance, then stored in the freezer. In this chapter, you'll find smooth, velvety ice cream and refreshing sorbets. Some ices are only part of the dessert, such as in Dark Chocolate and Coffee Mousse Cake, a rich chocolate sponge with an ice cream centre.

Cinnamon and Coffee Swirl Ice Cream

LIGHT ICE CREAM SUBTLY SPICED WITH CINNAMON AND RIPPLED WITH A SWEET COFFEE SYRUP.

SERVES SIX

INGREDIENTS
- 300ml/½ pint/1¼ cups single cream
- 1 cinnamon stick
- 4 egg yolks
- 150g/5oz/¾ cup caster sugar
- 300ml/½ pint/1¼ cups double cream

For the coffee syrup
- 45ml/3 tbsp ground coffee
- 45ml/3 tbsp near-boiling water
- 90g/3½oz/½ cup caster sugar
- 50ml/2fl oz/¼ cup water

1 Pour the single cream into a small pan and add the cinnamon stick. Slowly bring to the boil. Turn off the heat, cover with a lid and leave to infuse for 30 minutes. Bring back to the boil and remove the cinnamon stick.

2 Whisk the yolks and sugar until light. Pour the hot cream over the egg mixture, whisking. Return to the pan and stir over low heat for 1–2 minutes, until it thickens. Allow to cool.

3 Whip the double cream until peaks form and fold into the custard. Pour into a container and freeze for 3 hours.

4 Meanwhile, to make the syrup, put the coffee in a bowl and pour the hot water over. Leave to infuse for 4 minutes, then strain through a sieve.

COOK'S TIP
Make sure that the cinnamon ice cream is sufficiently frozen before adding the coffee syrup.

5 Gently heat the sugar and cold water in a pan until completely dissolved. Bring to the boil and gently simmer for 5 minutes. Cool, then stir in the coffee.

6 Turn the cinnamon ice cream into a chilled bowl and briefly whisk to break down the ice crystals.

7 Spoon a third back into the container and drizzle some of the coffee syrup over. Repeat in this way until all is used.

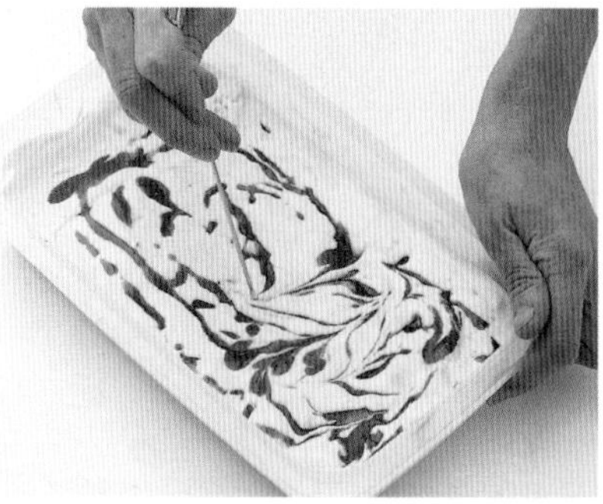

8 Drag a skewer through the mixture a few times to achieve a marbled effect. Freeze for 4 hours, or until solid. Allow to soften slightly before serving.

Toasted Nut and Coffee Ice Cream in Brandy Snap Baskets

Scoops of crushed caramel and toasted nut ice cream are served in crisp cases, then drizzled with a warm coffee and cognac sauce.

SERVES SIX

INGREDIENTS
- 75g/3oz/½ cup whole nuts, such as blanched almonds and hazelnuts
- 90g/3½oz/½ cup caster sugar
- 1 vanilla pod, split
- 30ml/2 tbsp ground coffee
- 200ml/7fl oz/scant 1 cup double cream
- 300ml/½ pint/1¼ cups Greek yogurt
- 6 brandy snap baskets, to serve

For the coffee and cognac sauce
- 115g/4oz/½ cup soft light brown sugar
- 50ml/2fl oz/¼ cup hot water
- 100ml/3½fl oz/½ cup strong brewed coffee
- 60ml/4 tbsp cognac

1 Put the whole nuts and caster sugar in a large heavy-based pan and heat gently until the sugar caramelizes to a light golden brown, shaking the pan only occasionally.

COOK'S TIP

To make brandy snap baskets, in a bowl, gently melt 50g/2oz/4 tbsp butter, 50g/2oz/¼ cup demerara sugar and 50g/2oz/¼ cup golden syrup. Stir in 50g/2oz/½ cup sifted plain flour and 5ml/1 tsp brandy. Drop well-spaced teaspoons on to oiled baking trays. Bake in a preheated oven at 160°C/325°F/Gas 3 for about 8 minutes. Cool for 1 minute, then lift with a palette knife and mould over the base of an inverted glass.

2 Pour on to an oiled baking sheet to cool and harden. Crush to a fine powder. Put the vanilla, coffee and cream in a pan. Heat almost to boiling, turn off the heat, cover and infuse.

3 After 15 minutes, strain through a sieve and leave to cool. Stir the coffee cream into the yogurt with the crushed nut mixture. Transfer to a freezerproof container and freeze for 4 hours.

4 To make the sauce, heat the sugar and water in a small heavy-based pan over a gentle heat until melted. Simmer for 3 minutes. Cool slightly, then stir in the coffee and cognac.

5 Meanwhile, allow the ice cream to soften in the fridge for 15 minutes. Scoop into the brandy snap baskets and serve immediately with the warm coffee and cognac sauce.

Coffee Ice Cream

Freshly ground coffee gives this classic ice cream a distinctive and sophisticated flavour. Choose a dark-roasted bean to ensure a rich, glossy colour to the ice cream.

SERVES EIGHT TO TEN

INGREDIENTS
- 60ml/4 tbsp dark-roasted ground coffee
- 600ml/1 pint/2½ cups milk
- 200g/7oz/scant 1 cup soft light brown sugar
- 6 egg yolks
- 475ml/16fl oz/2 cups whipping cream

1 Put the coffee in a jug. Heat the milk in a saucepan to near-boiling point and pour over the coffee. Leave to stand for 4 minutes.

2 Meanwhile, in a large bowl, beat the sugar and egg yolks until light. Pour the milk over, whisking all the time. Strain the mixture back into the pan through a fine sieve.

3 Cook the custard over a low heat for 1–2 minutes, stirring until it coats the back of a wooden spoon. Do not boil. Pour into a shallow freezer container and leave to cool, stirring occasionally.

COOK'S TIP
If using an ice cream maker, do not whip the cream: stir it into the coffee custard before adding to the machine.

4 Freeze for about 2 hours, then tip into a bowl and whisk with a fork until smooth. Whip the cream until peaks form and fold into the frozen mixture.

5 Return to the freezer for 1 more hour, then turn out and whisk again. Finally, freeze for 3–4 hours, until solid. Transfer to the fridge for 20 minutes, before scooping and serving.

Cappuccino Cones

Pretty white and dark chocolate cones are filled with swirls of cappuccino cream and topped with a light dusting of cocoa powder.

SERVES SIX

INGREDIENTS
- 115g/4oz each good quality plain and white cooking chocolate

For the cappuccino cream
- 30ml/2 tbsp ground espresso or other strong-flavoured coffee
- 30ml/2 tbsp near-boiling water
- 300ml/½ pint/1¼ cups double cream
- 45ml/3 tbsp icing sugar, sifted
- 15ml/1 tbsp cocoa powder, for dusting

1 Cut nine 13 x 10cm/5 x 4in rectangles from non-stick baking parchment, then cut each rectangle in half diagonally to make 18 triangles. Roll up each to make a cone and secure with sticky tape.

2 Heat the plain chocolate in a bowl over a pan of hot water until melted. Using a small pastry brush, thickly brush the insides of half the paper cones with chocolate. Chill until set. Repeat with the white chocolate. Carefully peel away the paper and keep the cones in the fridge until needed.

3 To make the cappuccino cream, put the coffee in a small bowl. Pour the hot water over. Leave to infuse for 4 minutes, then strain though a fine sieve into a bowl. Leave to cool. Add the cream and sugar and whisk until soft peaks form. Spoon into an icing bag fitted with a medium star nozzle.

4 Pipe the cream into the chocolate cones. Put on a baking sheet and freeze for at least 2 hours or until solid. Arrange on individual plates, allowing three cones per person and dusting with cocoa powder before serving.

COOK'S TIP
Make sure, when melting the chocolate, that the water doesn't boil or the chocolate will overheat and stiffen.

Maple Coffee and Pistachio Bombes

Real maple syrup tastes infinitely better than the synthetic varieties and is well worth searching for. Here it sweetens the dark coffee centre of these pretty pistachio bombes.

SERVES SIX

INGREDIENTS

For the pistachio ice cream
- 50g/2oz/¼ cup caster sugar
- 50ml/2fl oz/¼ cup water
- 175g/6oz can evaporated milk, chilled
- 50g/2oz/½ cup shelled and skinned pistachio nuts, finely chopped
- drop of green food colouring (optional)
- 200ml/7fl oz/scant 1 cup whipping cream

For the maple coffee centres
- 30ml/2 tbsp ground coffee
- 150ml/¼ pint/⅔ cup single cream
- 50ml/2fl oz/¼ cup maple syrup
- 2 egg yolks
- 5ml/1 tsp cornflour
- 150ml/¼ pint/⅔ cup whipping cream

1 Put six 175ml/6fl oz/¾ cup mini pudding basins or dariole moulds into the freezer to chill. Put the sugar and water in a heavy-based saucepan and heat gently until dissolved. Bring to the boil and simmer for 3 minutes.

2 Cool, then stir in the chilled evaporated milk, pistachio nuts and colouring, if using. Lightly whip the cream until it forms soft peaks and blend into the mixture.

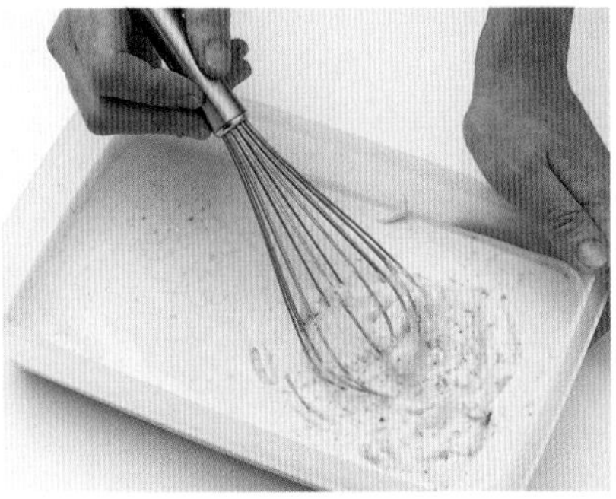

3 Pour the mixture into a freezerproof container and freeze for at least 2 hours. Whisk the ice cream until smooth, then freeze for a further 2 hours or until frozen, but not solid.

4 To make the centres, put the ground coffee in a jug. Heat the single cream to near-boiling point and pour over the coffee. Leave to infuse for 4 minutes. Whisk the maple syrup, egg yolks and cornflour together. Strain the hot coffee cream over the egg mixture, whisking continuously. Return to the pan and cook gently for 1–2 minutes, until the custard thickens. Leave to cool, stirring occasionally.

5 Meanwhile, line the moulds with the ice cream, keeping the thickness as even as possible right up to the rim. Freeze until the ice cream is firm again.

6 Beat the cream until peaks form, then fold into the custard. Spoon into the middle of the moulds. Cover and freeze for 2 hours. Serve immediately.

FROSTED RASPBERRY AND COFFEE TERRINE

A WHITE CHOCOLATE AND RASPBERRY LAYER AND A CONTRASTING SMOOTH COFFEE LAYER MAKE THIS ATTRACTIVE LOOKING DESSERT DOUBLY DELICIOUS.

SERVES SIX TO EIGHT

INGREDIENTS
- 30ml/2 tbsp ground coffee, e.g. mocha orange-flavoured
- 250ml/8fl oz/1 cup milk
- 4 eggs, separated
- 50g/2oz/¼ cup caster sugar
- 30ml/2 tbsp cornflour
- 150ml/¼ pint/⅔ cup double cream
- 150g/5oz white chocolate, roughly chopped
- 115g/4oz/⅔ cup raspberries
- shavings of white chocolate and cocoa powder, to decorate

1 Line a 1.5 litre/2½ pint/6¼ cup loaf tin with clear film and put in the freezer to chill. Put the ground coffee in a jug. Heat 100ml/3½fl oz/scant ½ cup of the milk to near-boiling point and pour over the coffee. Leave to infuse.

2 Blend the egg yolks, sugar and cornflour together in a saucepan and whisk in the remaining milk and the cream. Bring to the boil, stirring all the time, until thickened.

3 Divide the hot mixture between two bowls and add the white chocolate to one, stirring until melted. Strain the coffee through a fine sieve into the other bowl and mix well. Leave until cool, stirring occasionally.

COOK'S TIP
After decorating, allow the terrine to soften in the fridge for 20 minutes before slicing and serving.

4 Whisk two of the egg whites until stiff. Fold into the coffee custard. Spoon into the tin and freeze for 30 minutes. Whisk remaining whites and fold into the chocolate mixture with the raspberries.

5 Spoon into the tin and level before freezing for 4 hours. Turn the terrine out on to a flat serving plate and peel off the clear film. Cover with chocolate shavings and dust with cocoa powder.

Coffee and Minty-Lemon Sorbet

The flavours of fresh mint, sharp lemon and aromatic coffee are combined in this delicious icy sorbet. The lemon shells are an easy, but pretty, summery decorative touch.

SERVES SIX

INGREDIENTS

- 115g/4oz/generous ½ cup sugar
- 400ml/14fl oz/1⅔ cups water
- 15g/½oz fresh mint leaves
- 30ml/2 tbsp coffee liqueur, such as Tia Maria, Kahlúa or Toussaint
- 6 lemons
- 1 egg white
- sprigs of fresh mint, to decorate

1 Put the sugar in a large heavy-based saucepan with the water and heat gently until dissolved, stirring occasionally. Bring to the boil, and simmer for 5 minutes.

2 Remove from the heat, add the mint leaves, stir and leave to cool. Strain into a jug and stir in the liqueur.

3 Cut a thin slice from the base of each lemon so that they will stand upright, being careful not to cut through the pith. Cut the tops off the lemons and keep for lids. Scrape out the lemon flesh and squeeze the juice. Strain the juice into the mint and coffee syrup.

4 Pour into a freezerproof container and freeze for 3 hours. Whisk to break down the ice crystals, then freeze for 1 more hour. Whisk the egg white until stiff, then whisk into the ice. Scoop into the lemon shells and replace the lids.

5 Place upright on a tray and freeze for 2 hours, until solid. Transfer to the fridge 5 minutes before serving, to soften. Decorate with sprigs of mint.

COOK'S TIP

Fresh fruit sorbets will keep in the freezer for up to 2 months, but are best eaten within several days of making.

Espresso Granita

This famous frozen Italian ice makes a refreshing finish to a rich meal.

SERVES SIX

INGREDIENTS

- 90g/3½oz/½ cup sugar
- 600ml/1 pint/2½ cups espresso or other strong-flavoured coffee
- whipped cream, to serve (optional)

1 Add the sugar to the hot coffee and stir until dissolved. Leave to cool, then pour into a 900ml/1½ pint/3¾ cup shallow freezer container.

2 Freeze for at least 3 hours, or until ice crystals form around the edges. Whisk with a fork, then return to the freezer for another hour.

3 Whisk the mixture again with a fork and re-freeze. Repeat until the mixture is frozen and there is no liquid.

4 Transfer the granita to the fridge 20 minutes before serving. Break up the ice crystals with a strong fork and serve in glasses, topped with whipped cream, if you like.

COOK'S TIPS

- Don't whisk the granita too vigorously – it should have a rough granular texture, rather than a smooth one like a sorbet.
- After step 3, the granita can either be served at that stage or covered and stored in the freezer for up to 2 weeks.

Iced Coffee Mousse in a Chocolate Case

A dark chocolate bowl is filled with a light, iced coffee mousse. It looks a dramatic dessert, but isn't difficult to make.

SERVES EIGHT

INGREDIENTS
- 1 sachet powdered gelatine
- 60ml/4 tbsp very strong brewed coffee
- 30ml/2 tbsp coffee liqueur, such as Tia Maria, Kahlúa or Toussaint
- 3 eggs, separated
- 75g/3oz/scant ½ cup caster sugar
- 150ml/¼ pint/⅔ cup whipping cream, lightly whipped

For the chocolate bowl
- 225g/8oz plain chocolate squares, plus extra for decoration

1 Grease and line a deep 18cm/7in loose-based cake tin with non-stick baking parchment.

2 Melt the chocolate in a bowl over a pan of simmering water. Using a pastry brush, brush a layer of chocolate over the base of the tin and about 7.5cm/3in up the sides, finishing with a ragged edge. Allow the chocolate to set before repeating. Put in the freezer to harden.

3 Sprinkle the gelatine over the coffee in a bowl and leave to soften for 5 minutes. Put the bowl over a pan of simmering water, stirring until dissolved. Remove from the heat and stir in the liqueur. Whisk the egg yolks and sugar in a bowl over the simmering water until thick enough to leave a trail. Remove from the pan and whisk until cool. Whisk the egg whites until stiff.

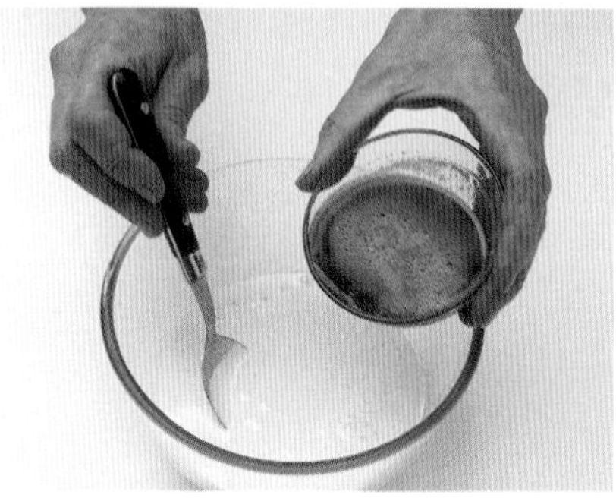

4 Pour the dissolved gelatine into the egg yolk mixture in a thin stream, stirring gently. Chill in the fridge for 20 minutes, or until just beginning to set, then fold in the cream, followed by the whisked egg whites.

5 Remove the chocolate case from the freezer and peel away the lining. Put it back in the tin, then pour in the mousse. Return to the freezer for at least 3 hours. To serve, remove from the tin and place on a plate. Allow to soften in the fridge for 40 minutes before serving. Decorate with grated chocolate. Use a knife dipped in hot water and wiped dry to cut into slices to serve.

Dark Chocolate and Coffee Mousse Cake

This double treat will prove irresistible – rich sponge filled with creamy coffee mousse.

SERVES EIGHT

INGREDIENTS
- 4 eggs
- 115g/4oz/generous ½ cup caster sugar
- 75g/3oz/⅔ cup plain flour, sifted
- 25g/1oz/¼ cup cocoa powder, sifted
- 60ml/4 tbsp coffee liqueur, such as Tia Maria, Kahlúa or Toussaint
- icing sugar, to dust

For the coffee mousse
- 30ml/2 tbsp dark-roasted ground coffee beans
- 350ml/12fl oz/1½ cups double cream
- 115g/4oz/generous ½ cup granulated sugar
- 120ml/4fl oz/½ cup water
- 4 egg yolks

1 Preheat the oven to 180°C/350°F/ Gas 4. Grease and line the bases of a 20cm/8in square and a 23cm/9in round cake tin with non-stick baking parchment. Put the eggs and sugar in a bowl over a pan of hot water and whisk until thick.

2 Remove from the heat and whisk until thick enough to leave a trail when the whisk is lifted. Gently fold in the flour and cocoa. Pour a third of the mixture into the square tin and the remainder into the round tin. Bake the square sponge for 15 minutes and the round for 30 minutes, until firm.

3 Cool on a wire rack before slicing the round cake in half horizontally. Place the bottom half back in the tin. Sprinkle with half the liqueur.

4 Trim the edges of the square sponge, cut into 4 equal strips and use to line the sides of the tin.

5 To make the mousse, put the coffee in a bowl. Heat 50ml/2fl oz/¼ cup of the cream to near-boiling and pour over the coffee. Leave to infuse for 4 minutes, then strain through a fine sieve.

6 Gently heat the sugar and water until dissolved. Increase the heat and boil steadily until the syrup reaches 107°C/ 225°F. Cool for 5 minutes, then pour on to the egg yolks, whisking until the mixture is very thick.

7 Add the coffee cream to the remaining cream and whip until soft peaks form. Fold into the egg mixture. Spoon into the sponge case and freeze for 20 minutes. Sprinkle the remaining liqueur over the second sponge half and place on top of the mousse. Cover and freeze for 4 hours. Remove from the tin and dust with icing sugar.

COOK'S TIP

Cover the seams of the cake with swirls of piped whipped cream and decorate with chocolate coffee beans, if you like.

CAKE AND TORTE RECIPES

From simple sponges to elaborate tortes and velvety cheesecakes, these are cakes to rival any shop-bought confection. Some, such as Coffee Almond Marsala Slice, are perfect with mid-morning coffee. Others, like Coffee Chocolate Mousse Cake and Cappuccino Torte, make unforgettable dinner party desserts.

Coconut Coffee Cake

Coconut and coffee are natural partners, as these little squares of iced cake prove.

SERVES NINE

INGREDIENTS
- 45ml/3 tbsp ground coffee
- 75ml/5 tbsp near-boiling milk
- 25g/1oz/2 tbsp caster sugar
- 175g/6oz/⅔ cup golden syrup
- 75g/3oz/6 tbsp butter
- 40g/1½oz/½ cup desiccated coconut
- 175g/6oz/1½ cups plain flour
- 2.5ml/½ tsp bicarbonate of soda
- 2 eggs, lightly beaten

For the icing
- 115g/4oz/8 tbsp butter, softened
- 225g/8oz/2 cups icing sugar, sifted
- 25g/1oz/⅓ cup shredded or flaked coconut, toasted

1 Preheat the oven to 160°C/325°F/Gas 3. Grease and line the base of a 20cm/8in square tin.

2 Put the ground coffee in a small bowl and pour the hot milk over. Leave to infuse for 4 minutes, then strain through a fine sieve.

3 Heat the caster sugar, golden syrup, butter and desiccated coconut in a pan, stirring with a wooden spoon, until completely melted.

4 Sift the flour and bicarbonate of soda together and stir into the mixture, along with the eggs and 45ml/3 tbsp of the coffee-flavoured milk.

5 Spoon the mixture into the prepared tin and level the top. Bake in the oven for 40–50 minutes until well-risen and firm. Allow the cake to cool in the tin for about 10 minutes, before running a knife around the edges to loosen. Turn out and cool on a wire rack.

6 To make the icing, beat the softened butter until smooth then gradually beat in the icing sugar and remaining coffee milk to give a soft consistency. Spread over the top of the cake and decorate with toasted coconut. Cut into 5cm/2in squares to serve.

VARIATION

Substitute 50g/2oz/½ cup chopped pecan nuts for the desiccated coconut and decorate the squares with pecan halves dusted with icing sugar.

MOCHA SPONGE CAKE

THE YEMENI CITY OF MOCHA WAS ONCE CONSIDERED TO BE THE COFFEE CAPITAL OF THE WORLD, AND STILL PRODUCES A COFFEE THAT TASTES A LITTLE LIKE CHOCOLATE. TODAY "MOCHA" MAY REFER TO THE VARIETY OF COFFEE OR MEAN A COMBINATION OF COFFEE OR CHOCOLATE, AS IN THIS RECIPE.

SERVES TEN

INGREDIENTS

- 25ml/1½ tbsp strong-flavoured ground coffee
- 175ml/6fl oz/¾ cup milk
- 115g/4oz/8 tbsp butter
- 115g/4oz/½ cup soft light brown sugar
- 1 egg, lightly beaten
- 185g/6½oz/1⅔ cups self-raising flour
- 5ml/1 tsp bicarbonate of soda
- 60ml/4 tbsp creamy liqueur, such as Baileys or Irish Velvet

For the glossy chocolate icing

- 200g/7oz plain chocolate, broken into pieces
- 75g/3oz/6 tbsp unsalted butter, cubed
- 120ml/4fl oz/½ cup double cream

1 Preheat the oven to 180°C/350°F/ Gas 4. Grease and line a 18cm/7in round fixed-base cake tin with greaseproof paper.

2 To make the cake, put the coffee in a jug. Heat the milk to near-boiling and pour over. Leave to infuse for 4 minutes, then strain through a sieve and cool.

3 Gently melt the butter and sugar until dissolved. Pour into a bowl and cool for 2 minutes, then stir in the egg.

4 Sift the flour over the mixture and fold in. Blend the bicarbonate of soda with the coffee-flavoured milk and gradually stir into the mixture.

5 Pour into the tin, smooth the surface, and bake for 40 minutes, until well-risen and firm. Cool in the tin for about 10 minutes. Spoon the liqueur over the cake and leave until cold. Loosen the edges with a palette knife and turn out on to a wire rack.

6 To make the icing, place the broken chocolate in a bowl over a pan of barely simmering water until melted. Remove from the heat and stir in the butter and cream until smooth. Allow to cool before coating the top and sides of the cake, using a palette knife. Leave until set.

Coffee Almond Marsala Slice

Roasted and crushed coffee beans are speckled throughout this delicious almond cake, distinctly flavoured with Italian Marsala wine.

SERVES TEN TO TWELVE

INGREDIENTS
- 25g/1oz/⅓ cup roasted coffee beans
- 5 eggs, separated
- 175g/6oz/scant 1 cup caster sugar
- 120ml/4fl oz/½ cup Marsala wine
- 75g/3oz/6 tbsp butter, melted and cooled
- 115g/4oz/1 cup ground almonds
- 115g/4oz/1 cup plain flour, sifted
- 25g/1oz/¼ cup flaked almonds
- icing sugar, to dust
- crème fraîche, to serve

1 Preheat the oven to 180°C/350°F/Gas 4. Grease and line the base of a 23cm/9in round loose-based tin with greaseproof paper. Put the coffee beans on a baking sheet and roast for about 10 minutes. Cool, then place in a large plastic bag and gently crush with a rolling pin.

2 Beat the yolks and 115g/4oz/generous ½ cup of the caster sugar until very pale and thick.

3 Stir in the crushed coffee, Marsala, butter and almonds. Sift the flour over, then carefully fold in.

4 Whisk the egg whites until they are stiff, then gradually incorporate the remaining caster sugar.

5 Fold into the almond mixture, a third at a time. Spoon into the tin and sprinkle the top with flaked almonds.

6 Bake for 10 minutes, then reduce the oven to 160°C/325°F/Gas 3 and cook for a further 40 minutes, or until a skewer inserted into the centre comes out clean. After 5 minutes, turn out and cool on a wire rack. Dust with icing sugar and serve with crème fraîche.

Sour Cherry Coffee Loaf

Dried sour cherries have a wonderfully concentrated fruit flavour and can be bought in supermarkets and health food shops.

SERVES EIGHT

INGREDIENTS
- 175g/6oz/12 tbsp butter, softened
- 175g/6oz/scant 1 cup golden caster sugar
- 5ml/1 tsp vanilla extract
- 2 eggs, lightly beaten
- 225g/8oz/2 cups plain flour
- 1.5ml/¼ tsp baking powder
- 75ml/5 tbsp strong brewed coffee
- 175g/6oz/1 cup dried sour cherries

For the icing
- 50g/2oz/½ cup icing sugar, sifted
- 20ml/4 tsp strong brewed coffee

1 Preheat the oven to 180°C/350°F/Gas 4. Grease and line a 900g/2lb loaf tin with greaseproof paper. Cream the butter, sugar and vanilla until fluffy.

2 Gradually add the eggs, beating well after each addition. Sift the flour and baking powder together.

3 Fold into the mixture with the coffee and 115g/4oz/⅔ cup of the sour cherries. Spoon the mixture into the prepared tin and level the top.

4 Bake for 1¼ hours or until firm to the touch. Cool in the tin for 5 minutes, then turn out and cool on a wire rack.

5 To make the icing, mix together the icing sugar and coffee and the remaining cherries. Spoon over the top and sides. Leave to set before slicing.

COFFEE AND MINT CREAM CAKE

GROUND ALMONDS GIVE THIS BUTTERY COFFEE SPONGE A MOIST TEXTURE AND DELICATE FLAVOUR. IT'S SANDWICHED TOGETHER WITH A GENEROUS FILLING OF CRÈME DE MENTHE BUTTERCREAM.

SERVES EIGHT

INGREDIENTS
- 15ml/1 tbsp ground coffee
- 25ml/1½ tbsp near-boiling water
- 175g/6oz/12 tbsp unsalted butter, softened
- 175g/6oz/scant 1 cup caster sugar
- 225g/8oz/2 cups self-raising flour, sifted
- 50g/2oz/½ cup ground almonds
- 3 eggs
- small sprigs of fresh mint, to decorate

For the filling
- 50g/2oz/4 tbsp unsalted butter
- 115g/4oz/1 cup icing sugar, sifted, plus extra for dusting
- 30ml/2 tbsp crème de menthe liqueur

1 Preheat the oven to 180°C/350°F/Gas 4. Lightly grease and base line two 18cm/7in sandwich tins with greaseproof paper.

2 Put the coffee in a bowl and pour the hot water over. Leave to infuse for about 4 minutes, then strain through a sieve.

3 Put the butter, sugar, flour, almonds, eggs and coffee in a large bowl. Beat well for 1 minute until blended. Divide the mixture evenly between the tins and level off. Bake for 25 minutes until well-risen and firm to the touch. Leave in the tins for 5 minutes, then turn out on to a wire rack to cool.

4 To make the filling, cream the unsalted butter, icing sugar and crème de menthe liqueur together in a bowl until light and fluffy.

COOK'S TIP
Make sure the butter is really soft and creamy before starting to mix the cake.

5 Remove the lining paper from the sponges and sandwich together with the filling.

6 Generously dust the top with icing sugar and place on a serving plate. Scatter with the fresh mint leaves just before serving.

Coffee and Walnut Swiss Roll with Cointreau Cream

Coffee and walnuts have a natural affinity. Here they appear together in a light and fluffy sponge enclosing a smooth orange cream.

SERVES SIX

INGREDIENTS
- 10ml/2 tsp ground coffee, e.g. mocha orange-flavoured
- 15ml/1 tbsp near-boiling water
- 3 eggs
- 75g/3oz/scant ½ cup caster sugar, plus extra for dusting
- 75g/3oz/⅔ cup self-raising flour
- 50g/2oz/½ cup toasted walnuts, finely chopped

For the Cointreau cream
- 115g/4oz/generous ½ cup caster sugar
- 50ml/2fl oz/¼ cup cold water
- 2 egg yolks
- 115g/4oz/8 tbsp unsalted butter, softened
- 15ml/1 tbsp Cointreau

1 Preheat the oven to 200°C/400°F/Gas 6. Grease and line a 33 x 23cm/13 x 9in Swiss roll tin with non-stick baking parchment.

2 Put the coffee in a bowl and pour the hot water over. Leave to infuse for about 4 minutes, then strain through a sieve.

3 Whisk the eggs and sugar together in a large bowl until pale and thick. Sift the flour over the mixture and fold in with the coffee and walnuts. Turn into the tin and bake for 10–12 minutes, until springy to the touch.

4 Turn out on a piece of greaseproof paper sprinkled with caster sugar, peel off the lining paper and cool for about 2 minutes. Trim the edges then roll up from one of the short ends, with the greaseproof paper where the filling will be. Leave to cool.

5 To make the filling, heat the sugar in the water over a low heat until dissolved. Boil rapidly until the syrup reaches 105°C/220°F on a sugar thermometer. Pour the syrup over the egg yolks, whisking all the time, until thick and mousse-like. Gradually add the butter, then whisk in the orange liqueur. Leave to cool and thicken.

6 Unroll the sponge and spread with the Cointreau cream. Re-roll and place on a serving plate seam-side down. Dust with extra caster sugar and chill in the fridge until ready to serve.

COOK'S TIP

Decorate the roll with swirls of piped whipped cream and walnuts, if you like.

COFFEE CHOCOLATE MOUSSE CAKE

Serve this dense, dark chocolate cake in small portions as it is very rich.

SERVES SIX

INGREDIENTS
- 175g/6oz plain chocolate
- 30ml/2 tbsp strong brewed coffee
- 150g/5oz/10 tbsp butter, cubed
- 50g/2oz/¼ cup caster sugar
- 3 eggs
- 25g/1oz/¼ cup ground almonds
- about 25ml/1½ tbsp icing sugar, for dusting

For the mascarpone and coffee cream
- 250g/9oz/generous 1 cup mascarpone
- 30ml/2 tbsp icing sugar, sifted
- 30ml/2 tbsp strong brewed coffee

1 Preheat the oven to 200°C/400°F/Gas 6. Lightly grease and line the base of a 15cm/6in square tin with greaseproof paper.

2 Put the chocolate and coffee in a small heavy-based pan and heat very gently until melted, stirring occasionally.

3 Add the butter and sugar to the pan and stir until dissolved. Whisk the eggs until frothy and stir into the chocolate mixture with the ground almonds.

4 Pour into the prepared tin, then put in a large roasting tin and pour in enough hot water to come two-thirds up the cake tin. Bake for 50 minutes, or until the top feels springy to the touch. Leave to cool in the tin for 5 minutes, then turn the cake out upside-down on to a board and leave to cool.

5 Meanwhile, beat the mascarpone with the icing sugar and coffee. Dust the cake generously with icing sugar, then cut into slices. Serve on individual plates with the mascarpone and coffee cream alongside.

COOK'S TIP

The top of this flourless cake, with its moist mousse-like texture, will crack slightly as it cooks.

CAPPUCCINO TORTE

The famous and much loved beverage of freshly brewed coffee, whipped cream, chocolate and cinnamon is transformed into a sensational dessert.

SERVES SIX TO EIGHT

INGREDIENTS
- 75g/3oz/6 tbsp butter, melted
- 275g/10oz shortbread biscuits, crushed
- 1.5ml/¼ tsp ground cinnamon
- 25ml/1½ tbsp powdered gelatine
- 45ml/3 tbsp cold water
- 2 eggs, separated
- 115g/4oz/½ cup soft light brown sugar
- 115g/4oz plain chocolate, chopped
- 175ml/6fl oz/¾ cup brewed espresso
- 400ml/14fl oz/1⅔ cups whipping cream
- chocolate curls and ground cinnamon, to decorate

1 Mix the butter with the biscuits and cinnamon. Spoon into the base of a 20cm/8in loose-based tin and press down well. Chill in the fridge while making the filling.

2 Sprinkle the gelatine over the cold water. Leave to soften for 5 minutes, then place the bowl over a pan of hot water and stir to dissolve.

3 Whisk the egg yolks and sugar until thick. Put the chocolate in a bowl with the coffee and stir until melted. Add to the egg mixture, then cook gently in a pan for 1–2 minutes until thickened. Stir in the gelatine. Leave until just beginning to set, stirring occasionally.

4 Whip 150ml/¼ pint/⅔ cup of the cream until soft peaks form. Whisk the egg whites until stiff. Fold the cream into the coffee mixture, followed by the egg whites. Pour the mixture over the biscuit base and chill for 2 hours.

5 When ready to serve, remove the torte from the tin and transfer to a serving plate. Whip the remaining cream and place a dollop on top. Decorate with chocolate curls and a little cinnamon.

Baked Coffee Cheesecake

This rich, cooked and chilled cheesecake, flavoured with coffee and orange liqueur, has a wonderfully dense, velvety texture.

SERVES EIGHT

INGREDIENTS
- 45ml/3 tbsp near-boiling water
- 30ml/2 tbsp ground coffee
- 4 eggs
- 225g/8oz/generous 1 cup caster sugar
- 450g/1lb/2 cups cream cheese, at room temperature
- 30ml/2 tbsp orange liqueur, such as Curaçao
- 40g/1½oz/⅓ cup plain flour, sifted
- 300ml/½ pint/1¼ cups whipping cream
- 30ml/2 tbsp icing sugar, to dust
- single cream, to serve

For the base
- 115g/4oz/1 cup plain flour
- 5ml/1 tsp baking powder
- 75g/3oz/6 tbsp butter
- 50g/2oz/¼ cup caster sugar
- 1 egg, lightly beaten
- 30ml/2 tbsp cold water

1 Preheat the oven to 160°C/325°F/Gas 3. Lightly grease and line a 20cm/8in loose-based tin with greaseproof paper.

2 Sift the flour and baking powder into a bowl. Rub in the butter until the mixture resembles fine breadcrumbs. Stir in the sugar, then add the egg and water and mix to a dough. Press the mixture into the base of the tin.

3 To make the filling, pour the water over the coffee and leave to infuse for 4 minutes. Strain through a fine sieve.

4 Whisk the eggs and sugar until thick. Using a wooden spoon, beat the cream cheese until softened, then beat in the liqueur, a spoonful at a time.

5 Gradually mix in the whisked eggs. Fold in the flour. Finally, stir in the whipping cream and coffee.

6 Pour the mixture over the base and bake in the oven for 1½ hours. Turn off the heat and leave in the oven to cool with the door ajar. Chill the cheesecake in the fridge for 1 hour. Dust the top with the icing sugar. Remove from the tin and place on a serving plate, Serve with single cream.

IRISH COFFEE CHEESECAKE

THE FLAVOURS OF WHISKEY, COFFEE AND GINGER GO WELL TOGETHER, BUT YOU CAN RING THE CHANGES BY USING ALMOND OR DIGESTIVE BISCUITS FOR THE BASE OF THIS CHEESECAKE.

SERVES EIGHT

INGREDIENTS
- 45ml/3 tbsp ground coffee
- 1 vanilla pod
- 250ml/8fl oz/1 cup single cream
- 15ml/1 tbsp powdered gelatine
- 45ml/3 tbsp cold water
- 450g/1lb/2 cups curd cheese, at room temperature
- 60ml/4 tbsp Irish whiskey liqueur, such as Millars or Irish Velvet
- 115g/4oz/½ cup soft light brown sugar
- 150ml/¼ pint/⅔ cup whipping cream

To decorate
- 150ml/¼ pint/⅔ cup whipping cream
- chocolate-covered coffee beans
- cocoa, for dusting

For the base
- 150g/5oz gingernut biscuits, finely crushed
- 25g/1oz/¼ cup toasted almonds, chopped
- 75g/3oz/6 tbsp butter, melted

1 To make the base, mix together the crushed gingernut biscuits, toasted almonds and melted butter and press firmly into the base of a 20cm/8in loose-based tin. Chill in the fridge.

2 Heat the coffee, vanilla and single cream in a pan to near-boiling point. Cover and leave to infuse for 15 minutes. Strain through a fine sieve. Sprinkle the gelatine over the water in a bowl and leave for 5 minutes. Place over a pan of simmering water until dissolved. Stir into the coffee cream.

3 Mix the curd cheese, liqueur and sugar together, then gradually blend in the coffee cream. Leave until just beginning to set.

4 Beat the whipping cream until soft peaks form, and fold into the coffee mixture. Spoon into the tin and chill for 3 hours, until set.

5 To decorate, whisk the whipping cream until soft peaks form and spread lightly over the top. Chill for at least 30 minutes, then transfer to a serving plate. Decorate with chocolate-covered coffee beans and cocoa.

VARIATION

Instead of a smooth layer of cream on top of the cheesecake, pipe swirls of cream around the edge of the cake.

Pies, Tarts and Pastries

The flavour and aroma of real coffee transforms perennial family favourites into something special, as you'll discover when you taste a slice of Coffee Custard Tart or Crunchy Topped Coffee Meringue Pie. Along with these much-loved pies and tarts are classic pastries from around the world.

WALNUT PIE

SWEETENED WITH COFFEE-FLAVOURED MAPLE SYRUP, THIS PIE HAS A RICH AND STICKY TEXTURE. THE WALNUTS CAN BE REPLACED BY PECANS FOR AN AUTHENTIC AMERICAN PIE.

SERVES EIGHT

INGREDIENTS

- 30ml/2 tbsp ground coffee
- 175ml/6 fl oz/¾ cup maple syrup
- 25g/1oz/2 tbsp butter, softened
- 175g/6oz/¾ cup soft light brown sugar
- 3 eggs, beaten
- 5ml/1 tsp vanilla extract
- 115g/4oz/1 cup walnut halves
- crème fraîche or vanilla ice cream, to serve

For the pastry

- 150g/5oz/1¼ cups plain flour
- pinch of salt
- 25g/1oz/¼ cup golden icing sugar
- 75g/3oz/6 tbsp butter, cubed and cubed
- 2 egg yolks

1 Preheat the oven to 200°C/400°F/Gas 6. To make the pastry, sift the flour, salt and icing sugar into a bowl. Rub in the butter until the mixture resembles fine breadcrumbs.

2 Add the egg yolks and mix to a dough. Turn out and knead on a lightly floured surface for a few seconds until smooth. Wrap in clear film and chill for 20 minutes.

3 Roll out the pastry and use to line a 20cm/8in fluted flan tin. Line with greaseproof paper and baking beans and bake for 10 minutes. Remove the paper and beans and bake for a further 5 minutes. Take out the pastry case and turn the oven to 180°C/350°F/Gas 4.

4 To make the filling, put the coffee and maple syrup in a small pan and heat until almost boiling. Remove from the heat and leave until just warm. Mix together the butter and sugar, then gradually beat in the eggs. Strain the maple syrup mixture through a fine sieve into the bowl and stir in with the vanilla extract.

5 Arrange the walnuts in the pastry case, then carefully pour in the filling. Bake for 30–35 minutes or until lightly browned and firm. Serve warm with crème fraîche or vanilla ice cream.

MISSISSIPPI PIE

THIS AMERICAN FAVOURITE WAS NAMED AFTER THE MUDDY BANKS OF THE MISSISSIPPI RIVER. IT HAS A DENSE LAYER OF CHOCOLATE MOUSSE, TOPPED WITH A MURKY COFFEE TOFFEE LAYER AND, FLOATING ON TOP, LOTS OF LOVELY FRESHLY WHIPPED CREAM.

SERVES EIGHT

INGREDIENTS

For the base

- 275g/10oz digestive biscuits, crushed
- 150g/5oz/10 tbsp butter, melted

For the chocolate layer

- 10ml/2 tsp powdered gelatine
- 30ml/2 tbsp cold water
- 175g/6oz plain chocolate, broken into squares
- 2 eggs, separated
- 150ml/¼ pint/⅔ cup double cream

For the coffee toffee layer

- 30ml/2 tbsp ground coffee
- 300ml/½ pint/1¼ cups double cream
- 200g/7oz/1 cup caster sugar
- 25g/1oz/4 tbsp cornflour
- 2 eggs, beaten
- 15g/½oz/1 tbsp butter
- 150ml/¼ pint/⅔ cup whipping cream and chocolate curls, to decorate

1 Grease a 21cm/8½in loose-based tin. Mix together the biscuit crumbs and butter and press over the base and sides of the tin. Chill for 30 minutes.

2 To make the chocolate layer, sprinkle the gelatine over the cold water and leave for 5 minutes. Put the bowl over a pan of hot water and stir until dissolved. Melt the chocolate in a bowl over hot water. Stir in the gelatine.

3 Blend the egg yolks and cream and stir into the chocolate. Whisk the egg whites and fold into the mixture. Pour into the biscuit case and chill for 2 hours.

4 To make the coffee layer, put the coffee in a bowl. Reserve 60ml/4 tbsp of cream. Heat the remaining cream to near-boiling and pour over. Leave to infuse for 4 minutes. Strain through a sieve back into the pan. Add the sugar and heat gently until dissolved.

5 Mix the cornflour with the reserved cream and the eggs. Add to the coffee and cream mixture and simmer gently for 2–3 minutes, stirring.

6 Stir in the butter and leave to cool for 30 minutes, stirring occasionally. Spoon over the chocolate layer. Chill in the fridge for 2 hours.

7 To make the topping, whip the cream until soft peaks form and spread thickly over the coffee toffee layer. Decorate with chocolate curls and chill until ready to serve.

CRUNCHY TOPPED COFFEE MERINGUE PIE

A SWEET PASTRY CASE IS FILLED WITH A COFFEE CUSTARD AND A MERINGUE TOPPING – CRISP AND GOLDEN ON THE OUTSIDE AND SOFT AND "MARSHMALLOWY" UNDERNEATH.

SERVES SIX TO EIGHT

INGREDIENTS

For the pastry
- 175g/6oz/1½ cups plain flour
- 15ml/1 tbsp icing sugar
- 75g/3oz/6 tbsp butter
- 1 egg yolk
- finely grated rind of ½ orange
- 15ml/1 tbsp orange juice

For the filling
- 30ml/2 tbsp ground coffee
- 350ml/12fl oz/1½ cups milk
- 25g/1oz/4 tbsp cornflour
- 130g/4½ oz/½ cup caster sugar
- 4 egg yolks
- 15g/½ oz/1 tbsp butter

For the meringue
- 3 egg whites
- 1.5ml/¼ tsp cream of tartar
- 150g/5oz/¾ cup caster sugar
- 25g/1oz/¼ cup skinned hazelnuts
- 15ml/1 tbsp demerara sugar

1 Preheat the oven to 200°C/400°F/Gas 6. Sift the flour and icing sugar into a bowl. Rub in the butter until the mixture resembles breadcrumbs. Add the egg yolk, orange rind and juice and mix to a firm dough. Wrap in clear film and chill for 20 minutes. Roll out and use to line a 23cm/9in loose-based fluted flan tin. Cover with clear film and chill for 30 minutes.

COOK'S TIP

The pastry case can be made up to 36 hours in advance, but once filled and baked the pie should be eaten on the day of making.

2 Prick the pastry all over, line with greaseproof paper and baking beans and bake for 15 minutes, removing the paper and beans for the last 5 minutes. Turn the oven to 160°C/325°F/Gas 3.

3 To make the filling, put the coffee in a bowl. Heat 250ml/8fl oz/1 cup of the milk until near-boiling and pour over the coffee. Leave to infuse for 4 minutes, then strain. Blend the cornflour and sugar with the remaining milk in a pan and whisk in the coffee-flavoured milk.

4 Bring the mixture to the boil, stirring until thickened. Remove from the heat.

5 Beat the egg yolks. Stir in a little of the hot coffee mixture into the egg yolks, then add to the remaining coffee mixture with the butter. Cook the filling over a low heat for 3–4 minutes, until very thick. Pour into the pastry case.

6 To make the meringue, whisk the egg whites and cream of tartar until stiff. Whisk in the caster sugar a spoonful at a time.

7 Spoon the meringue over the filling and spread right to the edge of the pastry, swirling into peaks. Sprinkle with hazelnuts and demerara sugar and bake for 30–35 minutes, or until golden brown and crisp. Serve warm, or cool on a wire rack and serve cold.

COFFEE CUSTARD TART

A CRISP WALNUT PASTRY CASE, FLAVOURED WITH VANILLA, IS FILLED WITH A SMOOTH CREAMY COFFEE CUSTARD, BAKED UNTIL LIGHTLY SET AND TOPPED WITH CREAM.

SERVES SIX TO EIGHT

INGREDIENTS
- 1 vanilla pod
- 30ml/2 tbsp ground coffee
- 300ml/½ pint/1¼ cups single cream
- 150ml/¼ pint/⅔ cup milk
- 2 eggs, plus 2 egg yolks
- 50g/2oz/¼ cup caster sugar
- icing sugar, for dusting
- lightly whipped double cream, to serve

For the pastry
- 175g/6oz/1½ cups plain flour
- 30ml/2 tbsp icing sugar
- 115g/4oz/8 tbsp butter, cubed
- 75g/3oz/½ cup walnuts, finely chopped
- 1 egg yolk
- 5ml/1 tsp vanilla extract
- 10ml/2 tsp iced water

1 Preheat the oven to 200°C/400°F/Gas 6. Put a baking sheet in the oven. Sift the flour and sugar into a bowl. Rub in the butter until the mixture resembles breadcrumbs. Stir in the walnuts. Mix together the egg yolk, vanilla and water. Add to the dry ingredients and mix to a dough. Wrap in clear film and chill for 20 minutes.

2 Roll out the dough and use to line a deep plain or fluted 20cm/8in flan ring, using a knife to smooth the edges. Chill again for 20 minutes. Prick the base with a fork. Fill with greaseproof paper and baking beans and bake on the hot baking sheet for 10 minutes. Remove the paper and beans and bake for a further 10 minutes. Turn the oven to 150°C/300°F/Gas 2.

3 Meanwhile, split the vanilla pod and scrape out the seeds. Put both in a pan with the coffee, cream and milk. Heat until near-boiling point, cover and infuse for 10 minutes. Whisk the eggs, egg yolks and caster sugar together.

4 Bring the cream back to boiling point and pour on to the egg mixture, stirring. Strain into the pastry case.

5 Bake the tart for 40–45 minutes or until lightly set. Take out of the oven and leave on a wire rack to cool. Remove the tart from the tin, pipe cream rosettes around the edge and dust with icing sugar to serve.

BLUEBERRY FRANGIPANE FLAN

A TANGY LEMON PASTRY CASE IS FILLED WITH A SWEET ALMOND FILLING DOTTED WITH RIPE BLUEBERRIES. THE JAM AND LIQUEUR GLAZE ADDS AN INDULGENT FINISH.

SERVES SIX

INGREDIENTS

- 30ml/2 tbsp ground coffee
- 45ml/3 tbsp near-boiling milk
- 50g/2oz/4 tbsp unsalted butter
- 50g/2oz/¼ cup caster sugar
- 1 egg
- 115g/4oz/1 cup ground almonds
- 15ml/1 tbsp plain flour, sifted
- 225g/8oz/2 cups blueberries
- 30ml/2 tbsp seedless blackberry jam
- 15ml/1 tbsp liqueur, such as Amaretto or Cointreau
- mascarpone, crème fraîche or soured cream, to serve

For the pastry

- 175g/6oz/1½ cups plain flour
- 115g/4oz/8 tbsp unsalted butter
- 25g/1oz/2 tbsp caster sugar
- finely grated rind of ½ lemon
- 15ml/1 tbsp chilled water

1 Preheat the oven to 190°C/375°F/Gas 5. Sift the flour into a bowl and rub in the butter. Stir in the sugar and lemon rind, then add the water and mix to a firm dough. Wrap in clear film and chill for 20 minutes.

2 Roll out the pastry on a lightly floured surface and use to line a 23cm/9in loose-based flan tin. Line the pastry with greaseproof paper and baking beans and bake for 10 minutes. Remove the paper and beans and bake for a further 10 minutes. Remove from the oven.

3 Meanwhile, to make the filling, put the coffee in a bowl. Pour the milk over and leave to infuse for 4 minutes. Cream the butter and sugar until pale. Beat in the egg, then add the almonds and flour. Strain in the coffee through a fine sieve and fold in.

COOK'S TIP

This flan can also be made in individual tartlets. Use six 10cm/4in tartlet tins and bake for 25 minutes.

4 Spoon the coffee mixture into the pastry case and spread evenly. Scatter the blueberries over the top and push them down slightly into the mixture. Bake for 30 minutes, until firm, covering with foil after 20 minutes.

5 Remove from the oven and allow to cool slightly. Heat the jam and liqueur in a small pan until melted. Brush over the flan and remove from the tin. Serve warm with a scoop of mascarpone or with crème fraîche or soured cream.

TIA MARIA TRUFFLE TARTS

THE IDEAL DESSERT FOR A TEA OR COFFEE BREAK, THESE MINI COFFEE PASTRY CASES ARE FILLED WITH A CHOCOLATE LIQUEUR TRUFFLE CENTRE AND TOPPED WITH FRESH RIPE BERRIES.

SERVES SIX

INGREDIENTS

- 300ml/½ pint/1¼ cups double cream
- 225g/8oz/generous ¾ cup seedless bramble or raspberry jam
- 150g/5oz plain chocolate, broken into squares
- 45ml/3 tbsp Tia Maria liqueur
- 450g/1lb mixed berries, such as raspberries, small strawberries or blackberries

For the pastry

- 225g/8oz/2 cups plain flour
- 15ml/1 tbsp caster sugar
- 150g/5oz/10 tbsp butter, cubed
- 1 egg yolk
- 30ml/2 tbsp very strong brewed coffee, chilled

1 Preheat the oven to 200°C/400°F/Gas 6. Put a baking sheet in the oven to heat. To make the pastry, sift the flour and sugar into a large bowl. Rub in the butter. Stir the egg yolk and coffee together, add to the bowl and mix to a stiff dough. Knead lightly on a floured surface for a few seconds until smooth. Wrap in clear film and chill for about 20 minutes.

2 Use the pastry to line six 10cm/4in fluted tartlet tins. Prick the bases with a fork and line with greaseproof paper and baking beans. Put on the hot baking sheet and bake for 10 minutes. Remove paper and beans and bake for 8–10 minutes longer, until cooked. Cool on a wire rack.

3 To make the filling, slowly bring the cream and 175g/6oz/generous ½ cup of the jam to the boil, stirring continuously until dissolved.

COOK'S TIP

When making the pastry, blend the egg yolk and coffee together until well mixed to ensure an evenly coloured pastry.

4 Remove from the heat, add the chocolate and 30ml/2 tbsp of the liqueur. Stir until melted. Cool, then spoon into the pastry cases, and smooth the tops. Chill for 40 minutes.

5 Heat the remaining jam and liqueur until smooth. Arrange the fruit on top of the tarts, then brush the jam glaze over it. Chill until ready to serve.

Coffee Cream Profiteroles

Crisp-textured coffee choux pastry puffs are filled with cream and drizzled with a white chocolate sauce. For those with a sweet tooth, there is plenty of extra sauce.

SERVES SIX

INGREDIENTS
- 65g/2½oz/9 tbsp plain white flour
- pinch of salt
- 50g/2oz/4 tbsp butter
- 150ml/¼ pint/⅔ cup brewed coffee
- 2 eggs, lightly beaten

For the white chocolate sauce
- 50g/2oz/¼ cup sugar
- 100ml/3½fl oz/scant ½ cup water
- 150g/5oz good quality white dessert chocolate, broken into pieces
- 25g/1oz/2 tbsp unsalted butter
- 45ml/3 tbsp double cream
- 30ml/2 tbsp coffee liqueur, such as Tia Maria, Kahlúa or Toussaint

To assemble
- 250ml/8fl oz/1 cup double cream

1 Preheat the oven to 220°C/425°F/ Gas 7. Sift the flour and salt on to a piece of greaseproof paper. Cut the butter into pieces and put in a pan with the coffee.

2 Bring to a rolling boil, then remove from the heat and tip in all the flour. Beat until the mixture leaves the sides of the pan. Leave to cool for 2 minutes.

3 Gradually add the eggs, beating well between each addition. Spoon the mixture into a piping bag fitted with a 1cm/½in plain nozzle.

4 Pipe about 24 small buns on to a dampened baking sheet. Bake for 20 minutes, until well risen and crisp.

5 Remove the buns from the oven and pierce the side of each with a sharp knife to let out the steam.

6 To make the sauce, put the sugar and water in a heavy-based pan and heat gently until dissolved. Bring to the boil and simmer for 3 minutes. Remove from the heat. Add the chocolate and butter, stirring until smooth. Stir in the cream and liqueur.

7 To assemble, whip the cream until soft peaks form. Using a piping bag, fill the choux buns through the slits in the sides. Arrange on plates and pour a little of the sauce over, either warm or at room temperature. Serve the remaining sauce separately.

DANISH COFFEE PASTRIES

THESE WORLD FAMOUS CRISP PASTRIES ARE TIME-CONSUMING TO MAKE, BUT WELL WORTH THE EFFORT.

MAKES SIXTEEN

INGREDIENTS

- 45ml/3 tbsp near-boiling water
- 30ml/2 tbsp ground coffee
- 115g/4oz/generous ½ cup caster sugar
- 40g/1½ oz/3 tbsp unsalted butter
- 1 egg yolk
- 115g/4oz/1 cup ground almonds
- beaten egg, to glaze
- 275g/10oz/1 cup apricot jam
- 30ml/2 tbsp water
- 175g/6oz/1½ cups icing sugar
- 50g/2oz/½ cup flaked almonds, toasted
- 50g/2oz/¼ cup glacé cherries

For the pastry

- 275g/10oz/2½ cups plain flour
- 1.5ml/¼ tsp salt
- 15g/½oz/1 tbsp caster sugar
- 225g/8oz/1 cup butter, softened
- 10ml/2 tsp easy-blend dried yeast
- 1 egg, beaten
- 100ml/3½fl oz/scant ½ cup cold water

1 Sift the flour, salt and sugar into a bowl. Rub in 25g/1oz/2 tbsp butter. Stir in the yeast. Stir the egg and water, add to the bowl and mix to a soft dough. Lightly knead for 4–5 minutes. Put in a plastic bag and chill for 15 minutes.

2 Put the remaining butter between 2 sheets of greaseproof paper and beat with a rolling pin to make a 18cm/7in square. Roll out the dough to about 25cm/10in square. Put the butter in the middle, like a diamond, then bring up each corner of dough to fully enclose it.

3 Roll out the pastry to about 35cm/14in long. Turn up the bottom third of the pastry, then fold down the top third. Seal the edges together with a rolling pin. Return the pastry to the plastic bag and chill for 15 minutes.

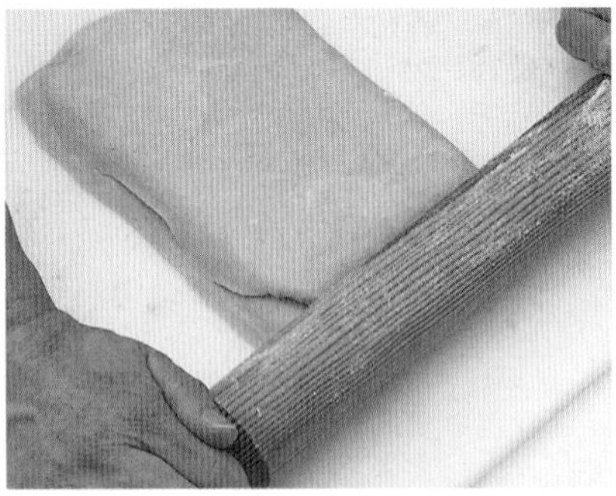

4 Repeat the rolling and folding three more times, each time turning the pastry so that the short ends are at the top and bottom. Allow a 15 minute rest between each turn.

5 To make the filling, pour the hot water over the coffee and infuse for 4 minutes. Strain through a fine sieve. Cream the sugar and butter together. Beat in the egg yolk, ground almonds and 15ml/1 tbsp of the coffee.

6 Divide the dough and filling equally into three. Roll one dough portion to an 18 x 35cm/7 x 14in rectangle. Spread with filling and roll up from a short end. Cut into six equal slices. Roll another portion into a 25cm/10in square; cut into a 25cm/10in round, remove the trimmings and cut into six segments.

7 Put a spoonful of filling at the widest end of each triangle, then roll up towards the point into a crescent.

8 Roll out the remaining dough into a 20cm/8in square; cut into four. Put some filling into the centre of each. Make cuts from each corner almost to the centre and fold four alternate points to the centre.

9 Preheat the oven to 220°C/425°F/Gas 7. Put the pastries on greased baking sheets, spaced apart. Cover loosely with oiled clear film and leave to rise for 20 minutes, until almost doubled in size. Brush with beaten egg and bake for 15–20 minutes, until lightly browned and crisp. Cool on wire racks.

10 Put the jam in a pan with the water; bring to the boil, then sieve. Brush the jam over the warm pastries. Mix the icing sugar with the remaining coffee, adding more water if necessary to make a thick icing. Drizzle the icing over some of the pastries and decorate some with flaked almonds or chopped glacé cherries. Leave to set before serving.

Greek Fruit and Nut Pastries

Aromatic sweet pastry crescents, known as "Moshopoungia" in Greece, are packed with candied citrus peel and walnuts, soaked in a coffee syrup.

MAKES SIXTEEN

INGREDIENTS

- 60ml/4 tbsp clear honey
- 60ml/4 tbsp strong brewed coffee
- 75g/3oz/½ cup mixed candied citrus peel, finely chopped
- 175g/6oz/1 cup walnuts, chopped
- 1.5ml/¼ tsp freshly grated nutmeg
- milk, to glaze
- caster sugar, for sprinkling

For the pastry

- 450g/1lb/4 cups plain flour
- 2.5ml/½ tsp ground cinnamon
- 2.5ml/½ tsp baking powder
- pinch of salt
- 150g/5oz/10 tbsp unsalted butter
- 30ml/2 tbsp caster sugar
- 1 egg
- 120ml/4fl oz/½ cup chilled milk

1 Preheat the oven to 180°C/350°F/Gas 4. To make the pastry, sift the flour, ground cinnamon, baking powder and salt into a bowl. Rub in the butter until the mixture resembles fine breadcrumbs. Stir in the sugar. Make a well in the middle.

2 Beat the egg and milk together and add to the well in the dry ingredients. Mix to a soft dough. Divide the dough into two and wrap each in clear film. Chill in the fridge for 30 minutes.

3 Meanwhile, to make the filling, mix the honey and coffee. Add the peel, walnuts and nutmeg. Stir well, cover and leave to soak for at least 20 minutes.

4 Roll out a portion of dough on a lightly floured surface until about 3mm/⅛in thick. Stamp out rounds using a 10cm/4in round cutter.

5 Place a heaped teaspoonful of filling on one side of each round. Brush the edges with a little milk, then fold over and press the edges together to seal. Repeat with remaining pastry until all the filling is used.

6 Put the pastries on lightly greased baking sheets, brush with milk and sprinkle with caster sugar.

7 Make a steam hole in each with a skewer. Bake for 35 minutes, or until lightly browned. Cool on a wire rack.

BAKLAVA

TURKISH COFFEE IS BLACK, THICK, VERY SWEET AND OFTEN SPICED. HERE IT IS USED IN THIS FAMOUS PASTRY CONFECTION, TRADITIONALLY SERVED ON RELIGIOUS FESTIVAL DAYS IN TURKEY.

MAKES SIXTEEN

INGREDIENTS
- 50g/2oz/½ cup blanched almonds, chopped
- 50g/2oz/½ cup pistachio nuts, chopped
- 75g/3oz/scant ½ cup caster sugar
- 115g/4oz filo pastry
- 75g/3oz/6 tbsp unsalted butter, melted and cooled

For the syrup
- 115g/4oz/generous ½ cup caster sugar
- 7.5cm/3in piece cinnamon stick
- 1 whole clove
- 2 cardamom pods, crushed
- 75ml/5 tbsp strong brewed coffee

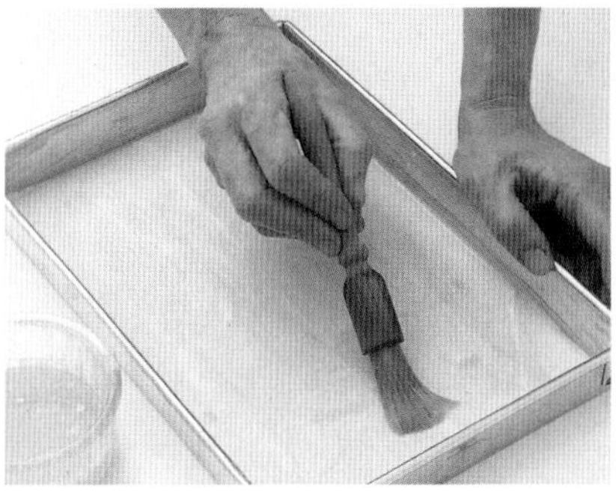

1 Preheat the oven to 180°C/350°F/Gas 4. Mix the nuts and sugar together. Cut the pastry to fit a tin measuring 18 x 28cm/7 x 11in. Brush the tin with a little butter. Lay a sheet of pastry in the tin and brush with melted butter.

2 Repeat with three more sheets and spread with half the nut mixture.

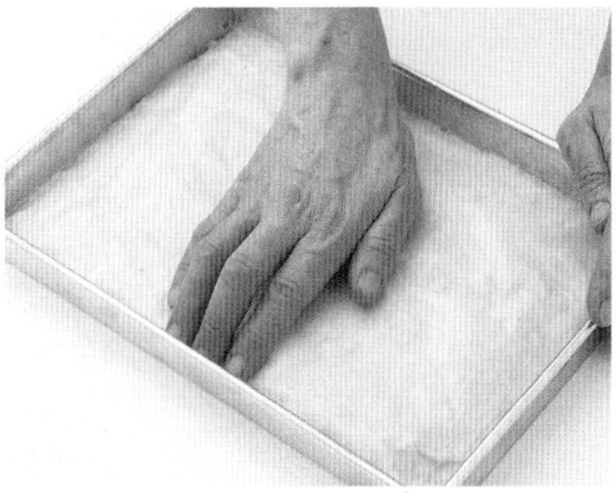

3 Layer up three more sheets of pastry, lightly brushing butter between the layers, then spread the remaining nut mixture over them, smoothing it over the entire surface. Top with the remaining pastry and butter. Gently press down the edges to seal.

4 With a sharp knife, mark the top into diamonds. Bake for 20–25 minutes until golden brown and crisp. Meanwhile, put the syrup ingredients in a small pan and heat gently until the sugar has dissolved. Cover with a lid and leave to infuse for 20 minutes.

5 Remove the baklava from the oven. Re-heat the syrup and strain over the pastry. Leave to cool in the tin. Cut into diamonds, remove from the tin and serve.

COOK'S TIP

While assembling the baklava, keep the pile of filo pastry covered with a damp cloth to stop it drying out and becoming brittle, which makes it difficult to use.

Sweets, Biscuits and Breads

Few people can resist the tantalizing display of biscuits and breads in the baker's shop window, but it's easy to recreate those delectable bakes at home. Here, you'll find a selection of traditional and Continental recipes from rich and gooey truffles to a stunning candied fruit plait.

STUFFED PRUNES

CHOCOLATE-COVERED PRUNES, SOAKED IN LIQUEUR, HIDE A MELT-IN-THE-MOUTH COFFEE FILLING.

MAKES APPROXIMATELY THIRTY

INGREDIENTS
- 225g/8oz/1 cup unstoned prunes
- 50ml/2fl oz/¼ cup Armagnac
- 30ml/2 tbsp ground coffee
- 150ml/¼ pint/⅔ cup double cream
- 350g/12oz plain chocolate, broken into squares
- 10g/¼oz/½ tbsp vegetable fat
- 30ml/2 tbsp cocoa powder, for dusting

1 Put the unstoned prunes in a bowl and pour the Armagnac over. Stir, then cover with clear film and set aside for 2 hours, or until the prunes have absorbed the liquid.

COOK'S TIP
Fresh dates can be used instead of prunes, if preferred.

2 Make a slit along each prune to remove the stone, making a hollow for the filling, but leaving the fruit intact.

3 Put the coffee and cream in a pan and heat almost to boiling point. Cover, infuse for 4 minutes, then heat again until almost boiling. Put 115g/4oz of the chocolate into a bowl and pour over the coffee cream through a sieve.

4 Stir until the chocolate has melted and the mixture is smooth. Leave to cool, until it has the consistency of softened butter.

5 Fill a piping bag with a small plain nozzle with the chocolate mixture. Pipe into the cavities of the prunes. Chill in the fridge for 20 minutes.

6 Melt the remaining chocolate in a bowl over a pan of hot water. Using a fork, dip the prunes one at a time into the chocolate to give them a generous coating. Place on non-stick baking parchment to harden. Dust each with a little cocoa powder.

COFFEE CHOCOLATE TRUFFLES

BECAUSE THESE CLASSIC CHOCOLATES CONTAIN FRESH CREAM, THEY SHOULD BE STORED IN THE FRIDGE AND EATEN WITHIN A FEW DAYS.

MAKES TWENTY-FOUR

INGREDIENTS
- 350g/12oz plain chocolate
- 75ml/5 tbsp double cream
- 30ml/2 tbsp coffee liqueur, such as Tia Maria, Kahlúa or Toussaint
- 115g/4oz good quality white dessert chocolate
- 115g/4oz good quality milk dessert chocolate

1 Melt 225g/8oz of the plain chocolate in a bowl over a pan of barely simmering water. Stir in the cream and liqueur, then chill the mixture in the fridge for 4 hours, until firm.

2 Divide the mixture into 24 equal pieces and quickly roll each into a ball. Chill for one more hour, or until they are firm again.

3 Melt the remaining plain, white and milk chocolate in separate small bowls. Using two forks, carefully dip eight of the truffles, one at a time, into the melted milk chocolate.

4 Repeat with the white and plain chocolate. Place the truffles on a board, covered with wax paper or foil. Leave to set before removing and placing in a serving bowl or individual paper cases.

VARIATIONS

Ring the changes by adding one of the following to the truffle mixture:

Ginger – Stir in 40g/1½oz/¼ cup finely chopped crystallized ginger.

Candied fruit – Stir in 50g/2oz/⅓ cup finely chopped candied fruit, such as pineapple and orange.

Pistachio – Stir in 25g/1oz/¼ cup, chopped skinned pistachio nuts.

Hazelnut – Roll each ball of chilled truffle mixture around a whole skinned hazelnut.

Raisin – Soak 40g/1½oz/generous ¼ cup raisins overnight in 15ml/1 tbsp coffee liqueur, such as Tia Maria or Kahlúa and stir into the truffle mixture.

CHOCOLATE AND COFFEE MINT THINS

THESE COFFEE-FLAVOURED CHOCOLATE SQUARES CONTAIN PIECES OF CRISP MINTY CARAMEL AND ARE IDEAL FOR SERVING WITH AFTER-DINNER COFFEE.

MAKES SIXTEEN

INGREDIENTS
- 75g/3oz/scant ½ cup sugar
- 75ml/5 tbsp water
- 3 drops oil of peppermint
- 15ml/1 tbsp strong-flavoured ground coffee
- 75ml/5 tbsp near-boiling double cream
- 225g/8oz plain chocolate
- 10g/¼oz/½ tbsp unsalted butter

COOK'S TIP
Don't put the chocolate in the fridge to set, or it may lose its glossy appearance and become too brittle to cut easily into neat squares.

1 Line a 18cm/7in square tin with non-stick baking parchment. Gently heat the sugar and water in a heavy-based pan until dissolved. Add the peppermint, and boil until a light caramel colour.

2 Pour the caramel on to an oiled baking sheet and leave to harden, then crush into small pieces.

3 Put the coffee in a small bowl and pour the hot cream over. Leave to infuse for about 4 minutes, then strain through a fine sieve. Melt the chocolate and unsalted butter in a bowl over barely simmering water. Remove from the heat and beat in the hot coffee cream. Stir in the mint caramel.

4 Pour the mixture into the prepared tin and smooth the surface level. Leave in a cool place to set for at least 4 hours, preferably overnight.

5 Carefully turn out the chocolate on to a board and peel off the lining paper. Cut the chocolate into squares with a sharp knife and store in an airtight container until needed.

COFFEE AND HAZELNUT MACAROONS

MACAROONS ARE TRADITIONALLY MADE WITH GROUND ALMONDS. THIS RECIPE USES HAZELNUTS, WHICH ARE LIGHTLY ROASTED BEFORE GRINDING, BUT YOU CAN USE WALNUTS INSTEAD, IF PREFERRED.

MAKES TWENTY

INGREDIENTS
- edible rice paper
- 115g/4oz/⅔ cup skinned hazelnuts
- 225g/8oz/generous 1 cup caster sugar
- 15ml/1 tbsp ground rice
- 10ml/2 tsp ground coffee, e.g. hazelnut-flavoured
- 2 egg whites
- caster sugar, for sprinkling

1 Preheat the oven to 180°C/350°F/Gas 4. Line two baking sheets with rice paper. Place the skinned hazelnuts on a baking sheet and cook for 5 minutes. Cool, then place in a food processor and grind until fine.

2 Mix the ground nuts with the sugar, ground rice and coffee. Stir in the egg whites to make a fairly stiff paste.

3 Spoon into a piping bag fitted with a 1cm/½in plain nozzle. Pipe rounds on the rice paper, leaving room to spread.

4 Sprinkle each macaroon with a little caster sugar then bake for 20 minutes, or until pale golden in colour. Transfer to a wire rack to cool. Remove excess rice paper when completely cold. Serve immediately or store in an airtight tin for up to 2–3 days.

VIENNESE WHIRLS

THESE CRISP, MELT-IN-THE-MOUTH PIPED BISCUITS ARE FILLED WITH A CREAMY COFFEE BUTTERCREAM.

MAKES TWENTY

INGREDIENTS
- 175g/6oz/12 tbsp butter
- 50g/2oz/½ cup icing sugar
- 2.5ml/½ tsp vanilla essence
- 115g/4oz/1 cup plain flour
- 50g/2oz/½ cup cornflour
- icing sugar and cocoa powder, to dust

For the filling
- 15ml/1 tbsp ground coffee
- 60ml/4 tbsp single cream
- 75g/3oz/6 tbsp butter, softened
- 115g/4oz/1 cup icing sugar, sifted

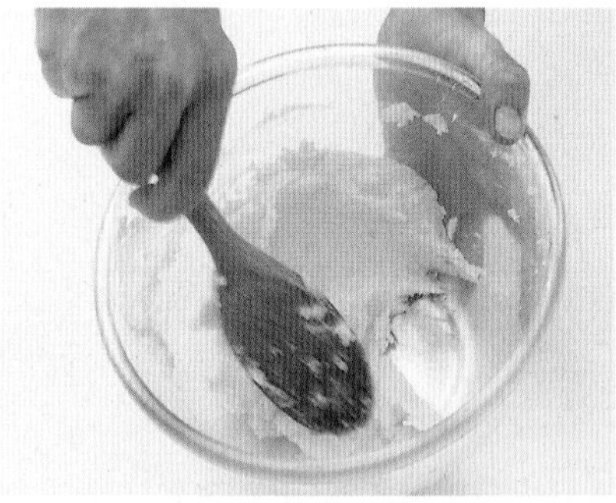

1 Preheat the oven to 180°C/350°F/Gas 4. Cream together the butter, icing sugar and vanilla essence until light. Sift in the flour and cornflour and mix in until smooth.

2 Using two tablespoons, spoon the mixture into a piping bag fitted with a 1cm/½in fluted nozzle.

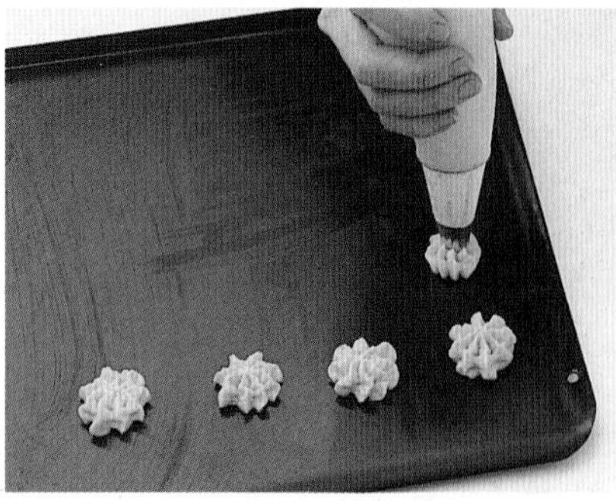

3 Pipe small rosettes well apart on greased baking sheets. Bake in the oven for 12–15 minutes until golden. Transfer to a wire rack to cool.

4 To make the filling, put the coffee in a bowl. Heat the cream to near-boiling and pour it over. Infuse for 4 minutes, then strain through a fine sieve.

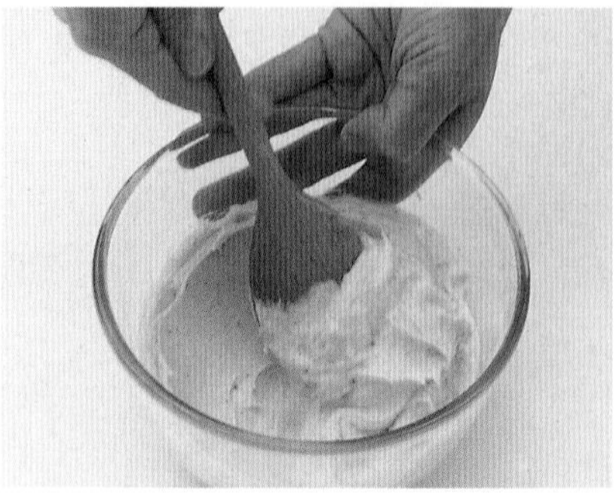

5 Beat the butter, icing sugar and coffee-flavoured cream until light. Use to sandwich the biscuits in pairs. Dust with icing sugar and cocoa powder.

VARIATION

For mocha Viennese whirls, substitute 25g/1oz/¼ cup cocoa powder for 25g/1oz/¼ cup of the flour.

BLACK RUSSIAN COOKIES

THE INGREDIENTS OF THE FAMOUS COCKTAIL – COFFEE AND VODKA – FLAVOUR THESE FABULOUS COOKIES.

MAKES SIXTEEN

INGREDIENTS
- 30ml/2 tbsp ground espresso or other strong-flavoured coffee
- 60ml/4 tbsp near-boiling milk
- 115g/4oz/8 tbsp butter
- 115g/4oz/½ cup soft light brown sugar
- 1 egg
- 225g/8oz/2 cups plain flour
- 5ml/1 tsp baking powder
- pinch of salt

For the icing
- 115g/4oz/1 cup icing sugar
- about 25ml/1½ tbsp vodka

1 Preheat the oven to 180°C/350°F/Gas 4. Put the coffee in a small bowl and pour the hot milk over. Leave to infuse for 4 minutes, then strain through a fine sieve and leave to cool.

2 Cream the butter and sugar together until light and fluffy. Gradually beat in the egg. Sift the flour, baking powder and salt together and fold in with the coffee-flavoured milk to make a fairly stiff mixture.

3 Place dessertspoonfuls of the mixture on greased baking sheets, spacing them slightly apart to allow room for a little spreading. Bake the cookies for about 15 minutes, until lightly browned. Cool on a wire rack.

4 To make the icing, mix the icing sugar and enough vodka together to make a thick icing. Spoon into a small greaseproof paper piping bag.

5 Snip off the end of the piping bag and lightly drizzle the icing over the top of each cookie. Allow the icing to set before serving.

COFFEE AND MACADEMIA MUFFINS

THESE MUFFINS ARE DELICIOUS EATEN COLD, BUT ARE BEST SERVED STILL WARM FROM THE OVEN.

MAKES TWELVE

INGREDIENTS
- 25ml/1½ tbsp ground coffee
- 250ml/8fl oz/1 cup milk
- 50g/2oz/4 tbsp butter
- 275g/10oz/2½ cups plain flour
- 10ml/2 tsp baking powder
- 150g/5oz/10 tbsp light muscovado sugar
- 75g/3oz/½ cup macadamia nuts
- 1 egg, lightly beaten

1 Preheat the oven to 200°C/400°F/ Gas 6. Lightly grease a 12-hole muffin or a deep-bun tray with oil. Alternatively, line with paper muffin cases.

2 Put the coffee in a jug or bowl. Heat the milk to near-boiling and pour it over. Leave to infuse for 4 minutes, then strain through a sieve.

3 Add the butter to the coffee-flavoured milk mixture and stir until melted. Leave until cold.

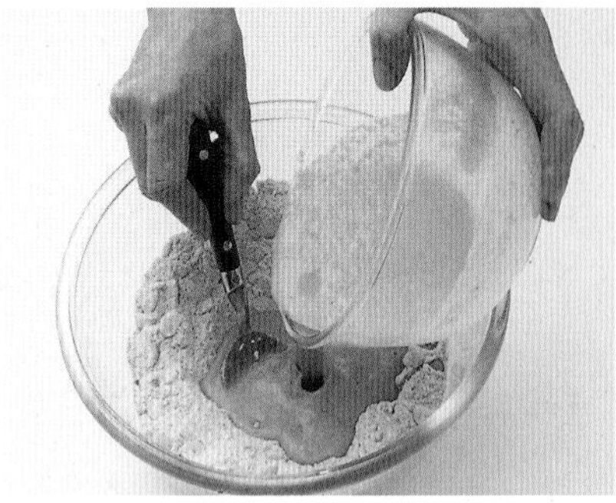

4 Sift the flour and baking powder into a large mixing bowl. Stir in the sugar and macadamia nuts. Add the egg to the coffee-flavoured milk mixture, pour into the dry ingredients and stir until just combined – do not over-mix.

5 Divide the coffee mixture between the prepared muffin tins and bake for about 15 minutes until well risen and firm. Transfer to a wire rack and serve warm or cold.

COOK'S TIP

To cool the coffee-flavoured milk quickly, place the jug in a large bowl of iced or cold water.

CHUNKY WHITE CHOCOLATE AND COFFEE BROWNIES

BROWNIES SHOULD HAVE A GOOEY TEXTURE, SO TAKE CARE NOT TO OVERCOOK THEM – WHEN READY, THE MIXTURE WILL STILL BE SLIGHTLY SOFT UNDER THE CRUST, BUT WILL FIRM AS IT COOLS.

MAKES TWELVE

INGREDIENTS
- 25ml/1½ tbsp ground coffee
- 45ml/3 tbsp near-boiling water
- 300g/11oz plain chocolate, broken into pieces
- 225g/8oz/1 cup butter
- 225g/8oz/1 cup caster sugar
- 3 eggs
- 75g/3oz/⅔ cup self-raising flour, sifted
- 225g/8oz white chocolate, chopped

1 Preheat the oven to 190°C/375°F/ Gas 5. Grease and line the base of a 18 x 28cm/7 x 11in tin with greaseproof paper. Put the coffee in a bowl and pour the water over. Leave to infuse for 4 minutes, then strain through a sieve.

2 Put the plain chocolate and butter in a bowl over a pan of hot water and stir occasionally until melted. Remove from the heat and cool for 5 minutes.

3 Mix the sugar and eggs together. Stir in the chocolate and butter mixture and the coffee. Stir in the sifted flour.

4 Fold in the white chocolate pieces. Pour into the prepared tin.

5 Bake for 45–50 minutes, or until firm and the top is crusty. Leave to cool in the tin. When completely cold, cut into squares and remove from the tin.

PECAN TOFFEE SHORTBREAD

COFFEE SHORTBREAD IS TOPPED WITH PECAN-STUDDED TOFFEE. CORNFLOUR GIVES IT A CRUMBLY LIGHT TEXTURE, BUT ALL PLAIN FLOUR CAN BE USED IF YOU LIKE.

MAKES TWENTY

INGREDIENTS
- 15ml/1 tbsp ground coffee
- 15ml/1 tbsp near-boiling water
- 115g/4oz/8 tbsp butter, softened
- 30ml/2 tbsp smooth peanut butter
- 75g/3oz/scant ½ cup caster sugar
- 75g/3oz/⅔ cup cornflour
- 185g/6½oz/1⅔ cups plain flour

For the topping
- 175g/6oz/12 tbsp butter
- 175g/6oz/¾ cup soft light brown sugar
- 30ml/2 tbsp golden syrup
- 175g/6oz/1 cup shelled pecan nuts, roughly chopped

1 Preheat the oven to 180°C/350°F/Gas 4. Lightly grease and line the base of a 18 x 28cm/7 x 11in tin with greaseproof paper.

2 Put the ground coffee in a small bowl and pour the hot water over. Leave to infuse for 4 minutes, then strain through a fine sieve.

3 Cream the butter, peanut butter, sugar and coffee together until light. Sift the cornflour and flour together and mix in to make a smooth dough.

4 Press into the base of the tin and prick all over with a fork. Bake for 20 minutes. To make the topping, put the butter, sugar and syrup in a pan and heat until melted. Bring to the boil.

5 Allow to simmer for 5 minutes, then stir in the chopped nuts. Spread the topping over the base. Leave in the tin until cold, then cut into fingers. Remove from the tin and serve.

COFFEE BISCOTTI

THESE CRISP BISCUITS ARE MADE TWICE AS DELICIOUS WITH BOTH FRESHLY ROASTED GROUND COFFEE BEANS AND STRONG AROMATIC BREWED COFFEE IN THE MIXTURE.

MAKES ABOUT THIRTY

INGREDIENTS
- 25g/1oz/⅓ cup espresso-roasted coffee beans
- 115g/4oz/⅔ cup blanched almonds
- 200g/7oz/scant 2 cups plain flour
- 7.5ml/1½ tsp baking powder
- 1.5ml/¼ tsp salt
- 75g/3oz/6 tbsp unsalted butter, cubed
- 150g/5oz/¾ cup caster sugar
- 2 eggs, beaten
- 25–30ml/1½–2 tbsp strong brewed coffee
- 5ml/1 tsp ground cinnamon, for dusting

1 Preheat the oven to 180°C/350°F/Gas 4. Put the espresso coffee beans in a single layer on one side of a large baking sheet and the almonds on the other. Roast in the oven for 10 minutes. Leave to cool.

2 Put the coffee beans in a blender or food processor and process until fairly fine. Tip out and set aside. Process the almonds until finely ground.

3 Sift the flour, baking powder and salt into a bowl. Rub in the butter until the mixture resembles fine breadcrumbs. Stir in the caster sugar, ground coffee and almonds. Add the beaten eggs and enough brewed coffee to make a fairly firm dough.

COOK'S TIP
Store the biscotti in an airtight tin for at least a day before serving.

4 Lightly knead for a few seconds until smooth and shape into two rolls about 7.5cm/3in in diameter. Place on a greased baking sheet and dust with cinnamon. Bake for 20 minutes.

5 Using a sharp knife, cut the rolls into 4cm/1½in slices on the diagonal. Arrange the slices on the baking tray and bake for a further 10 minutes, or until lightly browned. Cool on a rack.

Cappuccino Panettone

This light bread is served in Italy as part of their Christmas fare. It's traditionally a tall loaf with a dome on the top, formed by the rich yeasted dough as it rises.

SERVES EIGHT

INGREDIENTS

- 450g/1lb/4 cups strong plain flour
- 2.5ml/½ tsp salt
- 75g/3oz/scant ½ cup caster sugar
- 7g/¼oz sachet easy-blend dried yeast
- 115g/4oz/8 tbsp butter
- 100ml/3½fl oz/scant ½ cup very hot strong brewed espresso coffee
- 100ml/3½fl oz/½ cup milk
- 4 egg yolks
- 115g/4oz/⅔ cup plain chocolate chips
- beaten egg, to glaze

1 Preheat the oven to 190°C/375°F/Gas 5. Lightly grease and line a deep 14–15cm/5½–6in cake tin with greaseproof paper. Sift the flour and salt into a large bowl. Stir in the sugar and yeast.

2 Add the butter to the coffee and stir until melted. Stir in the milk, then add to the dry ingredients with the egg yolks. Mix together to make a dough.

COOK'S TIP
Unlike commercial varieties, home-made panettone should be eaten within a day or two of baking.

3 Turn the dough out on to a lightly floured surface and knead for 10 minutes, until smooth and elastic. Knead in the chocolate chips.

4 Shape into a ball, place in the tin and cover with oiled clear film. Leave to rise in a warm place for 1 hour or until the dough reaches the top of the tin. Lightly brush with beaten egg and bake for 35 minutes.

5 Turn down the oven to 180°C/350°F/Gas 4 and cover the panettone with foil if it has browned enough. Cook for a further 10–15 minutes, or until done.

6 Allow the panettone to cool in the tin for 10 minutes, then transfer to a wire rack. Remove the lining paper just before slicing and serving.

Candied Fruit Bread

THE CENTRE OF THIS COFFEE-FLAVOURED YEASTED PLAIT CONTAINS BRIGHTLY COLOURED CANDIED FRUITS, MOISTENED BY SOAKING IN RICH COFFEE LIQUEUR.

SERVES SIX TO EIGHT

INGREDIENTS

- 175g/6oz/1 cup mixed candied fruit, such as pineapple, orange and cherries, chopped
- 60ml/4 tbsp coffee liqueur, such as Tia Maria, Kahlúa or Toussaint
- 30ml/2 tbsp ground coffee
- 100ml/3½fl oz/½ cup near-boiling milk
- 225g/8oz/2 cups strong plain flour
- 1.5ml/¼ tsp salt
- 25g/1oz/2 tbsp soft light brown sugar
- ½ x 7g/¼oz sachet easy-blend dried yeast
- 1 egg, beaten
- 50g/2oz white almond paste, grated
- 65g/2½oz/¼ cup apricot jam
- 15g/½oz/1 tbsp unsalted butter
- 15ml/1 tbsp caster sugar
- 15ml/1 tbsp clear honey

1 Put the candied fruit in a small bowl and spoon the coffee liqueur over. Stir to coat the fruit, then cover with clear film and leave to soak overnight.

2 Preheat the oven to 200°C/400°F/Gas 6. Put the coffee in a bowl; pour the hot milk over and leave until tepid. Strain through a fine sieve. Sift the flour and salt into a bowl. Stir in the brown sugar and yeast. Make a well in the centre, add the coffee-flavoured milk and the egg and mix to a soft dough.

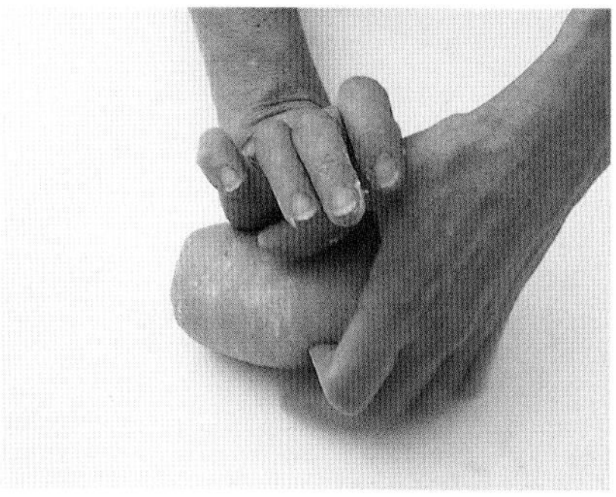

3 Knead for 10 minutes. Put the dough in a clean bowl, cover with clear film and leave to rise for 1 hour.

4 Meanwhile, mix the soaked fruit, almond paste and jam together. Lightly knead the dough again for 1 minute, then roll out to a rectangle 35 x 30cm/14 x 12in.

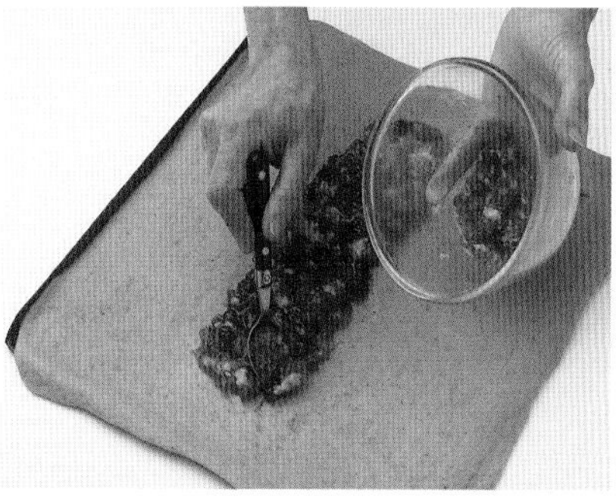

5 Spread the filling in a 7.5cm/3in strip lengthways down the middle to within 5cm/2in of each end. Make 14 diagonal cuts about 2cm/¾in wide in the dough either side of the filling.

6 Fold the ends of the dough up over the filling, overlapping alternate strips, Tuck in the last two strips neatly. Place on a greased baking tray.

7 Cover with clear film and leave to rise for 20 minutes. Melt the butter, sugar and honey in a small pan, then brush over the braid. Bake for 20–25 minutes. Allow to cool before slicing and serving.

USEFUL ADDRESSES

Good coffee is sold in countless places all over the world. The following addresses are intended as a starting point for those in search of quality coffee – either in coffee houses or as freshly roasted beans to brew at home.

UNITED KINGDOM

Coffee suppliers

Algerian Coffee Stores
52 Old Compton Street
London W1V 6PB
Tel: (020) 7437 2480
www.algeriancoffeestores.com

The Drury Tea & Coffee Co. Ltd
46-47 iO Centre
Armstrong Road
London SE18 6AT
Tel: (020) 7740 1100
www.drurycoffee.com

Ferns Coffee
Fern House
4 Onslow Close
Basingstoke RG24 8QL
Tel: (01256) 355 661
www.coffeeisferns.co.uk

Fortnum & Mason
181 Piccadilly
London W1A 1ER
Tel: (020) 7734 8040
www.fortnumandmason.com

Harrods
87–135 Brompton Road
Knightsbridge
London SW1X 7XL
Tel: (020) 7730 1234
www.harrods.com

Harvey Nichols
109–125 Knightsbridge
London SW1X 7RJ
Tel: (020) 7201 8088
www.harveynichols.com

H. R. Higgins
79 Duke Street
London W1K 5AS
Tel: (020) 7629 3913
www.hrhiggins.co.uk

Monmouth Coffee Company
27 Monmouth Street
London WC2H 9EU
Tel: (020) 7232 3010
www.monmouthcoffee.co.uk

Selfridges
400 Oxford Street
London W1A 1AB
Tel: (0800) 123 400
www.selfridges.com

Spinelli Coffee Company
College Road
Brighton, East Sussex BN2 1JB
Tel: (01273) 818 819
www.spinellicoffee.com

Wilkinson's Tea and Coffee Merchants
5 Lobster Lane
Norwich NR2 1DQ
Tel: (01603) 625 121
www.wilkinsonsofnorwich.com

Whittard of Chelsea
Head Office
Windrush House
Windrush Park Road
Witney, Oxfordshire OX29 7DX
Tel: (0800) 015 4395
www.whittard.co.uk

Coffee equipment supplier

Lakeland
Alexandra Buildings
Windermere
Cumbria LA23 1BQ
Tel: (01539) 488 100
www.lakeland.co.uk

Coffee houses and cafés

Aroma
273 Regent Street
London W1 2EZ
Tel: (020) 7495 4911

Bar Italia
22 Frith Street
London W1D 4RF
Tel: (020) 7437 4520
www.baritaliasoho.co.uk

Caffè Nero
43 Frith Street
London W1V 5TE
Tel: (020) 7434 3887
www.caffenero.co.uk

Maison Bertaux
28 Greek Street
London W1D 5DQ
Tel: (020) 7437 6007
www.maisonbertaux.com

Prêt à Manger
143 Fleet Street
London EC4Y 1HY
Tel: (020) 7932 5323
www.pret.com

Coffee museums and organizations

Bramah Tea and Coffee Museum
40 Southwark Street
London SE1 1UN
Tel: (020) 7403 5650
www.teaandcoffeemuseum.co.uk

International Coffee Organization
222 Gray's Inn Road
London WC12 8HB
Tel: (020) 7612 0600
www.ico.org

AUSTRIA

Café Central
Palais Ferstel
Herrengasse and Strauchgasse
Vienna, Austria
Tel: (1) 53 33 76 30
www.cafecentral.wien

Café Museum
Operngasse 71010
Vienna, Austria
Tel: (1) 241 00620
www.cafemuseum.at

Café Sacher
Philharmonikerstrasse 4
1010 Vienna, Austria
Tel: (1) 512 14 87
www.sacher.com

Demel's
Kohlmarkt 14
1010 Vienna, Austria
Tel: (1) 53 51 71 70
www.demel.com

BELGIUM

Cafés Knopes
Grand-Place 24
Arlon, Belgium 6700
Tel: (63) 22 7407
www.knopes.com

Corica
49 rue du Marché aux Poulets
Brussels, Belgium 1000
Tel: (2) 511 88 52
www.corica.be

CZECH REPUBLIC

Café Savoy
Vitezna 124/5, Vitezna 5
Prague, Czech Republic
Tel: 420 731 136 144
www.cafesavoy.ambi.cz

FRANCE

Brûlerie de L'Odéon
6 rue de Crébillon
Paris, France 75006
Tel: (01) 43 26 39 32
www.cafedelodeon.fr

Café Beaubourg
43 rue Saint-Merri
Paris, France, 75004
Tel: (01) 48 87 63 96
www.cafebeaubourg.com

Cafés Estrella
34 rue Saint-Sulpice
Paris, France 75006
Tel: (01) 46 33 16 37

Café de Flore
172 boulevard Saint-Germain
Paris, France 75006
Tel: (01) 45 48 55 26
www.cafedeflore.fr

Café de La Paix
5 Place de l'Opéra
Paris, France 75009
Tel: (01) 40 07 30 20
www.cafedelapaix.fr

Le Café Richelieu
Musée du Louvre

Paris, France 75001
Tel: (01) 47 03 93 31
www.louvre.fr/le-cafe-richelieu-angelina

Couleur Café
60 rue de Sèvres
Paris, France 75007
Tel: (01) 75 42 91 96
www.couleur-cafe.fr

Les Deux Magots
6 Place Saint-Germain des Prés
Paris, France 75006
Tel: (01) 45 48 55 25
www.lesdeuxmagots.fr

La Grande Épicerie de Paris
38 rue de Sèvres
Paris, France 75007
Tel: (01) 44 39 81 00
www.lagrandeepicerie.com

Lapeyronie
9 rue Brantôme
Paris, France 75003
Tel: (01) 40 27 97 57
www.lapeyronie.fr

GERMANY

Café Einstein
Kurfürstendamm 58
Berlin, 108885
Germany
Tel: (30) 2639 190
www.cafeeinstein.com

Alois Dallmayr
Dienerstrasse 14–15
Munich, 80331
Germany
Tel: (89) 21 35 0
www.dallmayr.com

Eilles
Residenzstrasse 22
Munich, Germany 80333
Tel: (89) 22 61 84
www.eilles.de

ITALY

Caffè Florian
Piazza San Marco 56–59
30124 Venice, Italy
Tel: (41) 528 53 38
www.caffeflorian.com

Caffè Concerto Paszkowski
Piazza della Republica 35R
Florence, Italy
Tel: (55) 21 02 36
www.caffepaszkowski.com

Caffè Pedrocchi
Via Otto Febbraio 15
Padua, Italy
Tel: (49) 878 1231
www.caffepedrocchi.it

Caffè Rivoire
Piazza della Signoria 5R
Florence, Italy
Tel: (55) 21 44 12
www.rivoire.it

Caffè San Carlo
Piazza San Carlo 156
Turin, Italy
Tel: (11) 532 586

Caffè degli Specchi
Piazza dell'Unità d'Italia 7
Trieste, Italy
Tel: (40) 661 973
www.caffespecchi.it

Caffè Torino
Piazza San Carlo 204
Turin, Italy
Tel: (11) 547 356
www.caffe-torino.it

La Casa del Caffè Tazza D'Oro
Via degli Orfani 84
Rome, Italy
Tel (6) 6678 97 92
www.tazzadorocoffeeshop.com

Sant'Eustachio Il Caffè
Piazza di Sant'Eustachio 82
Rome, Italy
Tel: (6) 688 02 048

UNITED STATES

Coffee roasters and suppliers

Ancora Coffee Roasters
107 King Street
Madison, WI 53703
Tel: 608-255-0285
www.ancoracoffee.com

Armeno Coffee Roasters Ltd
75 Otis Street
Northborough
MA 01532
Tel: 508-393-2821
www.armeno.com

Bean Central Coffee Roasters
4825 Trousdale Dr Ste 215
Nashville TN37 220
www.beancentral.com

Daybreak Coffee Roasters, Inc.
2377 Main Street
Glastonbury, CT 06033
Tel: 860-657-4466
www.daybreakcoffee.com

The Kona Coffee Council
P.O. Box 2077
Kealakekua, HI 96750
www.kona-coffee-council.com

Maui Coffee Roasters
444 Hana Highway
Kahului
Maui, HI 97669
Tel: 808-877-2877
www.mauicoffeeroasters.com

The Original San Juan Coffee Roasting Company
18 Cannery Landing
Friday Harbor, WA 98250
Tel: 360-378-4443
www.coffeesanjuan.com

Peet's Coffee & Tea
2124 Vine Street
Berkeley, CA 94709
Tel: 510-841-0564
www.peets.com

Storyville Coffee Company
9459 Coppertop Loop NE
Bainbridge Island
WA 98110
Tel: 206-780-5777
storyville.com

US Coffee
51 Alpha Plaza
Hicksville, NY 11801
Tel: 800-776-2866
www.uscoffee.com

Coffee houses and cafés

Blue Bottle
3081 S Delaware St
San Mateo CA94403
Tel: 510-653-3394
www.bluebottlecoffee.com

Boxcar Coffee Roasters
1825 Pearl Street B
Boulder CO 80302
www.boxcarcoffee.com

Café Grumpy
224 West 20th Street
New York, NY 10011
Tel: 212-255-5511
www.cafegrumpy.com

La Colombe Fishtown
1335 Frankford Avenue
Philadelphia
PA 19125
Tel: 267-479-1600
www.lacolombe.com

Crema Coffee
15 Hermitage Avenue
Nashville, TN 37204
Tel: 615-255-8311
www.crema-coffee.com

Culture Espresso
72 West 38th Street
New York, NY 10018
Tel: 212-302-0200
www.cultureespresso.com

Intelligentsia Coffee
3123 North Broadway
Chicago, IL 60657
Tel: 773-348-8058
www.intelligentsiacoffee.com

Panther Coffee
2390 North West 2nd Avenue
Miami, FL 33127
Tel: 305-677-3952
www.panthercoffee.com

Peregrine Espresso
660 Pennsylvania Avenue SE
Washington, DC 20003
Tel: 202-629-4381
www.peregrineespresso.com

Philz Coffee
3101 24th Street
San Francisco, CA 94110
Tel: 415-875-9370
www.philzcoffee.com

Spyhouse Coffee Roasting Co.
907 North Washington Avenue
Minneapolis, MN 55401
www.spyhousecoffee.com

Star Lounge Coffee Bar
2521 West Chicago Avenue
Chicago, IL 60622
Tel: 773-384-7827
www.darkmattercoffee.com

Thou Mayest Coffee Roasters
419 East 18th Street
Kansas City, MO 64108
Tel: 816-897-0505
www.thoumayest.com

Thunderbird Coffee
2200 Manor Road
Austin, TX 78722
Tel: 512-472-9900
www.thunderbirdcoffee.com

Water Avenue Coffee
1028 SE Water Avenue #145,
Portland, OR 97214
Tel: 503-808-7083
www.wateravenuecoffee.com

CANADA

Coffee houses and cafés

Bridgehead Roastery and Coffeehouse
130 Anderson Street
Ottawa, ON K1R 6T7
Tel: 613-233-1221
www.bridgehead.ca

Cafe Myriade
1432 Rue Mackay
Montreal, QC H3G 2H7
Tel: 514-939-1717
www.cafemyriade.com

Credo Coffee
10134 104 Street NW
Edmonton, AB T5J 1A7
www.credocoffee.ca

Revolver
325 Cambie Street
Vancouver BC V6B 2N4
Tel: 604-558-4444
www.revolvercoffee.ca

Rooster Coffee House
343 King Street East
Toronto, ON M5A 1L1
Tel: 416-995-1530
www.roostercoffeehouse.com

AUSTRALIA

Coffee suppliers

Arabicas Coffee Australia Pty Ltd
Unit 2 65 Meadow Ave
Coopers Plains QLD 4108
Tel: (07) 3277 9926
www.arabicacoffee.com.au

Aromas Tea and Coffee Merchants
60 Alexandra Place
Murarrie QLD 4172
Tel: (07) 3393 9324
www.aromas.com.au

Bay Coffee
2/214 Military Road
Neutral Bay NSW 2089
Tel: (61) 2 9953 6215
www.baycoffee.com.au

Vittoria Coffee
118 Wetherill Street
Silverwater NSW 2128
Tel: (02) 9748 0299
www.vittoriacoffee.com

Zentveld's Coffee
193 Broken Head Road
Newrybar NSW 2479
Tel: (02) 6687 2045
shop.zentvelds.com.au

Coffee exporter

Skybury Coffee Estate
136 Ivicevic Road
Mareeba QLD 4880
Tel: (07) 4093 2190
www.skybury.com.au

Coffee equipment suppliers

Belaroma Coffee Centre
75 Kenneth Road
Manly Vale NSW 2093
Tel: (02) 9948 0221
www.belaromacoffee.com.au

Boema
Unit 8/1 Cow Pasture Pl
Wetherill Park NSW 2164
www.boema.com.au

Segafredo Zanetti Australia Pty Ltd
Unit 8–9 4 Huntley Street
Alexandria NSW 2015
Tel: (02) 9310 3664
www.segafredo.com.au

Coffee houses and cafés

Coffee Alchemy
24 Addison Road
Marrickville NSW 2204
Tel: (02) 9516 1997
www.coffeealchemy.com

Dandelion and Driftwood Shop
20 Doncaster St
Hendra QLD 4011
Tel: (07) 3667 8388
www.dandeliondriftwood.com

Epic Espresso
5/1297 Hay Street
West Perth WA 6005
Tel: (61) 501 112649
www.epicespresso.com.au

Proud Mary Coffee Roasters
172 Oxford Street
Collingwood VIC 3066
Tel: (03) 9417 5930
www.proudmarycoffee.com.au

NEW ZEALAND

Coffee roasters and suppliers

Allpress Espresso Coffee Roasters
Tel: (09) 358 3121
www.allpressespresso.com

Altura Coffee Company Ltd
23 Douglas Alexander Parade
Albany, North Shore
Auckland 0632
Tel: (09) 448 1414
www.alturacoffee.co.nz

Atomic Coffee Roasters
420c New North Road
Kingsland
Auckland 1021
Tel: 0800 286 642
www.atomiccoffee.co.nz

Chiasso Coffee Roasters
20 Wynyard Street
Devonport
Auckland 0624
Tel: (09) 445 1816
www.chiasso.co.nz

Columbus Coffee
201a Victoria Street West
Freemans Bay Auckland
Tel: (09) 520 1044
www.columbuscoffee.co.nz

Millers Coffee
31 Cross Street
Newton
Auckand 1011
Tel: (09) 356 7322
www.millerscoffee.co.nz

Santos Coffee Limited
77 Carlton Gore Road
Newmarket Auckland 1023
Tel: 0800 500 008
www.santoscoffee.co.nz

BIBLIOGRAPHY

Adler C., Ramsay A., *Told in the Coffee House* (Macmillan Co. NY, 1898)

Alcott, Dr W.A., *Tea and Coffee: their physical, intellectual and moral effects on the human system* (Stoke-upon-Trent, UK, 1859)

Angell, John. *Health Lectures 8-10 Tea, Coffee and Cocoa.* (John Heywood, London, 1886)

Beeton, Isabella. *The Book of Household Management* (Facsimile), (Jonathan Cape, London, 1968)

Bradshaw, Steve. *Café Society Bohemian Life from Swift to Bob Dylan* (Wiedenfeld & Nicholson, London 1978)

Boettcher, Jürgen (ed.). *Coffee Houses of Europe* (Thames and Hudson, London, 1980)

Bramah, Edward. *Tea & Coffee* (Hutchinson, London, 1972)

Campbell, Dawn and Smith, Janet. *The Coffee Book* (Pelican Publishing Company, Louisiana, USA, 1995)

Chamberlain, Lesley. *The Food and Cooking of Eastern Europe* (Penguin Books, London, 1989)

Chamberlayne, John (trans.). *The Manner of Making Coffee, Tea and Chocolate* (London, 1685)

Coffee Bar and Coffee Lounge, (Periodical Publications, London, 1959–60)

Coptic Press. *Coffee Houses of Old London* (London, 1965)

Davids, Kenneth. *The Coffee Book* (Whittet Books, Weybridge, UK, 1976)

Debry, Gérard. *Coffee and Health* (John Libbey Eurotext, Paris, 1994)

Douglas, Dr James. *Yemensis fructum Cofé ferens; or, a description and history of the Coffee tree* (London, 1727)

Food and Agriculture Organization of the United Nations. *Traditional Foods in the Near East* (Rome, 1991)

Food and Agriculture Organization of the United Nations, *Utilization of tropical foods: sugars, spices and stimulants* (Rome, 1989)

Harleian Miscellany, vol.8. *The Character of a Coffee-House.* (London, 1673)

Harleian Miscellany, vol.8. *Coffee Houses Vindicated* (London,1673)

Hattox, Ralph S. *Coffee and Coffee Houses: The origin of a Social Beverage in the Medieval Near East* (University of Washington Press, USA, 1985)

Heise, Ulla. *Coffee and Coffee Houses* (Schiffer Publishing, Pennsylvania, 1987)

Jobin, P., *Les Cafés produits dans le monde* (P. Jobin et Cie, Le Havre, 4th ed.

Joel, G.C.W. (compiler). *One Hundred Years of Coffee* (London, 1942)

Kolpas, Norman. *Coffee* (John Murray, London, 1979)

Kummer, Corby, *The Joy of Coffee* (Houghton Mifflin Company, New York, 1997)

Law, William. *History of Coffee* (London, 1850)

Librairie Larousse. *Larousse Gastronomique* (Hamlyn, London, 1988)

McCoy, Elin and Walker, John Frederick. *Coffee and Tea* (Signet, New York, 1976)

Mennell, Stephen. *All Manners of Food* (Blackwell, Oxford, UK, 1985)

Porter, Roy and Teich, Mikulás (eds.). *Drugs and Narcotics in History* (Cambridge University Press, UK, 1995)

Renner, H.D. *The Origin of Food Habits* (Faber and Faber, London, 1954)

Roden, Claudia. *Coffee* (Faber, London, 1977)

Roden, Claudia. *The Book of Jewish Food* (Viking, London, 1997)

Roland, Paul. *Revelations: The Wisdom of the Ages* (Carlton Books, London, 1995)

Shaida, Margaret. *The Legendary Cuisine of Persia* (Penguin Books, London, 1994)

Schapira, Joel, David and Karl. *The Book of Coffee and Tea* (St Martin's Press, New York, 1975)

Simmonds, P.L. *Coffee as It Is, and As It Ought To Be* (London, 1850)

Stein, Stanley J. *Vassouras, a Brazilian Coffee County 1850-1900* (Princeton University Press, USA, 1985)

Stella, Alain. *The Book of Coffee* (Flammarion, Paris, 1997)

Stobart, Tom. *Herbs, Spices and Flavourings* (Penguin Books, London, 1977)

The Men's Answer to the Women's Petition Against Coffee... (London, 1674)

The Times Atlas of World History (Times Books, London, 1981)

The Vertues of Coffee (London, 1663)

The Women's Petition Against Coffee... (London, 1674)

Thorn, Jon, *The Coffee Companion* (Quintet, London, 1995)

Toussaint-Samat, Maguelonne. *History of Food* (Blackwell, Oxford, UK. 1994)

Trager, James. *The Food Chronology* (Henry Holt and Company, New York, 1995)

Ukers, W. *The Romance of Coffee* (Tea and Coffee Trade Journal Co., New York, 1948)

Uribe, C.Andres. *Brown Gold* (Random House, New York, 1954)

Wrigley, Gordon, *Coffee* (Longman Scientific & Technical)

ACKNOWLEDGEMENTS

The publishers would like to thank the following people for their assistance with the preparation of this book: Tony Higgins of H.R. Higgins Ltd., London; Mehmet Kurukaveçi of Istanbul; Frank Neale; Celcius Lodder, Martin Wattam and the library staff of the International Coffee Organization, Coffee Information Centre, London.

The following companies provided helpful assistance, equipment and coffee bean samples: Algerian Coffee Company; Andronicus; Bramah Tea and Coffee Museum; Ecom; Fairfax Kitchens; Gala Tea and Coffee company; Heals Café, Tottenham Court Road London, UK; Master Roasts; Monmouth Coffee Company and The Priory Tea and Coffee Company.

Picture Acknowledgements: All pictures are by William Lingwood, Louisa Dare and Janine Hosegood, except for the following: Advertising Archives: 11b, 29t, 29b, 53t. akg-images: 10, 11t, 14, 28, 32, 33, 35t, 35b, 36t, 37, 38b, 39, 44, 45, 46b, 49. Cephas: 12, 36b, 95tl, 100b, 116. Bridgeman Images: 24, 27. Charmet: 13t, 13b, 17, 18, 19. E.T. Archive: 21, 23, 25, 26, 30, 34b, 40t, 40b, 42t, 43b. Hulton Getty: 22, 43t, 46t, 47, 48, 50. Lloyds: 41. Museum of London: 31, 42b.

INDEX

A
Abdel-Kader Anasari Djezeri Haubuli, Sheik, 15
Act One Scene One Bar, London, 47
Aden, 13
adulterated coffee, 27
Aeropress® 136
Africa, 74–81
African coffee, 153
Aga, Suleiman, 33
al fresco coffee, 120
alcohol, 141, 145–7, 151–53
almonds
  baklava, 233
  blueberry frangipane flan, 227
  chilled coffee and praline soufflé, 170
  coffee almond Marsala slice, 212
  coffee biscotti, 245
  Danish coffee pastries, 230
Alpinus, Prosper, 13
American Civil War, 44, 48
Amsterdam, 22–3, 26
Angel coffee house, London, 41
Angola, 74
antestia bug, 60
apples, caramelized, 194
apricot panettone pudding, 166
Arabia, 12, 13, 14, 20–1
arabica coffee, 58, 59, 64, 116
Arabs, 22
Argentina, 88
Armagnac
  stuffed prunes, 236
Armenia, 61
auctions, 27
Australia, 94
Austria, 26, 36–7, 52, 45
Aux Deux Magots, Paris, 34
Avicenna, 13

B
babas, plum and rum, 187
Bach, J.S., 39
baked coffee cheesecake, 216
baklava, 231
Baltic Exchange, London, 41
Balzac, Honoré de, 28, 29
bananas
  coconut and coffee

  trifle, 188
  flambéed bananas with Caribbean coffee sauce, 190
Banesius, 10
baskets, brandy snap, 199
bean to cup coffee machine 136
beans
  grading, 66–8
  harvesting, 63–4
  processing, 64–5
Beardsley, Aubrey, 46
Beeton, Isabella, 50
Belloy, Jean Baptiste de, 49
Benin, 74
Berlin, 38, 45
berries, 57
Bezzera, Luigi, 130
biscuits
  black Russian cookies, 241
  coffee and hazelnut macaroons, 238
  coffee biscotti, 245
  Viennese whirls, 240
black Russian cookies, 241
blending coffee, 104
Blount, Sir Thomas Pope, 10
Blue Mountain beans, 24
blueberry frangipane flan, 227
Blunt, Sir Henry, 16
Bolivia, 88
Boston Tea Party, 44
botany, 11, 56–9
Bourbon
  hot mint julep, 144
Bramah, Edward, 49
Brandenburg, 38
brandy
  coffee & brandy syllabub, 160
brandy snap baskets, 199
Brazil, 24, 25, 26, 30, 63, 64, 67, 73, 88–90
breads
  candied fruit bread, 247
  cappuccino panettone, 246
Bremen, 38
brewing coffee, 49–52, 113–15, 118–35
Britain, 31, 40–3, 46–7, 51, 73
British East India Company, 46, 73
brown blight, 61
brownies, chunky white chocolate and coffee, 242
Budapest, 37, 45
bulletproof coffee 137
burr mills, 110
Burundi, 74
Byron, Lord, 19, 32

C
café à l'orange, 146
café au lait, 142
café brûlot, 147
café Central, Prague, 45
café de Flore, Paris, 34
café Gresham, Budapest, 45
café New York, Budapest, 45
café de olla, 144
café de la Paix, Paris, 34
café Royal, London, 46
café Vigadó, Budapest, 45
cafés , 33–4, 39, 46
cafetières, 49
caffè americano, 135
Caffè Greco, Rome, 32
caffè latte, 142
caffè vermouth, 152
caffeine
  decaffeinated coffee, 53, 116–17
  stimulant effects, 29, 116
caffettiera napoletana, 122–3
cakes, 209–19
  chunky white chocolate and coffee brownies, 242
  coconut coffee cake, 210
  coffee and mint cream cake, 214
  coffee and walnut Swiss roll with Cointreau cream, 215
  coffee almond Marsala slice, 212
  coffee chocolate mousse cake, 216
  dark chocolate and coffee mousse cake, 207
  mocha sponge cake, 211
  sour cherry coffee loaf, 212
Calvados
  French toddy, 145
Cambodia, 94
Cameroon, 74
Camp coffee essence, 53
candied fruit
  candied fruit bread, 247
  Greek fruit and nut pastries, 232
candle auctions, 27
canephora coffee, 58
canned coffee, 53
Cape Verde, 74
cappuccino, 50, 130
  recipe, 142
cappuccino cones, 200
cappuccino panettone, 246
cappuccino torte, 216
capsule machine, coffee 136
capsules, coffee 136
caramel
  caramelized apples, 194
  classic coffee crème caramel, 158
Caribbean, 82–7
Caribbean coffee sauce, flambèed bananas with, 190
Casanova, Giacomo Girolamo, 32
catering trade, 49–50
Catholic Church, 30
Central African Republic, 74–5
Central America, 82–7
Ceylon (Sri Lanka), 22, 24, 98
Charles II, King of England, 42
cheese, soft
  baked coffee cheesecake, 218
  coffee coeur à la crème, 164
  coffee crêpes with

peaches and cream, 186
grilled nectarines with coffee mascarpone filling, 190
Irish coffee cheesecake, 219
mango and coffee meringue roll, 172
tiramisu, 157
cheesecakes
baked coffee cheesecake, 216
Irish coffee cheesecake, 217
cherries, coffee, 11, 57, 62–5
cherries
sour cherry coffee loaf, 212
chicory, 37
chilled coffee Caribbean, 149
China, 94
chocolate, 139
cappuccino cones, 200
cappuccino panettone, 246
cappuccino torte, 216
chilled chocolate and espresso mousse, 165
chocolate and coffee mint thins, 238
chunky white chocolate and coffee brownies, 242
classic chocolate and coffee roulade, 172
coffee chocolate mousse cake, 216
coffee-chocolate soda, 150
coffee chocolate truffles, 237
coffee cream profiteroles, 229
frosted raspberry and coffee terrine, 203
iced coffee mousse in a chocolate bowl, 206
Mexican coffee, 144
Mississippi pie, 223
mocha sponge cake, 211
stuffed prunes, 236
Tia Maria truffle tarts, 228
twice-baked mocha soufflé, 171
chunky white chocolate and coffee brownies, 242
cinnamon, 140
cinnamon and coffee swirl ice cream, 198
Clement VIII, Pope, 30
Clieu, Gabriel Mathieu de, 23
Cobbett, William, 41
coconut and coffee trifle, 188
coconut coffee cake, 210
coeur à la crème, coffee, 164
coffea arabica, 11, 56, 58
coffea dewevrei, 56
coffea liberica, 56
coffea robusta, 56, 58–9
coffee almond Marsala slice, 212
coffee and brandy syllabub, 162
coffee and hazelnut macaroons, 238
coffee and macadamia muffins, 242
coffee and mint cream cake, 214
coffee and minty-lemon sorbet, 204
coffee and walnut Swiss roll with Cointreau cream, 215
coffee bars, 47
coffee berry borer, 60
coffee berry disease, 61
coffee biscotti, 245
Coffee Cantata (Bach), 39
coffee cardamom zabaglione, 160
coffee chocolate mousse cake, 216
coffee-chocolate soda, 150
coffee chocolate truffles, 237
coffee coeur à la crème, 164
coffee colada, 153
coffee cream profiteroles, 229
coffee crêpes with peaches and cream, 186
coffee, cold brew 137
coffee custard tart, 226
coffee essence, 53
coffee frappé, 148
coffee houses, 30–1
Austria, 36–7, 45, 52
Britain, 41–3, 46–7
France, 51
Germany, 38–9, 45
Hungary, 45
Italy, 32–4
North America, 44, 48
Turkey, 15–18, 21
coffee ice cream, 200
coffee jellies, 162
coffee liqueurs
coffee cardamom zabaglione, 160
coffee chocolate truffles, 237
coffee maker, portable 136
coffee meringues with rose cream, 178
coffee mills, 27
coffee pavlova with exotic fruits, 179
coffee plants 56–9
diseases, 60–1
growing, 56–7
harvesting, 62–4
natural disasters, 61
pests, 60
species, 58–9
coffee pods 136
coffee-producing countries, 72–99
coffee stewards, 19
cognac
coffee and cognac sauce 199
coffee cognac cooler, 153
Cointreau
café brûlot, 147
coffee and walnut Swiss roll with Cointreau cream, 215
cold brew coffee maker 137
cold brew method 137
colletotrichum coffeanum, 61
Colombia, 24, 61, 67, 91–2
Coltelli, Francisco Procopio dei, 33
Comoros, 75
Cona, 50, 129
Congo, Democratic Republic of, 61, 75
Congo, Republic of, 76
Constantinople, 15–16, 19, 21, 26
contact time, brewing coffee, 114
cookies, black Russian, 241
Costa Rica, 66–7, 82
Cracow, 37
cream, 138
cream desserts, 157–65
crème Anglaise
floating islands, 176
crème caramel, classic coffee, 158
crêpes
coffee crêpes with peaches and cream, 186
crunchy topped coffee meringue pie, 224
Cuba, 83
cupping, 69
custard tart, coffee, 226
custards
coconut and coffee trifle, 188
floating islands, 176
petits pots de cappuccino, 161
Cybercafés, 47

D
Danish coffee pastries, 230
dark chocolate and coffee mousse cake, 207
decaffeinated coffee, 53, 116–17
diseases, 60–1
D'Israeli, Isaac, 33, 35
Dominican Republic, 83
Donegan, Lonnie, 47
Douglas, Dr James, 10, 11, 12, 17, 22
drinks recipes, 142–53
dry processing, 64

Dutch East India Company, 22
Dutch East Indies, 22, 30
Dutch West Indies, 24
Dutch Guiana, 23, 24, 25

E
earthquakes, 61
Ecuador, 92
egg nog, coffee, 151
Egypt, 21
El Salvador, 83
electric espresso machines,

132–3, 138
electric filter
machines, 126–7
electric grinders, 109
electric percolators, 128
Equatorial Guinea, 76
equipment, 107–11, 118–33
espresso coffee, 50, 130–35
espresso con panna, 135
espresso corretto, 135
espresso crema, 130
espresso doppio, 135
espresso granita, 202
espresso lungo, 135
espresso macchiato, 134
espresso ristretto, 134
espresso romano, 134
espresso tazza d'oro, 135
essences, 140
Ethiopia, 12–13, 24, 64,
67, 76
Evelyn, John, 40–1

F
fazendas, 25, 63
fermentation, 65
Festival of Britain (1951), 46
fig compote, fresh, 180
Fiji, 94

filters, 46, 124–7
mugs 137
Finland, 38
flambéed bananas with
Caribbean coffee
sauce, 190
flans *see* tarts
flavourings, 53, 138–41
floating islands, 174
Florian's, Venice, 32, 33
flowers, 57
fragrant fruit salad, 193
France, 22–3, 24, 31, 33–5,
49, 50, 51, 73
frangipane flan,
blueberry, 227
Frederick the Great, King of
Prussia, 31, 38, 39
Frederick William, Elector of
Brandenburg, 38
French Guiana, 92
French Polynesia, 94
French toddy, 145
French West Indies, 24
frost damage, 61
frosted raspberry and coffee
terrine, 203
frozen desserts, 197–207
fruit
coffee coeur à la
crème, 164
coffee pavlova with exotic
fruits, 179
flavourings, 141
fragrant fruit salad, 193
summer berries with
coffee sabayon, 194
Tia Maria truffle tarts, 228
fungal diseases, 61

G
Gabon, 76
Gaggia, Giovanni Achille,
50, 130
Galapagos Islands, 93
Galen, 28
Georgia n' ginger, 141
Germany, 31, 38–9, 45
Ghana, 77
ginger
Georgia n' ginger, 143
gingered coffee
meringues, 175
sticky coffee and ginger
pudding, 167
Goethe, Johann Wolfgang
von, 32
grading beans, 66–8
granitas
espresso granita, 204
granita di caffè, 150
grapes
coffee & brandy
syllabub, 162
grasshopper coffee, 147
Greek fruit and nut
pastries, 232
Greenwich Village, 48
Gregory, Dr William, 51
Griensteidl coffee house,
Vienna, 37
grinders, 108–11, 114
growing coffee, 56–61
Guadeloupe, 83
Guatemala, 67, 83–4
Guinea, 77
Guyana, 93

H
haciendas, 25
Hahnemann, Samuel, 28, 29
Haiti, 84
Hamburg, 38
hand mills, 108
Hanover, 38
harvesting coffee, 57, 62–4
Hawaii, 94–5
hazelnuts
coffee and hazelnut
macaroons, 238
health, 116
Heaven and Hell Coffee Bar,
London, 47
Helen of Troy, 10
Hemileia vastatrix, 24, 60–1
Hill, Benson, 52
history, 10–53
Homer, 10
Honduras, 84
Hope, Bob, 46
humours, doctrine of, 28
Hungary, 26
hurricanes, 61
hybrid coffee trees, 56,
59, 61

I
ibriks, 118–19
ice cream
cinnamon and coffee swirl
ice cream, 198
coffee-chocolate
soda, 150
coffee ice cream, 200
maple coffee and pistachio
bombes, 202
toasted nut and coffee ice
cream, 199
iced coffee mousse in a
chocolate bowl, 206
India, 95
Indonesia, 67, 96
insect pests, 60
instant coffee, 53
International Coffee
Organization (ICO), 72
Irish coffee cheesecake, 219
Italy, 32–3, 50
Ivory Coast, 61, 77

J
Jamaica, 24, 73, 84–5

Jamaican black coffee, 145
Japan, 47
Java, 22, 24, 96
jellies, coffee, 162
jug method, 120
juke boxes, 47

K
Kaffee Hag, 53
Kaffeeklatch, 39
Kaffeekränzschen, 39
Kafka, Franz, 45
Kato, Satori, 53
Kenya, 24, 77
Kolschitzky, Franz, 36
Konditorein, 39

L
Laos, 97
leaf rust, 60–1
legends 10–12
Leipzig, 38
lemon
coffee and minty-lemon
sorbet, 204
Liberia, 77
Lisbon flip coffee, 152
Liszt, Franz, 32
liver-bakers, adulterated
coffee, 27
Lloyds of London, 41
London, 26, 27, 41–3, 46–7
Louis XIV, King of France,
22–3, 33

M
Macabre Coffee Bar,
London, 47
macadamia nuts
coffee and macadamia
muffins, 240
macaroons, coffee and
hazelnut, 238
Madagascar, 77–8
Malawi, 78
Malaysia, 97